ND1
SKEGNESS

28. MAR 07

16. JUN 04

28. OCT 04

19. JUL 07

04. OCT 07

20. JUN 05.

30. JUL 05

08. SEP 05

11. JUL 08

05 AUG

31. OCT 05.

10. JAN 06

15. DEC 08

31. MAR 06

06 MAY 06

02. MAY 09

21. JUL 06

HARDING, MIKE

WALKING THE PEAK AND PENNINES

£17.99

L 5/9

D0236812

AD 01964242

SO1

Walking the Peak and Pennines

Walking the Peak and Pennines

Mike Harding

Michael Joseph
London

MICHAEL JOSEPH LTD

Published by the Penguin Group
27 Wrights Lane, London W8 5TZ

Viking Penguin Inc., 375 Hudson Street, New York, New York 10014, USA
Penguin Books Australia Ltd, Ringwood, Victoria, Australia
Penguin Books Canada Ltd, 10 Alcorn Avenue, Toronto, Ontario, Canada M4V 3B2
Penguin Books (NZ) Ltd, 182–190 Wairau Road, Auckland 10, New Zealand

Penguin Books Ltd, Registered Offices: Harmondsworth, Middlesex, England

First published in Great Britain in 1992

Typeset in 10/12pt Bembo by Goodfellow & Egan Ltd, Cambridge
Colour reproduction by Anglia Graphics, Bedford
Printed and bound in Spain by Cayfosa Industria Gráfica, Barcelona

A CIP catalogue record for this book is available from the British Library.

ISBN 0 7181 3358 7

The moral right of the author has been asserted.

Front endpaper: Pendle Hill from near Sawley
Back endpaper: Evening at Hen Cloud

The Secret Life of Stones

Blood from–
Heart of–
Cold as–
Hard as–

-mad
-broke
-faced
-drunk

Condemned, the words judge us to death.
But see how water flows from our groins,
how we rim the moor's edge
and dandle climbers from our lips.

See how we take the acid rain and sweeten it,
cup it and send it shivering and twitching
in crazed veils to the valley floor.
See how we stand in circles singing and

our carved heads grin through eternity.
No enemies words, just Time, and wind
and water, ice and fire. See how we melt
and pucker and fold when the weasel water gnaws

into our bones. See how the sun parches
and flakes us and the ice picks at our sores
lifting the scabs. Scoured and rubbed,
the Bridestones fall, the beaches rise, and stone,

from moor to estuary takes to the wind,
a whisper in the air, blown stone.

[v]

Acknowledgements

THANKS to my wife, Pat, who went with me on so many of these walks and who spent so much of her time mounting and indexing the photographs, and correcting all my spelling mistakes.

To those others who shared the way with me: my friends Eddie, Tony, Rod and Sue, Robert and Cynthia, Colin and Baz, and Sarah and Emma, all of whom I got lost, wet, tired and hungry, sometimes all at once, but who didn't moan much.

To Roly Smith and Ken Smith (no relation) at the headquarters of the Peak District National Park who gave me so much help and information, and to Alison and Andrea for the coffee.

The author and publishers wish to thank the following for permission to reproduce extracts from copyright material:

Peggy Seeger for *The Manchester Rambler* by Ewan MacColl (pp. 1 & 130); Faber and Faber Ltd for 'In Praise of Limestone' by W. H. Auden (p. 11); HarperCollins Publishers Ltd for *Sir Gawain and the Green Knight* by J.R.R. Tolkien (pp. 52 & 59); Pamela Monkhouse and Diadem Books Ltd for *On Foot in North Wales and the Peak* by Patrick Monkhouse (pp. 60, 105 & 127); Jarrold Publishing Ltd for *Ghosts and Legends of the Peak District* by David Clarke (p. 67); Cicerone Press Ltd for *The Devil's Mill* by Walter Unsworth (p. 74); David Higham Associates and Ceolfrith Press Ltd for 'Above Oldham' from *Best of Neighbours* by Glyn Hughes (p. 91); Peters, Fraser & Dunlop Ltd and André Deutsch Ltd for 'Day of These Days' from *Selected Poems* by Laurie Lee (p. 96); Willow Publishing Ltd for *The 1932 Kinder Trespass* by Benny Rothman (p. 106); Sidgwick & Jackson Ltd for 'The Joy of Living' from *Journeyman* by Ewan MacColl (p. 130); Victor Gollancz Ltd for *Millstone Grit* by Glyn Hughes (p. 148); Faber & Faber Ltd for 'The Pylons' from *Collected Poems 1928–1985* by Stephen Spender (p. 173); Element Books Ltd for the 'Carmina Gadelica' from *The Elements of the Celtic Tradition* by Caitlin Matthews (p. 184).

Every effort has been made to trace copyright material and the author apologizes for any omissions.

The maps were drawn by Chris Jesty.

Contents

A Note on Maps and Things

I hate cautionary notes and warnings but it is important that I say this. The hills are wonderful places, friendly and welcoming. But if you don't take a bit of sensible care they can kill you. Never go anywhere without a map and compass and the ability to use them. Wear boots (the new lightweight boots like the Brasher Boot and the KSB by Karrimor are excellent and really light), take a pack with spare warm clothing and waterproofs, and enjoy yourself.

But do remember that farmers work the land you're walking through, so don't make a difficult job harder. Close gates, take your litter back with you, walk through hay meadows single file and don't let your dog chase or worry sheep. If you do, the farmer may shoot it and it will be your fault and not the dog's.

End of sermon, now the maps. The Ordnance Survey have produced three wonderful maps in their Outdoor Leisure 1:50,000 series that cover almost all the areas touched on in this book; they are excellent maps for walkers with plenty of detail. The *White Peak* and *Dark Peak* maps cover the walks in parts one and two and the *South Pennines* covers most of 'Spindledom.' The Ordnance Survey Pathfinder series, which is to the same scale and has the same detail, covers fringe areas like Saddleworth which just manages to fall off the edge of the Dark Peak map.

There are a number of maps produced by specialist firms that are worth a mention. Harvey Map Services have produced two fine maps of the Dark Peak, North and South, at a scale of 1:40,000. They are double-sided single sheets complete with waterproof wallets and have been published specifically for walkers.

Saddleworth Local History Society has published a good map of the Saddleworth area with a fair deal of historical notes; it is available from the Tourist Information Centre at Uppermill.

Pendle used to be a problem for walkers when it came to maps for the only detailed maps of the hill, the Pathfinder series, overlapped to cover the area so that you had to buy four maps with a little bit of Pendle in each corner. Now there's a good detailed map of the hill produced by Duncan Armstrong and Associates which is available from most of the local bookshops and information centres. The Pendle Heritage Centre at Brierfield nearly always has them and you can treat yourself to one while you're eating your Sabden Treacle Tart and looking at the coddy-muck cannonballs in their glass cases.

No matter what your or my views might be on access to the uncultivated hills and moors of the Pennines, the fact is that much of the uplands of this fair isle are enclosed lands in private ownership. I have tried in this book to keep to public footpaths wherever possible; however, there were times when I wandered off the track. This does not imply in any sense a right of way or of access.

For those interested, the photographs were taken using a Nikon F3 camera in the main, with a variety of lenses from 16mm to 200mm. A small number of the shots were taken on a Widelux camera. The panorama shots were taken on a Hasselblad and the panorama shots were taken on a Widelux camera. The film throughout is Fuji; both Fuji 50 Pro and Velvia.

I've had some of the most wonderful times of my life in these hills and I hope a little of that comes across.

Born to Ramble

I'm a rambler I'm a rambler from Manchester way
I get all my pleasure the hard moorland way
I may be a wage slave on Monday
But I am a free man on Sunday

Ewan MacColl: *The Manchester Rambler*

THIS ISN'T A WALKING BOOK in the usual sense, in that there are no detailed maps and no graphic instructions telling you how to turn left by a byre or right by a hen hut or to look for a stile. There are enough good guide books and walking books of that kind on the Peak and the Pennines already and I don't see any sense in adding to the number. The first walking book I ever wrote contained maps that I'd drawn myself just to give an outline of the general direction of my wanderings. To indicate hills and their summits, I indulged in what I thought was a fairly tasteful form of shading, going in depth and colour from light green to dark green and then to a sort of ochre that finally became a rust red. An Irish friend of mine said they looked like inflamed pustules and, looking at them now, I think he's right. So the maps in this book are even sketchier and, as far as I know, there are no warts or boils.

So what kind of book is this then? Well, it's a book of wanderings I suppose, of stories and impressions, days out on the hills, the moors, and the valleys of that rib-cage and spine of white and dark rocks they call the Pennines. It's a book of things I've picked up along the way, fleeting things, some of them, like a white hare leaping the frosty heather or a farmer's wave across a field on a summer's evening; others are hard and lasting like a stump of pickled bog-oak or the millstone grit beneath. Some are bright as the brass buttons on a bandsman's coat, others are shades as dark and sour as the black breath of the moors on a grey winter's day.

I've walked the hills and valleys of the Peak and the Pennines since I was a child and though I wouldn't be so stupid as to claim that I know them all by heart I can find my way round pretty well. It's a great area to walk in, a place where the bones of dead Norsemen and Celts moulder in the bogs, where coiners hid to clip the King's mint in deep wooded gorges, and where mill poets left the factory after a day's work at the loom to ramble the moors, weaving the warp and weft of their verses. It's not a country-comfortable landscape like the Cotswolds or as wild and remote a place as Torridon, but it has a nature all of its own.

In the south is the old kingdom of Mercia and the dales of Dove and Miller, Manifold and Water Cum Jolly, while to the west and east the gritstone stands again in the Edges of Baslow, Curbar, Stanage and the Hen and the Roaches. In these southern Derbyshire dales, the

A farm near Chrome Hill, just inside the Staffordshire border

The Natural Arch in Dovedale

valleys are thickly wooded; gentle dales in the main, with good trout rivers and banks clotted with trees, for the south is limestone country, the land of the White Peak, good sweet grass and the teeth of the hills outcropping. It isn't without its scars, of course; the remains of lead mines lie everywhere on the plateaux and the ruins of old water-driven mills still stand where the first grumblings of the Industrial Revolution were heard on the banks of the Derwent at Cromford. Even today the land is being blown apart and then crushed and raked and riddled for minerals and road-fill on a scale no one could ever have imagined, even in the days when 'muck was brass'. Below the plateau, the land is hollow, its limestone belly gnawed out by the worm of the waters into caves and potholes and great caverns like Treecliffe, Peak and Speedwell. It was said by one writer that the land of the White Peak is so hollow that if you had a beater big enough, you could sound it out like the drum of the world.

To the north are the moors and crags of Elmet where great humps of hills, blanketed with peat bog and heather and topped with gritstone tors, ride above valleys whose bottoms are often a cluster of mills and factories. For it is a land where man has worked since before the Romans, where lead gave way to wool and wool made room for cotton and where now the great palaces of Spindledom, those

'dark Satanic Mills', are mostly silent and empty or turned to other uses. The northern valleys have felt the heavy hand of what William 'Billy' Holt, the Todmorden writer, called 'Massman'* and canal and railway follow the river through craggy 'deans' where, in parts, the light of day hardly glimmers, while above it all, unchanged but for the walls that came with the enclosures, the moors range to the edge of view. This land of the north, where the southern top of the Yorkshire Dales gives way to the forests of Trawden and Pendle and the moors above Haworth and Calderdale, is the old Kingdom of Elmet, the beginning of the great sheet of millstone grit that stretches from Ponden Kirk on the edge of Haworth Moor to Kinder, ending in a shiver above Castleton and the beginning of the limestone.

And running through it all go the hills, the ribs, the backbone of the country. I remember my teacher at primary school telling us they were called 'The Pennines' because somebody long ago had compared them to the Apennines. They were the spine of our country, he said, and we were lucky to live on the edge of them. But he

*'Massman' to Holt was that great, rolling, unstoppable force of industrialisation and development that so changed the face of the North, turning it from a land of small farms and huddled villages into a country of mills, factories and overcrowded and often squalid towns.

was a Northern Chauvinist of the old school who supported Rochdale Hornets and thought that anybody born south of Birmingham was soft mentally and physically, and tucked their shirt inside their underpants. Whether it was because of him or not, I don't know, but the Pennines have fascinated me from that day to this.

You could see them from the end of our street on clear days; purple-blue and hazy in summer, in winter, white-over and stark. But they were there all through my growing years, way off in the distance, and to someone who'd never strayed much beyond the smoky catacombs of the streets around, they seemed unattainable. As a child I would look at them and think them mountains. Later, as I grew older, I travelled all over those hills, from Leek to Lothersdale, working in the mills and factories, scaling the boilers that drove the mill engines and made the steam to bleach and colour the cloth. I came to know them and climb them on days out from Manchester, buses and trains taking me, either alone or with a handful of mates, into the folding hills, the striding moors and thrusting crags. Often we camped out for weeks on end, living high on the hills in old army tents, looking down at the valleys, smoking and clustered below us, as we cooked porridge, sausages and beans, or baked potatoes in the embers of the fire. Other days it was stolen time, freedom grabbed for a day, a few hours spent rambling the cloughs and the gills before the last bus home.

In the years since then, I've wandered them over and again, revisiting places I'd first known as a child, the high gritstone hills and the cloughs and deans of heathery moors whose waters run down into Spindledom, and to me now it is a landscape peopled with ghosts, for the hand and foot of man has long been felt on these hills.

Men wandered here before History, crossing the land-bridge from the continent and threading their way along the drier uplands, gathering their roots, nuts and berries, and hunting deer and bison, wild pig and bear. They took refuge in the high caves of the limestone country at Creswell Crags; there, at Pin Hole Cave and Robin Hood's Cave, were found some of the first signs of man in this country, his weapons, his tools and the remains of his food and, in the crudely carved bones he left behind, his first reachings towards art. Men of the Stone Ages settled here leaving behind little trace other than their tombs and henges. After them came the Celts who peopled these uplands, building forts and villages and bringing with them from Central Europe and North Africa a religion and a culture, the last traces of which were found preserved in the parchments of medieval Irish monks and in the strange stone heads that, even today, keep appearing in some of the more unknown valleys. With the Romans came the colonisation, the lead-mining, the imposition of the rule of the colonies and civitas, hypocausts and baths, roads and villas and strings of horses carrying Derbyshire lead for the gutters of Rome.

As the Romans' far-spread Empire slid into decline, as all empires must, there came German raiders from Saxony who saw the Roman remains and declared them to be the 'weird work of giants'. Their kingdoms of Mercia, Elmet and Northumbria turned to Christianity when the Irish monks came in their skin canoes, rolling in on the surf of Lancashire and Cheshire shores and sailing up the Ribble, Mersey and Dee. After them, Norsemen came from the east and west, scouring the land and driving up the valleys, raiding and laying waste. They drove the King of Mercia into exile overseas and settled the land, moving into the higher valleys where their axes cleared the forests and where their settlements still stand. And yet still, it is believed, the Celts lingered on in their hidden dales and out on the moss and boglands: the 'Welshmen' they came to be called, the word meaning 'foreigners' or 'strangers'.

The Normans came with William, and he, a feudal overlord of overlords, after fitting Harold with a feathered contact lens, declared each inch of the kingdom his and carved it up amongst his followers. On the high hills, at Castleton, Derby, Bakewell and Pilsbury, they

The hollow boulder at Pots and Pans

built their castles so that the serf could straighten up from his work and see the great house, power and dominance made solid in stone and glass, looking down on him as he laboured in the fields of his lord.

History books often tell us that conquerors came in 'waves', giving us to imagine that somehow those who were there before vanished with the 'mists of time'. Not so. Like the British in India, they adapted, lived alongside and intermarried with the in-comers as people have always done and always will, and thus there are groups of people living in the Pennines now who are unlike any people around. They are dark and short and are often taken for gypsies, but they are people who have lived on the lowland mosses and the remote valleys for thousands of years, perhaps before even the Celts came. There are said to be people in two of the valleys of the millstone grit country

Hardcastle Crags and Hebden Water in the autumn

who still carve stone heads and bury them in sacred springs where votive rags hang from branches, and at the old Celtic festivals of Beltane, Samhain, Oimelc and Lughnasa, fires still burn on the fells.

In a BBC television programme made in 1986, a woman from Glossop described herself as a Celt and went on to confirm what a great many other people had already suspected, that the 'old religion' is still practised in some parts of the North.

But the Celts linger on in other less obvious ways. The Derbyshire Well Dressing ceremonies, for example, are simply a Christianisation of the Celtic-Pagan custom of decorating wells and springs with flowers, while the rush-bearings and morris dancing of the gritstone valleys go directly back to the corn gods and fertility rites of the people who built Mam Tor and carved the stone heads that the Christian priests took in to church and called 'gargoyles'.

So this book is a book of rambles and meanders, folk-lore and history, gossip and conjecture. It travels afoot in the hills of Derbyshire, Lancashire and Yorkshire, with brief lurches into Staffordshire and Cheshire. It goes as far south as Wirksworth and Cromford,

where the land drops below 1,000ft while its northernmost wanderings stop just below the Aire Gap because beyond that lie the Yorkshire Dales, another piece of country entirely. In the main, the walks stay high, and all but one are along the backbone of England.

The one area that lies away from the central hills as an outlier to the Pennines is Pendle, but it is such a good hill and such good walking country that I couldn't leave it out. So as I said at the beginning, this isn't your usual sort of walking book. There are no detailed maps and there are no directions beyond don't get lost, don't get dead and don't walk across cultivated land or let your dog off near sheep. I suppose in a way it's a book of bits, a glimpse, a peek, a taste of what is there. The main thing is to use the book as a starting point, to enjoy and discover for yourself places that are perhaps not so well known. Unlike the wilderness areas of the world, this area of the Peak and

Pennines is only a semi-wilderness. It's probably impossible to find a stretch of land where nobody has been and laid his hand and foot, but that's the attraction of the place.

Tribesmen walked here before History, Roman legions with their scribes and engineers, monks and packmen, coiners and pedlars, ranting Methody parsons, highwaymen and murderers, rebels and Luddites, Irish and Scots migrant workers, hand-loom weavers forced from their cottages by the new steam power, farm-hands tramping for work, listed soldiers and Jack Tars home from the wars, lead miners and quarrymen, lurking criminals and choking millworkers sucking the free, clean air into their lungs; all these made their way across these moors and dales and wherever you walk, from the blunt nabs of the Roaches to the limestone above Tideswell, from the gritstone of Kinder to the sour peat bogs of Haworth Moor, you walk on the bones and shadows of the past and if you listen carefully enough you can hear the echoes of their voices still singing in the wind.

Carved stone heads dating from Saxon times, in Bakewell church

[7]

Eddie on the ridge of Chrome Hill

The White Peak

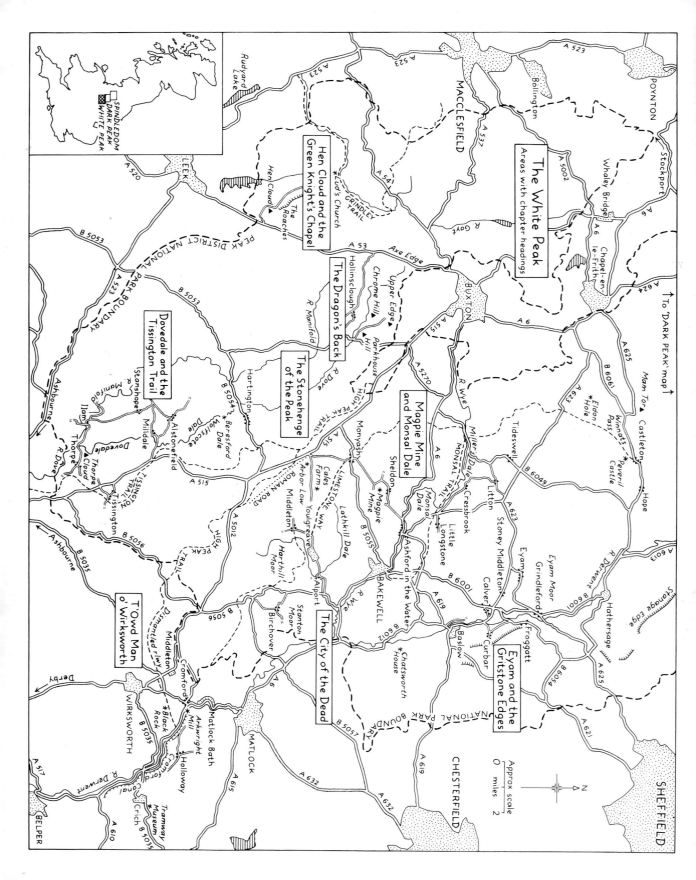

The Bones of the North – a prologue

Mark these rounded slopes
With their surface fragrance of thyme and beneath
A secret system of caves and conduits: hear these springs
That spurt out everywhere with a chuckle
Each filling a private pool for its fish and carving
Its own little ravine whose cliffs entertain
The butterfly and the lizard

W.H. Auden: 'In Praise of Limestone'

THE WHITE PEAK IS limestone country, a well-drained tableland with deep valleys scored into its face. Its grass is sweet and its caves are deep and since he first walked on its soil, man has hacked and rived at it, leaving his monuments behind in his lows and henges and earthworks, and now, in these most greedy and destructive of times, the scars of quarrying blight the land. Two things, it is said, could be seen from the moon as signs of the hand of man on the face of the Earth, one was the Great Wall of China, the other, the biggest of the Derbyshire limestone quarries.

The limestone extends southwards from Buxton, rolls out into the east and south, disappearing before Derby; while in the west, it gives way to gritstone just before the Roaches; there the rocks stand like a frozen wave that has rolled half across the country, to halt shuddering above the Cheshire plain. But from the shales of the Great Ridge to the Staffordshire grits, the country is limestone, the whitened bones of the world. Wild Bill Whalley, the geography teacher at my school, told us in one lesson how the bones of countless sea creatures in the warm primeval seas sank and were piled miles deep through the millennia, then crushed under incredible pressures until they became solid rock. 'Just as,' said Bill, 'when you crush a snowball in your hand all those little flakes turn to solid ice.'

Where the heat metamorphosed it, the rock became marble, coloured with the strains of metal, traces of cobalt, iron, copper, manganese. Elsewhere the bones lay sunk in slabs a mile thick. Then the rains came, scalding hot, a chemical soup of dissolved acids that sizzled across the stone and gouged out ginnels and runnels and

[11]

groins, and formed maggot-rivers that nibbled and burrowed their way inside, gnawing at the rock like a canker, hollowing it out into great holes and caverns.

When the ice came it stripped the land and gouged out valleys. Over and again it ebbed and flowed, a solid sea, with mammoth and sabre-toothed tiger and the first upright men coming and going with the wash of the ice. And forty to fifty thousand years ago, as it ebbed and flowed for the last two or so times, in the survivable interglacials when the ice sheets had drawn back from the land, the first people lit their fires in the magnesian limestone caves of Creswell, mated, gave

Derbyshire 'screws': crinoids in the limestone

birth and died, left behind the bones and pins that they had offered to their gods and melted away like the ice.

We'll never know, in spite of all the carbon dating and spectrum analysis, exactly what happened here, any more than we know with any certainty what happened at Watergate or in the General Strike. Once it's Yesterday we need to try to measure and fix it, but it's like trying to fill a sandy hole on the beach with water. So we guess and surmise and imagine and try and draw close to the truth.

The Peak District is the name properly given to that area south of Kinder, north of Wirksworth. According to the *Oxford English Dictionary*, 'Peaclond' appears first in AD 924 and is the name of the district where Peveril had his stronghold. But why 'Peak', since there isn't a hill of any note between Castleton and Wirksworth? Rather the land is a limestone plateau, with deep valleys gouged into it. Some suggest that Peak is a corruption of 'Puck' which, like 'Pixie', is thought to be a corruption of Pict. In Irish Gaelic the word for spirit or ghost is 'Pooka'. Perhaps the Celtic newcomers to the area, seeing the small dark people who fled before them thought of them as spirit people, what we would call fairies. Thus we have the legends of children stolen by fairies, fairy forts or circles and little people coming from the woods or from below the ground to steal and make mischief.

It became part of the lore of the folk that the only protection against the little people was iron; one reason for this could be that the people driven west by the invaders had no iron, only stone and flints and they therefore feared the metal. Within living memory in some country districts, flint arrow-heads were called 'elf-bolts' and iron was placed on milk churns to prevent the fairies from interfering with the butter coming. Horseshoes were nailed above doors and horseshoe nails were also thought lucky; a sure way to break a 'witch's' power was to boil these nails in her urine. Thus smith and smithy, iron and horse became symbols of the 'luck' and power of the Celts and, even today, belief in the horseshoe's power lingers on.

Typical limestone landscape: a pattern of walls near Youlgreave

Peveril Castle near Castleton: a ruined Norman castle set on rocky limestone

So, there you go, a hill country with no hills or a country inhabited by a people called Peacs or Picts. You pays your money and you takes your choice, and as my kids used to say, 'Don't ask him any more questions for God's sake, he's a mine of useless information.'

The White Peak is fine walking country, well-drained uplands and pleasant, wooded dales and its stoney acres are home to the lime-loving wildflowers, thyme, speedwell, tormentil, herb Robert and saxifrage. It is almost too good a country and the danger is that we might kill it by loving it too much. Getting there by train and bus is difficult but not impossible and if more of us left our cars and walked, then the honeypot-type pressure on the place might be just that bit less.

The caves of the White Peak are well worth a visit, Peak Cavern in Castleton in particular is an immense hole stretching back into the hill on which stands Peveril Castle. I've sat amongst six hundred people and seen concerts and audio-visual displays in there, complete with pie and peas supper. Castleton lies just under the Greek Ridge which divides the White Peak from the Dark Peak.

People lived in the cave from the earliest times and Celia Fiennes, arriving there on her tour found 'several poor little houses in it built of stone and thatch'd like little Styes . . . now none but poor people live there which makes some small advantage by begging and by lighting the strangers into the Cave.' The cave was used by ropemakers, their ropewalk having been in use until recently, but like Treak Cliff, Blue John and Speedwell, it is now just a show cave. Though there is no way through, water-dye tests have shown that it connects with the massive pot of Eldon Hole, above on the limestone beyond Winnats, and a local legend tells of a woman losing a goose down Eldon Hole that, two months later, came wadding out of Peak Cavern, its feathers singed by the fires of Hell. Blue John – a purplish fluorospar whose name is said to be a corruption of the French *bleu et jaune* because of its two main colours – is still mined here and some good examples of fine local craftsmanship can be seen in the jewellery,

ornaments and inlaid table tops for sale around the village of Castleton.

The Peak Park was the first of Britain's National Parks. Formed in 1951, it struggles to maintain a balance between local and national needs with less money per year than is spent on creating five miles of motorway. Pressure of visitors on the Peak is enormous; within easy reach of Manchester, Birmingham, Sheffield and Derby it takes a tremendous hammering, with up to twenty million visitors a year and most of them coming by car. It is the lungs and playground of four major cities and, at the same time, it is the workplace of the farmers and quarrymen of the Peak.

Turning it over to tourism would destroy the very thing that people come to see, yet much of the farming is marginal and only sustainable by grant aid. Now the grants may be going and the farmers may be forced off the land. If we want the landscape preserved then we must be prepared to pay for it. Grants should be available to keep upland farmers in business, as farmers and conservationists; they could preserve traditional hay meadows, maintain drystone walls and reduce stocks so that moorland heather regenerates after over-grazing. There are many things that could be done but the political will doesn't seem to be there. Brussels spends millions maintaining butter and beef mountains and wine and milk lakes, yet doesn't seem to want to spend on real mountains and lakes and the people who live amongst them and maintain them.

Matlock and Bakewell, Buxton and Hathersage are good jumping off points for most of the White Peak and providing you don't go in high season you should be able to find reasonable places to stay in the area that don't cost an arm and a leg, although English hotels with their boring 'British Breakfast' and 'Meat and Two Veg' dinners do seem to delight in charging prices for a night's kip and food that would buy you a week's holiday on one of the Greek islands. There are Youth Hostels, camping barns and bunkhouse barns and, of course, many good camp sites too; and for those hardy enough, plenty of good bivvy sites.

Dovedale and the Tissington Trail

Was you ever in Dovedale? I assure you there are things in Derbyshire as noble as in Greece or Switzerland.

Lord Byron

Izaak Walton's *Compleat Angler*, apart from being one of the first books ever written on fishing, is also one of the first books ever written about this area, and if people know little else, they know that it was at Dovedale and the home of James Cotton that Walton first experienced the joy of the angle. Though millions of feet have followed the paths that Piscator and Viator travelled, and though those same paths are largely artificial now with hard-core and duckboards along much of the trail to Milldale, the dale is hardly changed since that time when the two proponents of 'the angle' sat discussing the best way to tie a fly and the many ways to cook a fish.

Dovedale is such a gentle meandering dale now that it is difficult to imagine the forces that went into its making, but the isolated fangs of Ilam Rock and Pickering Tor and the cliffs above the Natural Arch give some indication of the way the dale has been gouged out of the Earth. For the stone of this area is great Reef limestone, formed when a coral reef in the hot lagoons of those primeval seas froze into stone, and the 'peaks' of Bunster Hill and Thorpe Cloud, and further north the humps of Parkhouse Hill and Chrome Hill, are knuckles of that reef. The dale has some of the oldest woodlands in the Peak and is a grade one Site of Special Scientific Interest because of its ash woods. For much of its length, Dovedale is now in the hands of the National Trust and although it suffers tremendously at its southern end from

being greatly over-visited (more than 3,000 people walk its paths in each direction *every hour* on a busy weekend day in summer), few people venture much above the stepping stones or Milldale. If you're lucky enough to be able to go out of season, on a weekday, particularly in winter, you'll often find it relatively quiet.

There is some argument concerning the name Dovedale, which most scholars feel is derived from the Celtic *dubh* or *dobh* meaning 'dark', but the dale, even under its high cliffs is hardly dark, and when it was less wooded the white limestone would have made it a much lighter place. In any case, the River Dove rises on Axe Edge where it certainly is not dark, and has that name for forty-five miles. My guess is that Dove is derived from the same root as Derwent and Dee and comes from the name of the Celtic river goddess Deva. It seems about as sensible as anything else I've heard but I wait to be shot down in flames.

On a bright May morning long ago, I walked the footpath beneath Thorpe Cloud which, with Bunster Hill, forms what William Adam, the Victorian writer on Derbyshire, called 'the massive portals of the Dale', and walked what was then an unmade footpath to the stepping stones. It was so early that, as yet, there was no one else in the dale, and by the stepping stones, obviously taking advantage of the peace

The stepping stones over the River Dove, Dovedale

was a heron, one of my favourite of all birds, mooching in the shallows. As I disturbed it, it half ran, half flew, looking comic and clumsy on the water's edge until, with enough lift, it took to the air. Then the true grace of the bird showed and with slow, long wing strokes, it moved sweetly along the surface of the river and rose curving above the new green of the trees until it was lost to sight.

Much of the river's length runs over weirs which were constructed as trout pools in the last century since, in very dry summers, the Dove becomes the laziest of babbles. The stepping stones were built for Victorian day-trippers who delighted in the natural rock formations in the dale, to which they gave names such as The Twelve Apostles, Jacob's Ladder, Tissington Spires, Pickering Tor and Reynard's Cave. The most impressive rock formations at the lower end of the dale are the Natural Arch and Ilam Rock. The rock is a formidable stone tooth, isolated and rising a hundred feet above the small footbridge. A woman once remarked to a National Park officer that she'd looked all over Dovedale but hadn't been able to find 'the eleven a.m. rock'.

The Arch, across the river from the rock and just in front of Reynard's Cave, is a curved limestone bow some forty feet in span, and both arch and cave are probably all that are left of a massive river-worn hollow gouged out by glacial melt over aeons. It is best seen from the mouth of the cave which, according to local legend, was at one time the haunt of foxes, though like all good places it doesn't just saddle itself with the one legend. Another tale has it that the cave was the home of a robber called Reynard. It is equally likely that the cave has some connection with the legend of Reynardine, the shape-changer who, in the form of a handsome young man, ensnares the heart of a beautiful young woman. As he is leading her over the mountains to his 'home', she notices his eyes and teeth strangely shining – by which time of course it is too late and he has turned back into a fox. The legend has affinity with the were-wolf legends of Eastern Europe and at nursery level with Red Riding Hood. A lovely

Ilam Rock, Dovedale

The old packhorse bridge in Milldale, called either Wheelbarrow Bridge or Viator's Bridge

English folk-song tells the story of Reynardine far better than ever I could.

Oh his hair was black as the night sky
His teeth so bright did shine
And she followed him over the mountains
That bold young Reynardine.

On a more prosaic note, a woman called Annie Brassington, who died aged eighty-one in 1950, used to travel from Milldale every day

Poppies at Alstonefield

carrying two baskets of sweets, mineral waters and postcards to Reynard's Cave where she would set up a stall at the foot of the steep climb. She fixed a rope along the 150-feet slippery slope to the cave and charged people a penny to haul themselves up.

I followed the path from the cave and down to the river where it curves beneath the massive arched caves of Dove Holes and on to the hamlet of Milldale. The old packhorse bridge at Milldale, called variously Wheelbarrow Bridge and Viator's Bridge after the character in *The Compleat Angler*, is slender indeed, but a bit wider than the 'scarce three fingers' suggested by Izaak Walton. According to the book, when Viator came to this bridge he crawled over it on hands and knees. It has parapets now, which weren't there during packhorse days when they would have got in the way of the panniers but, even so, it could hardly have been dangerous. Milldale is a tidy hamlet with a shop and a telephone and seats and a tribe of very aggressive ducks. From Milldale I followed the path to Alstonefield for a pub lunch and then ambled back to Ilam where I spent a good hour looking at the village and the church.

Ilam village was originally part of the Burton-on-Trent Abbey estates until Henry VIII stole it and gave it to one of his followers. In the nineteenth century, it was bought by a businessman called Jesse Watts Russell who knocked down the village because it spoilt his view and rebuilt it in alpine style further from the hall. He built a family mausoleum, a new school and vicarage, and renovated the church. Now the hall is a Youth Hostel and the estate is owned by the National Trust. The riverside walks are lovely and the church has a beautiful Saxon font and crosses as well as the tomb of St Bertram who lived as a hermit in a cave above Ilam after his wife and child were killed by wolves. It's a quiet village with no shop and no pub although, in season, the tea-room in the hall is open.

I walked the length of Dovedale one summer with Eddie, an old friend from Dentdale; he is our village shopkeeper, disc jockey,

Evening light on the bridge at Ilam, and the River Manifold

cricket team captain and head philosopher. It was a warm, soft morning with the first murmurings of summer's end in the air, and we'd planned to walk the complete round following the Dove to just below Hartington where we would turn and come back by the Tissington Trail; not a hard day, no climbing, just a lengthy ramble.

The footpath from Thorpe Cloud to the stepping stones was busy but people were thinning out by Ilam Rock and by the time we reached Wolfscote Dale we had the place much to ourselves. Wolfscote has nothing to do with Reynardine. The name simply means 'the dale of the cottage of Wulfstan', one of the Norsemen who settled here long years ago and who has left behind nothing but his name.

Wolfscote Dale opens out after the narrow straits of middle Dovedale; it has high overhanging limestone bluffs and the river runs lackadaisically, peopled with ducks and fringed by trees thick with squirrels. The ducks have become so used to walkers that they'll come and take bread from your hand, although on the day Eddie and I walked through the dale, we had no bread and gave them chocolate instead, which is probably bad for them.

At its head, Wolfscote Dale opens out into broad meadows, flanked by spinneys of broadleafed trees and as we walked we saw ahead of us

Stone font, Ilam church

unheard of in the area now and the golden eagle, once found in some parts of the White Peak is now only to be found much further north. The path through Beresford Dale threads its way by fishing weirs and moss-draped cliffs. It is dark and wooded and its pools at one time

a group of people with a Jack Russell terrier walking along the river bank. Without any warning, there was a sudden explosion of noise and fur, the dog let out a howl, jumped three feet in the air and set off like a little, fat, brown-and-white, short-legged bullet along the bank. Inches ahead of it was a very frightened grey squirrel. The squirrel turned and dived into the water, and swam desperately across the river to the trees on the far side. It scrambled rapidly up the bank and climbed a tree vanishing from sight, leaving a quizzical dog on the other side of the river, his head cocked, his ears expressing his confusion.

'He can't swim,' said his owner in explanation as we passed.

'If you ask the squirrel nicely, it might teach him,' said Eddie, leaving behind a group of puzzled people who didn't know whether to shout things or look around for something to throw at us.

Beyond Wolfscote is Beresford Dale which means 'the dale of the beaver's ford', although beavers, like many other precious and lovely things, went from England long ago. Otters are almost contained the best fishing for miles around. On the far bank, hidden in a spinney, is the fishing house of Charles Cotton which is not open to the public. Cotton was the Squire of Beresford and a poet.

> O, my beloved nymph, fair Dove,
> Princess of rivers, how I love
> Upon thy flowery banks to lie,
> And view thy silvery stream
> When gilded by the summer's beam:
> And in it all thy wanton fry,
> Playing at liberty!

Together with Izaak Walton, he developed the craft of angling with the rod, fly and line and the two men could be said to have been the first philosophers of the angle.

(As an aside and another piece of useless information, there is a very beautiful stained glass window in Winchester Cathedral celebrating Izaak Walton and a host of other fisherman-saints, erected at the expense of Victorian anglers. One of the panels depicts Walton seated in Dovedale beneath its limestone cliffs.)

I spent much of my childhood fishing for roach, perch and gudgeon, old wellies and bicycle frames on the mill lodges and canals of Lancashire and can well understand the fishing bug. I would be out for hours in those days when parents didn't have to worry about children out alone and would wander home with the night, whistling up our street, having drowned a pint of maggots and had a handful of bites, but happy, supremely happy. Since then I've fished for trout and salmon but only for the pot since I can't understand the idea of killing anything for sport, and if I had to rely on my skill as a piscator I'd have been a vegetarian long ago. I did hear one funny fishing story a number of years ago, however, sworn to be 'true as he was standing there', by a rare old friend.

A party of senior fishermen from Manchester had gone fishing in a

boat on Rudyard Lake, taking with them a crate of ale and some sandwiches. One of them, having eaten his snap, took out his false teeth to wash them in the water. As he leaned over the boat, the teeth slipped from his grasp and spiralled down into the peaty deeps of the lake. You can imagine with what sympathy and understanding his misfortune was met. When his mates had picked themselves up from the bottom of the boat and dried their eyes, they carried on fishing, hiccuping now and then and shaking their heads with sympathy as the tragedy passed once again before their minds' eyes. One wag, who himself had shares in Sterodent, took out his own top set and, unseen by the rest of the crew and in particular by the exceedingly glum person in the stern, fastened them to his line, and lowered them gently into the depths.

'Fish on!' he shouted, as a warning to the others to watch their lines, and very carefully he wound in the teeth, now realistically covered with a frond of duckweed. The fangless angler took the dentures from the hook while the rest of the boat cooed in amazement. Expectant silence gripped them all as the teeth went in. He sucked them for a while, thoughtfully, took them out, looked at them, tried them again, then with a snort pulled them out and slung them across the lake where they plopped and sank, watched by puzzled pike and finny roach no doubt.

'They're not mine,' he said, and went on fishing.

That night in the pub, two gummy piscators sucked their potato crisps, staring into the fire as people all round them found bones in their beer and wiped their eyes on their sleeves.

At the head of Beresford Dale the country opens out into woods and farmland. Eddie and I cut across country, following the path under Pennilow, through to the dry valley of Dalehead and by field paths and stiles to the Tissington Trail. The Trail follows the line of an old disused railway and is easy walking along what has become an ecological corridor. At the height of summer, it is almost choked with flowers and herbs because nitrates and weedkillers were never used on the embankments and cuttings. The Peak District National Park have done a very good job with their footpaths and most of them are clear and defined and not over waymarked (too many yellow arrows and posts and information boards can turn a ramble into a guided tour). In particular, they've successfully negotiated with land-owners and business interests to turn disused railway lines into cycling and walking routes. The Monsal Trail, the High Peak Trail, the Manifold Way and the Tissington Trail all use old permanent ways for most of their length and it's a shame that some of the other National Parks don't follow suit.

For short walks and long cycle rides, or even for longer walks linking villages and dale, the Trail is fine, but at the end of a long day, five miles of it can become a monotonous plod. Light was failing at the close of a hot and windless afternoon, and the road, as Tolkien says, went ever on and

The Tissington Trail

landmarks that should have been miles behind us were still way ahead; feet were hot and tongues were cracked and the arid stone trail ran far into the distance like something Dante would have conjured up for trespassers in his triple-circled Hell. Eddie began to mutter about mugging passing cyclists for their bikes. It was all I could do to restrain him.

It is at such moments that I begin to understand Einstein's Theory of Relativity and how it applies to Time and Space – we seemed to be spending a lot of time getting nowhere. Eventually we made a quantum leap and crossed the fields to the road to Thorpe where we'd left the car. There we had a pint that didn't even touch the sides. It had been a great walk, but on a hot dusty day it's a long one and I seriously consider that the Peak National Park should build

oases along the Tissington Trail or at least have St Bernard dogs padding up and down the track with large barrels of Marston's Pedigree round their necks.

T'Owd Man o' Wirksworth

Every rural sound is sunk in the clamour of cotton works; and the simple peasant . . . is changed into the impudent mechanic.

John Byng, eighteenth-century traveller writing on Cromford Mill

B ECAUSE IT LIES JUST OUTSIDE the National Park, the area below Matlock Bath is often missed by walkers and that is a pity; because, although it doesn't offer the isolation of the northern peak and the hard walking of the gritstone moors, if you're interested in history, you can get a different kind of fulfilment wandering from village to village looking at the archaeological and industrial remains. The handful of miles you can cover in the round trip from Cromford to Wirksworth and back is an example of what I mean.

Cromford has some claim to have been in at the birth pangs of the Industrial Revolution because it was here that Sir Richard Arkwright built his first mill and created the world's first cotton town. Much of the old mill is intact and is being repaired slowly and painfully by the Arkwright Society with whatever funding they can get, although the later, red-brick Masson Mill, built like a castle to repel the machine wreckers – notice there are no breakable windows at floor level – is more familiar to drivers who pass it on the road.

Cromford is a fascinating village with a good pub, a good bookshop, a village pond and a waterwheel. A road called the Via Gellia ends here. For years I thought that this road, which goes west and up into the limestone plateau, was, because of its name, a Roman road. It is in fact a mineral way built by a quarry owner called Gell

who obviously wished posterity to see him as some kind of patrician nobleman. In the other direction, out of Cromford, going south-east, an easy road walk takes you to Crich and the tram museum where there are trams of all shapes and sizes and colours. On the way to Crich, the road passes Holloway where Lea Hurst was once the home of Florence Nightingale, the lady who held candles under soldiers' armpits to revive them, while Lea, half a mile to the north was the home of Alison Uttley the writer of *The Country Child* and *Little Grey Rabbit*.

So Cromford can be the beginning of any number of excursions and explorations, although it's doubtful that Cromford would have existed as anything other than a huddle of houses if it weren't for a fat man from Preston. Richard Arkwright, described by one writer as 'a bag-cheeked, pot-bellied Lancashire man' came to Crompton in 1771 to build his mill away from the spying eyes of competitors and the wrecking hammers of frame-breakers.

It was the secrecy of the place and the River Derwent with its powerful constant flow that brought him there; that and the fact that there was plenty of cheap labour to be had because of the slump in the lead industry. He built a model village and by the standards of the time is reckoned to have been a benevolent man, although Peel's

Committee of 1816, set up to enquire into the state of health of children employed in the cotton industry, did hear a report from Arkwright's son which admitted that the children 'mostly of seven to thirteen years' had become deformed from working long hours at the low-placed spinning frames. Arkwright's workers were largely pauper families shipped in bulk to Cromford and, although they were housed well, they were bound to the mill which worked twenty-four hours a day and which paid its adult workers fourpence for a twelve-hour shift while, at the same time, Arkwright spent £20,000 purchasing an estate above the mill. By his death, he would boast that his personal fortune could liquidate the National Debt. Not bad for a man who had once been a semi-literate barber and wigmaker, the thirteenth child of a poor Preston family.

On a ragged October morning with brassy leaves and sooty rooks being scrubbed all over the sky by a wind that never let up all day, my wife Pat and I left Cromford past the pond and the trundling waterwheel of what once was a mill but is now a basket warehouse, and followed the road out of the village along the valley bottom. The valley, once beautiful and peaceful, is now busy with thunderous lorries shipping the limestone of the Peak out by the forty-ton load.

Tram Museum at Crich

A few yards out of the village, we took a footpath across a mill stream and into the woods. It was good to be away from the busy highway, and the noise of the traffic diminished as we followed the damp and tangled path between trees that were just beginning to turn with the year. Below the path, to our right, we noticed a deserted mill with a ruined and mossy church font in the overgrown garden, and we stopped for a few moments to look around. There was, about that old stone mill, falling to ruin in a damp and mossy wood, a strong feeling of death and decay, 'ineluctable mutability' as James Joyce called it, made even stronger by the strange font, abandoned miles from any church and full of weeds.

From the mill, the path climbed through a clump of beeches and followed a lovely narrow, walled packhorse lane to Middleton. As we walked through the village, the last of the gardeners were out creosoting fences, tying up the roses, giving the lawns a final barbering and doing other odd bits and bobs, before oiling the shears and the mower and putting them away for the winter. The pale golden light of late autumn lay on the land as we crossed the fields, and a couple walking hand in hand passed with a 'hello' and became two dots on the skyline behind us.

At Middleton Top, the winding-house was open and we went in to

Cromford's mill pond in the spring

The winding wheel at Middleton Top winding-house

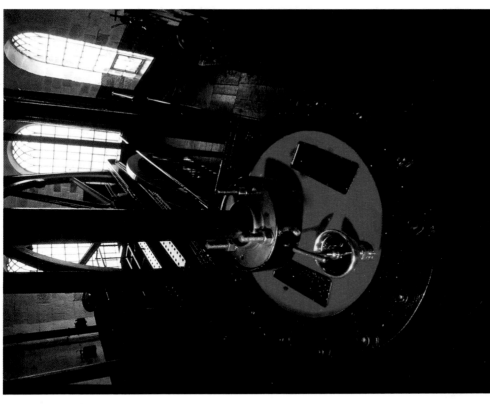

Machinery in the winding house at Middleton Top

look at the beam engine and its massive wheel with all its brass and huge steel piston rods, its red paint and glinting gun-metal. The engine was used to haul the wagons of the Cromford and High Peak Railway up the fierce incline from the Cromford Canal below. As you stand beneath the great wheel, you can see the window that the engine-man looked out of to check if the train was coupled on the cable, and the brass-notched disc that turned with the cable to tell him just how far the train had come. It's a wonderful engine, beautifully preserved.

Originally there had been plans to build a canal along this route, linking the Cromford Canal with the Peak Forest Canal at Whaley Bridge, but because the limestone of the plateau would have made finding water a near impossibility, and because the undulating landscape would have meant constructing more locks and aqueducts per linear mile than any other canal in the country, the proposers decided instead to construct one of the new railways that were becoming popular at the time.

The line was built on canal principles, using ropes to haul the trains up the savage inclines instead of a series of locks, and it served that purpose from 1830 until 1967 when it was closed. At Sheep Pasture, the lowest part of the incline, there was a 'catchpit' to prevent runaways; it was built after the near-disaster of 1888 when two wagons broke away from the haul and shot off down the 1,320 yards of the incline, gathering speed with every yard. They hit the bottom with a thundering crack and left the rails, clearing the canal and the main Manchester railway line before landing harmlessly in a field. After the closure of the line, the Peak Park, in partnership with Derbyshire County Council, bought the line and turned it into a long-distance footpath and cycle route. It's a really good walking route through delightful country and there are various cycle hire-points too, Middleton Top winding-house being one.

From Middleton Top, we walked down the road to Wirksworth to

The 'king and queen' carving in Wirksworth church, and (right) 'T'Owd Man'

get some lunch. Wirksworth was once the centre of Derbyshire's lead-mining industry and still has an ancient Barmote lead-mine court. It also has one of my favourite Peakland churches, a wonderfully quiet, still pool in the heart of a busy place. Its delights include an Anglo-Saxon sarcophagus lid, a 'king and queen' carved on a stone plaque above a door in the western wall and, my favourite, a carving of an Anglo-Saxon lead miner complete with tools and butty box on his way to work. Local people call him 'T'Owd Man' – the Old Man – and he's said to represent the ghost or spirit of the mine.

The mythology of mines and mining is fascinating. Probably because it meant descending into the Earth Mother and therefore violating her, miners were held in awe, and treated with a respect bordering on fear, from the earliest times. In some societies, they are still seen as almost a race apart. In Zanskar and Ladakh, and amongst the Pueblo Native Americans of Arizona, mining is seen as an affront to the spirits of the Earth. Perhaps because of this, a body of lore has grown up around miners and the underground world.

In Derbyshire, noises heard in the levels and workings were said to

Black Rock, above Dimons Dale

be caused by 'T'Owd Man' and in the north-east of England within the last ten years, miners were still telling stories of a mythical figure called the Big Hewer who could bite a wagonload of coal from the pit face and spit it into the wagons. So the little Saxon plaque up on the church wall has, for as long as anyone can remember, simply been known as 'T'Owd Man'. Another ancient custom takes place every year in Wirksworth: the people of the village join hands to form a ring around their church in what they call 'Clipping the Church'. I'm sure there must be echoes there of rites that go back to maypoles, standing stones, stone circles and beyond.

We wandered round the streets of the village for a while before walking back via the road to the High Peak Trail and following it through the afternoon sun to the tea-rooms at Steeplehouse Station which was doing screaming business and where, even though it was late October, people were sitting outside in the sun with their tea.

Beyond the old station there are relics of steam days, water troughs and cable runs overgrown and full of weed. We dawdled on, coming a few hundred yards further to Black Rock, a massive outcrop that looms above the trail and the woods of Dimons Dale (the name Dimons perhaps meaning demons as it does at Demon's Dell in Monsal Dale?). There were baby crag-rats swarming all over Black Rock, worming their way up on finger- and toe-holds, hanging off on ropes and abseiling down. Their average age must have been twelve and there were dozens of them with their instructors, all fastened together with ropes and, with their red helmets and spandex tights, they looked like a lot of dayglo caterpillars caught in a spider's web.

We dropped down towards Cromford and saw, through the late afternoon light, Arkwright's mansion high above the woods, looking down on his mill, canal and factory snuggled in amongst the trees. The incline enters a steep wooded cutting just above the canal: the path was mossy and the tunnel of trees had more than a hint of the rusts and bronzes of autumn in their leaves. We passed the spot where the runaway wagon had shot through the air and we crossed the water more sedately at the bridge by the old pumping house that drew water up from the Derwent to the Cromford canal. The steam engine that drove the pump is still operational and is fired up in the high season, and on special days when the volunteers who run it can get the coal. We followed the canal towpath back to the mill, the last of the afternoon sun catching in the high trees of the opposite bank, and by the time we reached Cromford the sun was gone and the western sky was shot through with blood-red and magenta as the last of the day's walkers made their way back home.

The City of the Dead

I will consider the outnumbering dead:
For they are husks of what was rich seed.
Now, should they come together to be fed,
They would outstrip the locusts' covering tide.

Arthur, Elaine, Mordred; they are all gone
Among the raftered galleries of bone,
By the long barrows of Logres they are made one,
And over the city stands the pinnacled corn.

Geoffrey Hill: 'Merlin'

THE AREA AROUND Stanton Moor and Birchover is one of the most magical places in all England. There is an air of mystery and timelessness about the place, a sense of air and light on the moor, of something shining and vibrating; and deep in the woods near the Nine Ladies stone circle, where moss-hung massive boulders lie amongst silver birch and fern, there is the feeling of something very, very old.

I first came to Stanton Moor when I was on tour and, being based in Derby for four days, had time, during the day, to get into the surrounding hills. With a friend, I drove out of Matlock and, parking the car above Birchover, walked by the weathered gritstone hulk of the Cork Stone to the moor. The Cork Stone is a natural outcrop and stands alone on the moor's edge with footholds cut into it and iron hoops to help you climb to the top. Now it's regarded as a bit of an oddity, a curiosity, something you climb up to have your photograph taken. But it has a much more noble past. At one time, historians believe, it was the centre stone of a larger stone circle, perhaps the largest circle on the moor, and was surrounded by other smaller monoliths. When the nearby quarry was opened, the stones were smashed and carted away and only the central stone, too big for the tools of the time, remains. (I'm puzzled by the name Cork; could it be a corruption of an older word? 'Cock' stone, perhaps? It certainly looks nothing like a cork.)

It was very early in the spring and snow still covered much of the countryside around as we walked the footpath by the numerous cairns. The moor was deserted and the King's Stone and Nine Ladies stood in the last of the winter snows. The Nine Ladies were turned to stone, of course, for dancing on the Sabbath, and the King's Stone is the fiddler who was playing for them. The Nine Maidens and Nine

The Reform Tower, built in 1832 as a tribute to Earl Grey

Ladies stone circles here in Derbyshire, Long Meg and Her Daughters in Cumbria and the stones of Stanton Drew in Somerset are all of a similar nature in that legend depicts them as people turned to stone, often after a wedding, for dancing on a Sunday – a nice way of Christianising a pagan sacred site and condemning dancing and music and merrymaking on the Sabbath at the same time. I only had a few hours to steal from the day but I made a mental note to return when I had more time.

A couple of years later, one morning towards the end of summer, Eddie and I left Stanton by the road and followed it south out of the village until we came to the footpath marked 'Stanton Moor by the Stone Circle'. It was a warm, cloudless but hazy morning, with the first hint of autumn in the soft air, winter waiting in the wings and in a hurry to yellow the leaves and strip the land bare. I assured Eddie I knew the way to the circle and that we didn't need to use the map. Oh folly, folly! We followed the pathway by the woods with, just visible far to our left, the tip of the old Reform Tower. The tower is a 'modern' multilith constructed in 1832 as a tribute to Earl Grey for carrying the Reform Bill through Parliament and for making such nice tea.

I decided that we should leave the main path and branch off into the woods, since I remembered the Nine Ladies as being surrounded by trees. We were soon completely lost, my fault entirely. Had we stayed on the path it would have led us straight to the stone circle, but I thought we could come on it through the trees. We wandered round for quite some time, although being lost had its advantages, for the narrow path we were following ran by vast deep holes where sandstone had been quarried lord only knows how long ago; these are now so overgrown, steep and mossy that it feels as though they've been there from the birth of forever. There is something about being in the heart of an old wood; a stillness and quietness surrounds you and the green breath of the forest is on your face. Light finds its way

The Nine Ladies stone circle

with difficulty to the forest floor and even then it is pale and tinged with green. Sit still long enough and you'll swear you can hear the forest breathing. We wobbled through bracken and over stones and under low branches for quite some time. I pretended that I was not actually lost but exploring, always a good ploy, but Eddie was not to be fooled.

'Piggin 'eck, Tommy, we've explored this rock three times now!' he pointed out correctly.

Eventually we scrambled our way back to the track and followed it to the stone circle. Some travellers ('bus people', a man we met walking his dog at the stones called them) had camped there that midsummer, and the ashes of their fires were evident in the heart of the circle. I've nothing against anybody camping or stopping near places like this, but they'd taken chain saws to some of the beautiful old silver birches to make their fires and that to me is sacrilege. Live and let live applies to trees as well as people. According to the man, one of their vans had backed into the King's Stone while reversing and had knocked it cockeyed.

'Two thousand years it's been there and they bugger it up in two seconds!'

The Nine Ladies and the King's Stone are aligned NNE to WSW which I would guess to be the sunrise and sunset of the winter solstice though that would be hard to check now because of the surrounding trees. When you go to the Nine Ladies, try to go when there are few people about, then sit for a while alone. It is a very, very special place.

The moor was bruised with heather, and a soft light moved across the land. All over the moor are the stone cairns and collapsed chambers, the grave mounds of the Bronze Age people that have turned the moor into a city of the dead. Half hidden in the heather, many of them are little more than gentle humps now and are hardly recognisable. The whole area is a true necropolis with five stone circles (only Nine Ladies being easily recognisable), and more than seventy cysts and burial mounds, many of which were used for multiple burials over a long period of time, this in an area not much more than 1200 yards by 600. Most of the burial mounds, which date from 2,200–1,400 BC, were found on

excavation to contain human remains and grave goods, indicating that the Bronze Age tribes that buried their dead and worshipped here believed, like the Egyptians of the Pharaohs, that the amber beads, bronze and flint daggers and richly decorated urns would accompany them into the afterlife. A local family, the Heathcotes of Birchover, began excavating some of the barrows in 1926 and urns and grave goods were taken to their private museum. Much of the collection has now gone to the City Museum in Sheffield.

Walking across the deserted moor is a tremendous experience. All around you are the stones and circles of this city of the ancient dead and above you a wide and open sky pulsing with life.

We walked down to Birchover where, behind the Druid Inn, stand Rowter Rocks (Rowter meaning 'Rough Tor') where the 150-feet high

The view from Robin Hood's Stride

outcrop has been carved into phantasmagorical shapes, popular myth attributing this to the work of Druids. Seats, steps, columns, tunnels and echoing chambers have all been cut out of the solid rock. It's a fascinating place but it can be a dangerous one too, the face drops away sheer, there are hidden holes and gullies and a school child fell to her death from the edge not long ago. There may be a connection with 'druids' here in that, like the rest of the area it was probably always 'holy' and of religious importance, but the rocks were actually carved out by local quarrymen on the instruction of the Reverend Thomas Eyre who, before he died in 1717 liked to sit in the specially carved out study composing his sermons. But, here again, legend intrudes, for the good parson is also said to have carried on the 'old religion' on the rocks and to have had dealings with Old Nick. It is also said that he constructed the chapel across the lane in atonement for his sins.

His chapel stands down the lane from the Druid Inn. It is a lovely building with Celtic heads incorporated into the porch and a stone dragon carved above the door that reminded me of the stone work on the wonderful church at Kilpeck in Herefordshire. Inside there are wood carvings and primitive paintings and the graveyard, apart from some interesting pieces of Norman stone, has two of the ugliest and most twee Victorian gravestones I've ever seen.

From Birchover, we walked by Rocking Stone Farm to the road and took the Limestone Way over Harthill Moor by Mock Beggar's Hall and the Nine Maidens stone circle. Mock Beggar's Hall, or Robin Hood's Stride, is a natural stone outcrop said to be where Robin Hood, in escaping from pursuers, jumped from stone to stone, although in fact it is more likely that the Robin Hood here is Robin Goodfellow, Jack in the Green, or, as he is also known, the

Carved steps on the Rowter Rocks

Green Man. Mock Beggar's Hall comes from the fact that from a distance and in some lights the stones look like the chimneys of a grand house and presumably beggars would be fooled into thinking that they'd get a warm welcome and a sup at what turned out to be a pile of stones. Begging was rife in earlier centuries as the enclosures of common lands forced poor cottagers onto the roads where begging was often their only means of survival.

On Harthill Moor, four standing stones are all that is left of the Nine Maidens, another unfortunate gang of Neolithic ravers who danced themselves rigid. The tallest stones in the Peak District, they stand not far from the Hermit's Cave under Cratcliff for, like Stanton Moor, Harthill is peppered with ancient remains. The Hermit's Cave, with its crucifix and bench-bed, stands by the Portway, an old Roman road that followed the line of what must have been a Neolithic track that goes on to Alport. Standing on Harthill Moor you are conscious again, as on Stanton Moor, of being in the centre of something very old and very important. For example, just north of Harthill Moor Farm, is the remains of an ancient fort which must have been quite sizeable and would have easily commanded this part of the Portway.

It was a lovely walk along the Limestone Way, through woods and meadowland to Youlgreave. I thought I had read somewhere that

The path to Mock Beggar's Hall, which is seen on the right of the skyline

The Nine Maidens stone circle on Harthill Moor

The Burne-Jones window in Youlgreave church

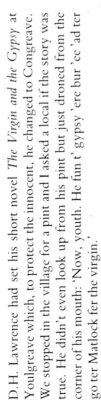

A knight's tomb in Youlgreave church

The little pilgrim, Youlgreave church

D.H. Lawrence had set his short novel *The Virgin and the Gypsy* at Youlgreave which, to protect the innocent, he changed to Congreave. We stopped in the village for a pint and I asked a local if the story was true. He didn't even look up from his pint but just droned from the corner of his mouth: 'Now, youth. He fun t' gypsy 'ere bur 'ee 'ad ter go ter Matlock fer the virgin.'

Before we left Youlgreave, we had a good look around the church. One of the loveliest churches in the Peak, it has a fine stained-glass window by Burne-Jones, a Celtic head, a little stone pilgrim carved in the wall and a wonderful alabaster tomb. The Cockayne tomb shows the dead knight resting, his hands closed in prayer, his head resting on a chicken, which is quite an amusing little pun on the family name.

We dropped back down to the River Bradford and followed it under the limestone bluffs to Alport where, the afternoon being well on and we being hot and thirsty, we queued behind some Cubs for two lollies at an ice cream van. They lasted us part of the way back by the road to Stanton where the pub, The Flying Childers, named after a favourite horse belonging to the Duke of Devonshire, looked open but was closed. We did however get to Matlock just as the pubs were opening and liked it so much that we stayed at the Station and County Hotel where, that night, we heard some very cool sixties rock and roll, which Eddie said was just his bag, 'Daddy O.'

[41]

An autumn evening near Youlgreave

The Stonehenge of the Peak

And see you the marks that show and fade,
Like shadows on the Downs?
O they are the lines the Flint Men made,
To guard their wondrous towns.

Trackway and Camp and City lost,
Salt marsh where now is corn –
Old wars old Peace, old Arts that cease,
And so was England born

Rudyard Kipling: 'Puck's Song'

IN THE COMIC BOOKS I read as a child, characters were always finding magic rings, or balls, or patches on the seat of their pants made from some old wizard's cloak which would zoom them out through space and time into exciting adventures. And, probably because of this, one of my greatest wishes, when I was very much younger, was that I could become a time-traveller like Jimmy and His Magic Patch, free to move through time and space – to mingle, perhaps, with the crowds in the bear-pit at Southwark watching the first performances of Shakespeare's plays, to march with the Roman legions along the wannie hills of Northumberland by Hadrian's Wall, or to travel back to the South America of Pizarro and Montezuma. But the fantasy-land I returned to time and again was the misty world of prehistoric man – the 'cave men' as we so ignorantly called them, because we thought anybody who lived in those dim pasts must have lived in caves and fought dinosaurs, armed with nothing but stone hammers. We didn't know then that, well before the coming of the Romans, British-Celtic civilisation had its own government, trade and art.

This fascination with pre-history was first fired off when I was seven or eight, by a school visit to Queen's Park Museum, then a scruffy little hall set in a park that held grimly onto a few acres of sooty, grass slopes above a poisoned industrial valley in north Manchester. There was a dug-out canoe and some flint arrow- and spear-heads in a glass case to which my hot little nose was applied like a snail's bum on an aquarium wall. There was another case, and within its glass world there lay a tiny model lake-village, said to represent the settlement that lived its life out in the swamps of the Irk Valley that now lay, poisoned by industrial filth, beneath the museum. Below the snail's bum of my nose, little model people tended fires, turned querns and skinned the catch of the hunt, while other little people paddled pea pod-sized canoes across a lake that was a real lake seen through the reverse telescope of Time.

Forty years on, I'm still fascinated by early man and, in particular, by the traces of his life in these Pennine uplands. The marks of his passing are everywhere and even a brief look at the Ordnance Survey map reveals pre-Roman settlements, burial cairns and chambered tombs, spattered in their thousands across the uplands and yet, although we have a reasonable idea, from classical writings, of life from Roman times onwards, much of the lives and ways of these first people remains a mystery. Every century has produced its theories, from Victorian romantic images of Druids with their golden sickles gathering mistletoe in the misty woods, to today's hi-tech, radio-active carbon dating, pollen analysis and electron spin resonance that can tell you not just what crops the earliest societies grew and when their hut timbers were first hammered into the earth, but what their last meals were and probably what the dog was called. But always, elusive and subtle, the true essence escapes. Only in the imagination, perhaps, through folk-lore and what anthropologists call the 'race memory', that great bulk of oral tradition, can we get close to understanding not just what happened here but to understanding more importantly that there are people here who have never left.

They came and sliced the turf from off
Dub Hill with surgeons' care, then peeled
it from the skull and laid bare brown,
clay, barrow rings, stone chambers, sunk
cyst walls. For months after, they came
and scraped and brushed and sliced and took
back shards and iron slag and yellow
brittle bone.

A field away Jack Sedgwick keeps
his yowes for tupping; Jack whose blood
first beat here in the barrow wrights
whose bones came from a mould laid down
when ice began to melt. Across
the field he watched them in the sun
dig up his people's grave beneath
the standing stones.

The author: 'Diggers'

Nowhere in the Pennines is the evidence of early man so densely found as in the area of limestone plateau to the north and west of Matlock Bath. Search the map of the White Peak and you will find, on the high dry lands where man first wandered and settled, the word 'low' in plenty. Sometimes it appears as a suffix, as in Ringham Low, Arbor Low, and the comically named High Low: at other sites, it appears as a word on its own as in Lowfield Farm, Low Wood and, simply, The Low. The upland plateau to the south of Monyash is peppered with them, Carder Low, Lean Low, Blake Low, End Low, Calling Low, Mining Low and Aleck Low.

'Low' itself comes from the Old English *hlaw* that has supplanted whatever Celtic name would have described these burial chambers, for the henge builders left little behind them save their henges and graves and the merest smear of their language. It is only in the names of some of the rivers, wells and hills that the old language has survived. 'Dove', as I have said before, possibly comes from Derva, the same river goddess who gave her name to the Cheshire and Yorkshire Dees, and perhaps 'Carder' as in Carder Low comes from the Celtic for 'castle', the same word that gave us Cader Idris, Carlisle and Caernarvon. For the rest, Anglo-Saxon and Danish and finally French as in Norman have smothered the tongue of the henge-

Arbor Low

builders over the centuries, language has been laid upon language, stone on stone, riddle on riddle.

Arbor Low (Arbor may come from the Anglo-Saxon *eordburh* meaning 'earth mound') is one of the most magical places in England, an impressive collapsed stone circle, its outer earthworks almost 300ft in diameter. Its great size and its position along major prehistoric trading routes, as well as its standing as the foci of so many other important lines, has caused it to be called 'The Stonehenge of the North', and as a henge it stands third in rank to Stonehenge and Avebury. All its stones are fallen now, and though no evidence of socket holes has been found that would prove once and for all that the stones were at one time upright, the Rev. Samuel Pegge, writing in 1783, quotes the words of a local man, William Normanshaw, who claimed to remember some of the stones being erect. He was fifty years old at the time, which would indicate that round about the mid eighteenth century the stones either fell or were pushed down. These 'orthostats', as the archaeologists call them, were dragged here a fair distance on wooden sledges or rollers. It surely isn't conceivable that millions of man hours were expended merely to drag a heap of stone half way across the plateau, only to leave them lying down.

I can just imagine the foreman of the hauling gang being asked what they were going to do with them now that they'd got them there.

'Oh, I think we'll leave them lying down, John.'

'Aren't we going to make them stand up, Silas?'

'No, they'd clash with the curtains.'

Had they (as most people now believe) been standing at one point, they could have been toppled by erosion and foul weather, but it is more than likely that they were pushed over. From the time of the first Christians, the standing stones and 'temples' of the old religion were purposefully destroyed. King Edwin of Northumbria (which then included this area) authorised Paulinus to destroy all 'altars and temples with the enclosures that are about them'. Ironically, until his

own conversion to 'the true faith', he had been one such worshipper himself. Whatever happened, the stones are now all lying, sprawled in a great circle in the grass, at its heart is another U-shaped arrangement of stones which may, as thought by some scholars, have been a symbolic entrance to the underworld. All of them are massive weathered blocks of limestone and the whole site is surrounded by a deep ditch and bank; if the stones were standing, to be here at a solstice would be a really powerful experience.

The last time I walked to Arbor Low, a group of people from the Rudolph Steiner Institute were sitting on the spring grass listening to their leader. He had such a broad German accent that I found what he was saying hard to follow. But I do think I heard him say that this is one of the most important archaeological and psychic sites in Britain. Stand here on a winter's day with the wind blowing rags of rooks all over the heavens as thick grey clouds are piling in out of the west, or sit here alone on a soft autumn evening as the sun is dropping behind the trees on the far edge of the plateau, and you'll find it does have a very special atmosphere.

On a chill day one early spring, with a razor-wind skimming the land and a hard blue sky above, I left Youlgreave and dropped down the hill to the path by the River Bradford which leads to Middleton. Here Bateman, the Barrow Knight, is buried. Famous as one of the first excavators of the burial mounds and tombs of the area, he had a habit of leaving a lead tag behind with his name stamped on it, a sort of 'Bateman Was Here' message to posterity. His grave in Middleton churchyard is surmounted by a copy of a Bronze Age funerary urn and is worth looking at. From Middleton I followed the road by Rake Wood and took a walled lane to Long Rake and then the road to Arbor Low. It's a shame that there isn't a footpath to the Low, but the Roman road that at one time ran to Gib Hill is now hidden, marked only by a long boundary fence: curiously, if you look at it on the map, it is the only long, totally straight fence in the area and you can trace it southwards for miles.

At Upper Oldham's Farm, a little boy ran out and took my admission fee and I walked across the fields to the henge. Each time I come on it, I feel a frisson of excitement; there is something here that even the cows and the fourteen cubs running after Akala round the ditch can't dispel. It is wonderful to sit here when everyone else has gone and to feel the special nature of the place, like a mist around you. I sat with my lunch, thinking on things of the past and then lay in what had become a warm sun for a while until some people with cameras arrived and, rather than get in the way, I walked over to Gib Hill which stands between Arbor Low and the old Roman road. Shaped like a miniature Silbury Hill, it was thought at one time to be a simple earth mound but Bateman, when he excavated it, found a Bronze Age burial, some important chieftain perhaps wishing to be buried near a magical site, just as we bury our dead now in churchyards.

I walked back to the road and followed the path by Cales Farm and One Ash Grange Farm, turning down to Lathkill Dale. One Ash Grange was originally a penitentiary for the monks of Roche Abbey (penitentiary not meaning prison, as in Alcatraz, but a place set aside for penitents to work off their sins). There is a camping barn there, one of the better ideas of the last few years: this has meant that a number of old barns for which there is no longer any agricultural use can be maintained and give a little bit of income to the farms that support them. Lathkill Dale is a National Nature Reserve and one of the most beautiful dales in the Peak but it wasn't always as quiet and untrammelled as it is now. For although industry has long departed, at one time the dale was busy with lead-mine shafts and workings and the main mine here had one of the largest waterwheels in the country, some 52ft in diameter. The river that springs from the cave at Lathkill Head is one of the clearest trout streams in the county with clear deep

Gib Hill, the tumulus at Arbor Low

pools and weirs and I followed it down to Alport where I took the lovely riverside path back to Youlgreave under the limestone cliff. It was a pull up the village street as the afternoon closed in and the only place open was the butchers where I got a pie and a carton of orange and as I sat on the wall eating my tea, I had a bit of a think about the henge.

To build such a monument as Arbor Low means that there must have been a long period of settlement in the northern uplands, equivalent to the period that produced the great henges of Woodhenge, Avebury and Stonehenge in the south. A powerful chieftain or chieftainess (the Celts were no chauvinists – remember Boudicca and her razor-blade hubcaps?) and a well entrenched aristocracy, as well as a stable, structured society, were necessary to release surplus man-

The River Lathkill in Lathkill Dale

Conksbury Bridge at the end of Lathkill Dale

Sunset over Youlgreave

power for the building of tombs and henges like Arbor Low. They took thousands of man-hours and must have been a fantastic drain on the local economy and yet, today, their use can really only be conjectured at. They were certainly aligned in such a way that they lay positional to the sun at the times of winter and summer solstice and to the cycles of the moon. (It is intriguing that the Egyptian temple of Abu Simmel, the Megalithic tomb at Newgrange, Co Meath in Eire, and the henges of the chalk and limestone uplands of Britain and Ireland were all aligned so that the sun at the summer solstice fell directly into their hearts.) For 'primitive' man to achieve such accuracy means that they were something other than the woad-painted savages we were taught about at school. Symbols, complex

Full moon over Arbor Low

calendars, mystical power houses, the first cathedrals – perhaps the henges were something of all of these, and they were built of stone rather than wood for two reasons.

First, stone will of course stand longer than any wooden henge but, more importantly, stone in itself has long been deemed to have magical qualities. Their use as sacred sites has, of course, long been forgotten by country people, but they have nevertheless always respected the stones and in many cases created stories to explain their significance. Stone has always been a highly respected material; England crowns her monarchs upon the Stone of Scone, Arthur drew Excalibur from the stone, the Church of Rome was founded on Peter's 'Rock' and today even the ruinous stones of henges, abbeys and churches draw people to them – why?

I mentioned in an earlier book a tentative thought I had (theory is too strong a word) that powerful emotions of fear, terror, even the ecstasy of religious fervour, perhaps generate energies that we have as yet no way of measuring, and that these energies could possibly be somehow stored in stone. Chartres Cathedral, Stonehenge, the great stone trough of Glencoe, and all the myriad ruins of the past, are tremendously powerful places to millions of people and create a great sense of something remote but powerful as you stand within their walls, so perhaps it is something that has soaked into the stone over the long march of the years, who knows? It's interesting that at all these powerful sites, the stone has a great quantity of quartz in it, and quartz, as any schoolboy knows, has electro-magnetic properties.

So that was what I thought about while sitting on the stone wall that day, eating my meat pie and drinking the E numbers and, before you laugh, remember that what you are reading now, though it originally came from my conscious and subconscious meanderings, first saw the light of day as a series of pulses and waves input and stored on a word processor using micro-chips, and what is a micro-chip but a minuscule sliver of silicon. In other words – stone.

Hen Cloud and the Green Knight's Chapel

For the head in his hand he held it up straight,
towards the fairest at table he twisted the face,
and it lifted up its eyelids and looked at them broadly,
and made such words with its mouth as may be recounted.
'See thou get ready Gawain, to go as thou vowedst,
and as faithfully seek till thou find me good sir,
as thou has promised in the presence of these knights.
To the Green Chapel go thou, and get thee, I charge thee'.

Sir Gawain and the Green Knight: Trans. J.R.R. Tolkien

THE LAST ROLLING WAVE of the gristone that was thrust up from the floor of ancient seas and the first battlements of upland Britain, Hen Cloud and The Roaches, beetle out over the valley of the Dane, looking towards Cheshire and its plains. Poor old Cheshire, solid and lush and full of fat cows and cheese, but not a hill you could spit from. The whole of the Edge from Hen Cloud to the Hanging Stone makes a superb walk, probably one of the great walks of Britain, and if you have time to wander off the direct route and cut through the forest to Lud's Church then you'll have made a day and a half of it.

Clud is a Celtic word meaning 'rock', and it can be found scattered all over the Pennines, from Hen Cloud and Five Clouds here in the south, to Skennersheugh Cloudes and Fell End Cloudes under Wild Boar Fell in the northern Yorkshire Dales. Hen could well be a corruption of 'Herne', the Celtic fertility god who has a clough and an

outcrop of stones named after him on Bleaklow. It is one of the handful of Celtic names to survive in the Peak, for though it is really part of the Staffordshire gristone, I still think that for the purposes of this book, this outcropping close to the Leek to Macclesfield road can be included in the White Peak as a sort of annexe or semi-detached gristone wart, to be less than poetic.

One early spring afternoon, and not a promising one at that, I hitched a lift up to the road below the Edge and, taking the access footpath, started climbing towards the Hen, hoping to traverse the whole ridge and see the church before the light went. Cheshire was grey and distant and there was a damp chill in the air as I pushed on up the path. Taking it nice and slowly and turning to watch the plain fall below, I came to the grit and scrambled through a gully to the summit. I clambered amongst great blackened bulks of gristone, worn and smoothed, and looked through a gap at the drop below.

[52]

Crag-rats on The Roaches: Hen Cloud in the distance

An easy path descends from the Hen to The Roaches' edge and, following it, I saw ahead of me, in spite of the chill grey day, a spatter of crag-rats (what other collective noun is there for them?) dotted across the rocks. The Roaches are great climbing ground, and at almost any time you'll find crag-rats in spandex ballet tights performing deeds of litho-terpsichorian derring-do on the various routes. I stood for a while watching one young climber free-climbing the face below the Sloth. Watching him move across that rock with nothing between him and disaster but a bag of chalk, a few hand holds and a pair of rubber soles was like watching a great dancer at work. His poise and balance, the rhythmic ease with which he scaled the face, the uncluttered symmetry of man and rock, were music to the eyes.

I scrambled past the climbers up onto the Edge path and walked along in a light that was pale and watery, with a strange shimmer to it. There are times when I enjoy walking with friends, glad of the company and the feelings of good fellowship you can get in a group of like-minded people, but there are other times when I'm happier on my own just thinking and soaking in whatever is around me. Today was one of those days. I could smell the newness of the earth, things waiting to come, but the spring was still bogus and fern and feather were coiled, waiting for the first real days of warmth.

Below the Edge, the plain looked washed out and unreal and, as I travelled, darker clouds moving from the west began to bunch and hover over the edge like fists. Further along the Edge, thankful for my fibre-pile jacket now that a cold wind had sprung up, I came, through encroaching gloom, to the strange black mere they call the Doxey Pool. Doxey is a funny word. 'Trim rig doxey' is a phrase that crops up once or twice in English folksong usually concerning a sailor and a lady he meets on shore, and, according to the *Oxford English Dictionary* is beggar's cant meaning trull, trollop or prostitute. I think it could well be a corruption of an earlier word, something like siren perhaps, which would tie in with the idea that a mermaid or sprite lives in this dark peaty pool, for legend has it that a water-sprite or undine has often been seen here.

Lest it be thought that such tales are the stock in trade of toothless old men who mumbled them out for Victorian scholars to collect, the following story was taken from Mrs Florence Pettit who visited the pool one morning in 1949, for a swim. She had a friend from Buxton with her who corroborated the story: 'A great "thing" rose up from the middle of the lake. It rose very quickly until it was 25 to 30 feet tall. Seeming to be part of the slimy weeds and water, yet it had eyes, and those eyes were extremely malevolent. It pointed its long fingers menacingly at me so there was no mistaking its hostility. I stood staring at the undine, water spirit, naiad or whatever it was while my heart raced. Its feet just touched the surface of the water, the weeds and the air. When I dared to look again the creature was dissolving back into the elements from which it had formed.'

Lake creatures are not uncommon in the Peak and Pennines. Mermaid's Pool on Kinder contains a naiad and there is another such creature in Blake Mere under Axe Edge, which is said to haul the unwary that venture there after dark into the acidic waters of the pool which, as in all good mere legends, is bottomless. Such stories find other parallels in the lake monsters of Scotland and in the very many Irish pesce legends, where the 'pesce' or water spirit appears often as a horse-head shape (shades of Nessie?) rising from the water. And after all, what is Grendel's mother in the Beowulf saga other than a water hag?

Well, on this particular day there were no pesces about, water or otherwise, though there was plenty of water because, at the trig point beyond the Doxey Pool, the weather finally broke and a mixture of lashing hail and rain sent me scuttling back through the shelter of the woods below the Edge to the road to thumb a lift. The church would wait for another day.

*

The path near Lud's Church

Later that year at the end of a hot summer, I climbed Hen Cloud again onto the Edge and walked along to the church. The lovely gritstone path rambles under you as you go and the smells of summer and the noise of larks were wonderfully healing. I'm often asked why I go out into the hills so much and I feel that if you have to ask, then perhaps you'll never know. It's something that can't necessarily be explained. The old thing about the inadequacy of human language to express emotion comes into it I suppose. As Gustave Flaubert said: 'Human language is a cracked kettle on which we beat out tunes for bears to dance to, when all the time we wish to move the stars to pity.'

I always feel that the longing most of us have to get back into the countryside – to walk where there is no concrete and jabbering traffic, no office blocks, no madding crowds – is something that goes very deep, something profoundly atavistic and bound up with all our origins. We came from the wilds, from the open country. Some of our ancestors were forced to leave the land to work in cities no more than a hundred or so years ago. If a swallow that has never seen Africa can find its way back there through all those miles of storms and mad Italian guns, is it too much to suggest that some hankering for the wilderness, for the wind and the rain, lurks in all our blood? It is this need that can only be met by the conservation of our last wilderness areas, our last semi-wildernesses and our National Parks. Turning them into forestry plots, urban parks and golf courses will destroy them and rip out our very roots.

What would the world be, once bereft
Of wet and wildness? Let them be left,
O let them be left, wildness and wet;
Long live the weeds and the wildness yet
Gerard Manley Hopkins: *Inversnaid*

As I approached the Doxey Pool, I kept a look-out for mermaids and actually thought I saw one ahead, lying on her side, beckoning me on

and into the pool, but it was only another walker cooling his feet in the water and wafting the flies away with his map. I skirted the pool and walked down by Bearstone Rock and over into Forest Wood where a path lead me to Lud's Church. Described on the map as a cave, it is nothing of the kind. It is a massive gritstone cleft sixty feet deep and two hundred feet in length, caused by faulting in the earth. Mossy and overgrown, wet and cool on the hottest of days, it is primeval and enters into the very root of things. Years ago, a wooden statue stood in a high niche in the cliff face. Called Lady Lud, it was said by some to be a statue of the Virgin, by others to be an old ship's figurehead put up there for a lark. But people generally don't do things for a lark in Lud's Church. It's not there any more but how, why or where it went is a mystery.

I stopped in the church to eat my sandwiches and to try and take a photograph of the interior. It's a difficult place to make anything of photographically because if you get the exposure right for the dark interior, the sky looks burnt out and likewise if you expose for the sky, the interior loses any detail and ends up as a black hole. One of these days I'm going to take up sketching. The pencil, unlike the camera can, and does, lie.

I've read more than a couple of times that local legend, if nothing else, gives Lud's Church as the site of the Green Chapel commemorated in the Arthurian poem *Sir Gawain and the Green Knight*. Some historians assert that this is nonsense, that 'Lud' is a corruption of 'Lollard' and the 'church' was simply a safe place where they held their religious ceremonies on their flight from persecution. I think that's much more far fetched than the Arthurian explanation.

Lud or Lug, the god celebrated at Lughnasa, was an old Celtic and pre-Celtic Nature God, a Corn God who can be seen in manifestations such as Cernunos, the horned God, the Herne the Hunter whose horns later metamorphosed into the foliage that entwines the many faces of the Green Man to be found on numerous churches and pub signs around the country. The Arthurian Romances, written down in the Middle Ages and imposing a chivalrous and romantic patina on the exploits of what was probably a northern Celtic chieftain (or chieftains), would quite easily take something like this green cleft sacred to Lug in the escarpment of The Roaches, and turn it from a pagan sacred green grove into a Christian green chapel.

The story of the Green Knight is a complete re-working of the Corn God, Green Man myth, the man who dies only to be reborn again each spring. While Arthur and his court of the Round Table are celebrating the New Year (Old Pagan New Year – Celtic Samhain?), a giant-like Green Knight appears carrying a massive axe and challenges anyone there present to strike him a blow with it. The only proviso is that the Green Knight must be able to return the blow a year later (year = one complete cycle of death and re-birth). Arthur's nephew, Sir Gawain, takes the axe and with one blow strikes off the head of the Green Knight. The still living body stoops and picks up the head which then speaks, telling Gawain that in a year's time he must meet him at the Green Chapel. Then, head under his arm, the Green Knight rides away. After many trials, including a near seduction which he resists, Gawain finds himself at the Green Knight's Chapel and, entering, finds the knight within. In keeping with his vow, he bows his head to accept the axe's blow; the Green Man swings the axe but pulls the blow short so that Gawain takes only a symbolic nick and is then sent away to tell his tale to Arthur's court.

There are so many elements of myth here, Green Man, Celtic head cults, sacred groves or chapels, that the story must be a prototype going back beyond fourteenth-century Staffordshire, where the tale is said to have been written, to the Celts and pre-Celts of the region. Who knows what winter's tale the writer of Gawain picked up at his grandmother's fireside to re-tell here in Arthurian form?

Lud's Church fits almost to perfection the description of the Green Knight's Chapel. When Gawain at length comes to the country of the

Lud's Church, or the Green Knight's Chapel

Green Knight, search as he may, he can find no trace of anything that looks like a church until he comes to a hill with a deep cleft that . . .

was overgrown with grass, a gorge of gloom,
A craggy crevice, nobut an old cave, he could not it explain
'Oh Lord!' quoth the gentle knight
'Is this the Green Chapel?
Here might about midnight
The Devil his matins tell.'

I would be prepared to accept that *Sir Gawain and the Green Knight* was written almost anywhere about anywhere were it not for that word 'nobut'. Nowhere outside this region would you hear that expression spoken and it is used even to this day. It means 'nothing but' as in 'nobut a lad', 'nobut a cockstride away'. The word places the poem firmly in the north-west and that coupled with Hen (Herne) Cloud, Lud's Church and the Green God in the Grove, seem to me to make this green gorge as likely a setting for the chapel of the Green Knight as anywhere else. It is thought possible by historians that the 'church' was used for Druid rites since a stone on the path from the church to the River Dane is supposed to be all that is left of an altar where human sacrifices were made in Celtic times. There are stories of ghosts in the rocky cleft too, and headless Green Men and floating lights are claimed to appear there at certain times.

Something else makes me suspect that the legends of Lady Lud and Green Knights in chapels have more than a flimsy basis in the truth. Not far from the chapel on the Cheshire Plain stands Lindow Moss where the famous body in the bog was discovered recently. 'Lindow Man' as he is often called, is now thought by historians like Dr Anne Ross to have been a druid prince (i.e. a magician), ritually murdered and thrown into the bog as an offering to the gods. No great distance away, at Alderley Edge where the gritstone outcrops over the plain, locals have long believed that a wizard called Merlin lies under the rock waiting for a call that will summon him back to the world. Magicians in a Cheshire bog, King Arthur's magician, Merlin, buried in Cheshire stone, King Arthur's nephew, Gawain, 'beheaded' in a 'chapel' under The Roaches – there are too many loose ends for there not to be a common thread somewhere.

I climbed the well-made steps out of the Green Chapel and followed the path through the woods back to the Edge above Paddock and Hangingstone Farm. It was a lovely afternoon, still and breathless, with a hazy sun dropping slowly westward and I bounced along through the heather. The Hanging Stone, a massive outcrop of rock some way off the path, has a sad plaque on it to commemorate the soldier-son of a local family killed in action in the Burma jungle in World War Two. It surely points to the madness of all war that a Staffordshire lad should have died halfway across the world to be remembered here, on this lonely rock above the Cheshire Plain.

The walk back along the edge from the Hanging Stone to The Roaches is superb, a good high trail, hard and dry underfoot with impressive gritstone outcrops not marked on the map. It's a joy to walk along. From Bearstone Rock I climbed back to the trig point, then dropped down to follow the path back to the Hen through the woods under The Roaches. The old house of Rockhall is a ruin now, but until recently it was lived in by a man people called 'King Doug, Lord of The Roaches'. Built into the rockface itself, it was designed originally as a hunting lodge by the Lord of The Roaches and, after it fell into disuse, it stood empty for years until it was taken over by 'King Doug'. This local character, with his black eye-patch and long coat, was well known by the climbers and walkers who came to the gritstone edge. The last I heard of him he had been moved out and rehoused in an old farmhouse by the Peak Park Board. The old lodge is a climbing hut now, dedicated to the memory of Don Whillans, though when I was last there, it had been vandalised and was boarded up. Sad that such an interesting building should be falling slowly to ruin.

Pat on The Roaches

The Dragon's Back

There remains one thing to be said. There has never been a time when more people were conscious of the beauty of hills and dales, or when more people thought it a matter of public importance that beauty should remain beautiful.

Patrick Monkhouse: *On Foot in North Wales and the Peak*

Like the giant fins or bleached domino-spine of some long-dead dinosaur, the hills of Chrome and Parkhouse rear up above Dowel Dale just inside the Staffordshire border, the last shake in the tail of the limestone serpent that lurks below the White Peak. Chrome Hill (pronounced 'Croome' by the locals) is also known as the Dragon's Back, and was strictly out of bounds to walkers until recently when the Peak Park, among the most enlightened of the National Parks, negotiated access with the landowner and a footpath along the ridge is now open to all. This top end of Dovedale is a peaceful, secretive, little-visited place and although much of the walking round about is easy, the ridge of Chrome Hill is an airy ramble with only a little exposure and is the single, true ridge walk in the Derbyshire Dales.

Eddie and I set out one glorious early autumn morning, and leaving Buxton cooking its breakfast, headed south and west for the hamlet of Hollinsclough. We pulled the car off the road by the telephone box, and sat on the bumper to put on our boots. Hollinsclough, a sleepy huddle of houses now, was once famous as a silk weavers' village and was an important and busy staging-post in packhorse days. In fact, the village chapel is said to have been built at the beneficence of one such packhorse man or 'jagger'. On this particular day, the place was deserted except for a big black-and-tan dog that looked at us with a leery eye and pulled back its lips to show an even leerier set of teeth.

With the sun seeing off the stragglers of the previous night's storm clouds, we took the road out of the village and followed it uphill for a while. The Dragon's Back, its gullies and folds looking like the fluting and ribs of a giant lizard, lurked across the valley to our right and, further behind, the sharp fin of Parkhouse Hill cut the sky. We climbed gently to where the footpath left the road and followed it down to the river and a fine packhorse bridge.

'The Dragon's Back,' I said, pointing towards the hill.

'I didn't know it had been away,' said Eddie, who can be really funny at times – although this wasn't one of them.

The Washgate Bridge, a little further upstream, is a fine single-span bridge standing at the junction of eight major routes and shows how vitally important this area was when packways were the only means of transporting goods and raw materials across the country. Our route lay downstream from the Washgate and, according to one local we met, it once served the salters who brought salt from the mines of Cheshire into Derbyshire and beyond to Yorkshire and the coast. Salt was one of the basics of life. It was the only way of preserving meat for the winter months and was also used in the burgeoning cotton,

Chrome Hill, a distant view of the Dragon

Chrome Hill, looking along the Dragon's Back

Eddie on the ridge of Chrome Hill

woollen, chemical and dyestuff industries. We followed the Saltersgate over the beck, then turned north along the track to Booth Farm. Broom and harebells lined the way and the sun, shining through broken clouds, swept over the land in patches of light, catching the far fells and white farms as it washed across the dales. September can be lovely for walking, particularly when the sun is mellow and golden. It never gets too hot and yet there is a bounce and a lift in the air that belies the dying of the year. I'm always conscious at such times of how immeasurably beautiful each moment in such a world can be.

Above Stoop Farm we had our first view of Chrome Hill end on, and it truly is a remarkable looking piece of limestone. When the rest of the bed of the seas which were to form the limestone dales of the White Peak had been formed, these reefs were still growing, giant coral atolls in the hot carboniferous lagoon, swarming with life, that covered much of Derbyshire. The coral reefs were made of harder calcium and were therefore more resistant to the weathering that ground down the rest of the landscape; this is why the hills of Thorpe and Bunster, Parkhouse and Chrome lord it above the dales today.

The scramble on to Chrome Hill is one of the most interesting routes in the White Peak. Never so exposed that you are in any real

Broom below Chrome Hill

danger, it is still the only hairy bit of a scramble you'll find for miles around and the only place we used our hands as well as our feet in the whole of a week of walking in the hills. White stone outcrops from the bright green grass, and falls swiftly away on either side. As you follow the ridge, it drops and rises in a series of small arêtes and on one of them you can look through a miniature natural arch at the dale below. Looking westward from a point just below the summit, we saw rags of sun and shadow whirling across the land. To the south-west was Hollinsclough, due south, the broad upper levels of the Manifold valley and Longnor; east was Dowel Dale and the infant River Dove and further east still, just visible over the crest of Upper Edge were the tips of the heavy plant of one of the quarries below Buxton. The quarries are just outside the National Park (if you look at the map you can see that the boundary was drawn very carefully to dip below Buxton, excluding both it and the quarries from the National Park's jurisdiction) and, although they are a terrible scar on the land, they provide much employment. Until alternative sources of work are found, there isn't much that can be done to phase them out. But the fact that most of the limestone of Derbyshire ends up being dumped in motorways is a terrible insult to an already raped and degraded landscape.

Parkhouse Hill from Chrome Hill

On the summit of the hill, a family sat in the lee of the wind, which up here was far sharper than on the valley floor below, and had just a tooth or two of winter in it. Below and ahead of us, the fin of Parkhouse stood above the dale, the stump of the Sugar Loaf sentinel before it: sadly the Peak Park has so far been unable to negotiate access to either of these so that they remain beautiful but tantalisingly forbidden territory. On our way up the ridge, we had met a middle-aged chap walking on his own, who told us how a few years previously he had walked over Parkhouse Hill assuming, since it is fairly rough open country with footpaths at either end, that there was open access along its ridge. He was disabused of this idea when, dropping down from the top, he was told he was trespassing, that the land was private and was made to feel, as he said, 'like a naughty schoolboy'.

The man was hardly a Hell's Rambler intent on rape, loot, mayhem and cups of tea, simply a walker out to enjoy the countryside and although I totally agree that a farmer has every right to expect people to respect his right and need to make a living in the country, I still feel that people should be allowed access to all open uncultivated uplands. Enclosed meadows and fields with growing crops in them are obviously not places where anybody should roam or ramble, any more than are farmyards and gardens. Sites that are proven to have rare wildlife or plants that would be endangered by the passage of walkers should also be sacrosanct, but for the rest, the open spaces of our moors and hills, the historical landscape of our great stone circles and packhorse ways, our sea shores and river banks, our ridges, caves and cliffs – surely these should be free for all to enjoy, providing they treat them with care and respect?

The argument is often made that opening a moor up to walkers encourages them to go there. This may be true, but opening up more of the country will surely, in the long run, take the burden off those 'honey pots' that have suffered so much from over use – Dovedale, the Three Peaks of Yorkshire, the Langdales, Snowdon and Crib Goch. When I'm writing about places I've enjoyed walking through, I often worry that, by making people aware of those places, I may be encouraging them to go there. But who am I to claim them only for myself? And what is the good of beauty if it can't be seen and shared? It has been argued that there are some places in the world that nobody should go to, places that should be left totally alone, places that would be destroyed by the very presence of humans, such as the Lascaux Caves or certain areas of the Mojave Desert. The very fact that we know that they exist, the argument goes, should be enough for us. Though I would agree with that, I don't think such an embargo can be placed on the open spaces of Britain, so many of which are still without any public right of access. We live on such a crowded island, surely the open spaces should be free for all to share. Anyway, that is my opinion.

We dropped slowly down from the summit of Chrome Hill to the track below Parkhouse Hill and the Sugar Loaf, taking a longing look at both of them as we passed by. Behind us, the hump of Chrome Hill looked very impressive. I've read that the word 'Chrome' is a corruption of the Old English 'crumb' meaning sickle-shaped, but it could equally well be a degraded version of Crom, the name of one of the most powerful of the Celtic Gods. In Irish lore, he was known as Crom Dubh, Crom the Black, so it could be argued (contrary to my suggestion earlier that Dove is a corruption of Derva) that both the words for river and hill come from the same root and garner their names from Crom Dubh. It's an interesting thought.

We left the farm track and followed a system of field paths through the sunshine back to Hollinsclough. We didn't say much, for a change, even Eddie was quiet. It was one of those golden afternoons you dream about long after it's over, when the old feel young and the young run round like mad rabbits. It was like that all the way back and we savoured every minute of it.

Magpie Mine and Monsal Dale

One of them reported that he had seen a man with a candle walking along a tunnel from which he had disappeared without trace. A photograph of another member of the party on a raft in a sough at the mine showed second man standing apparently on nine feet of water. The Old Man was clearly either trying to protect his ancient rights or to help twentieth-century searchers find the ore.

David Clarke: *Ghosts and Legends of the Peak District*

SOMEBODY ONCE DESCRIBED the Derbyshire limestone country as a giant cheese that first Nature and then Man had bored and hollowed out and riddled like a million maggots since the earliest of times. Nature scoured the bones of that coral sea with hot rains and glaciers to make the valleys and dales that we see today, while men, with the advent of metal-working, delved for the rich ores trapped in seams in the stone. Galena or lead sulphide was the ore they were after. Smelted, it produced an easily worked soft metal that could be used by early man for plates and drinking vessels. The Derbyshire leadfields were particularly rich and their ores comparatively easily won, so that it is reckoned that upwards of six million tons of ore have been taken from the area since the advent of mining.

The Romans took lead from Derbyshire, employing Brigante slaves captured in battle to work the open cast excavations and smelt the ore into metal which, cast into 'pigs' and stamped with the letters LVTVD (standing, some say, for *Lutudarum*, the mining camp at either Wirksworth or Matlock) have been found as far afield as Sussex.

After the Romans, the lead mines continued to be worked but seemingly on a smaller scale. The Saxons, when they filtered into the limestone dales, further exploited the ore veins and some of the richer mines – for example those at Wirksworth – passed into the hands of the abbeys and monastic granges. They, in turn, lost the leadfields to the Danish invaders who declared the mines the property of their king, Ceolwulf. The Odin Mine near Castleton is said to have been named after the Norse god by the men from the longships who settled there and took over the workings. Because those Scandinavian invaders declared the mines the King's property, the mineral duties in what is known as 'the King's Field' still belong to the Duchy of Lancaster today.

Lead from Derbyshire went to be mixed with tin to make the pewter crockery of the gentry and, more importantly, went to cover the roofs of many of the great abbeys and monastic houses of mediaeval England. So well considered were the mines of the limestone dales that a great deal of lead was exported overseas. Two hundred tons, for example, were sent late in the twelfth century to roof one of the great abbeys of France at Clairvaux.

With the expansion of the Spanish lead mines in the nineteenth century, the demand for English lead slumped and many of the Derbyshire lead mines were forced to close. Some mines managed to keep going into this century but the cost of finding new veins of ore and pumping out flooded levels were too high. Attempts were made to re-open old mines, even as recently as the middle of this century, but now they are all closed and nothing remains behind but their ruins, the marks of their hushes and the mouths of their adits where still, in some of the older workings, you can see the pickmarks of mediaeval miners.

Magpie Mine is the best preserved of all the Derbyshire mines and the walk from Ashford in the Water to the Magpie through Deep Dale, then on via the Monsal Trail and Cressbrook Mill to Litton, coming back by Monsal Head is, I've been told, a perverse way of looking at some of Derbyshire's most interesting industrial ruins.

Eddie and I walked to Magpie Mine one cold, grey, early autumn day when there was a crisp nip in the air and the leaves were just

Magpie Mine

beginning to yellow. We left Ashford in the Water and followed the track that climbs above the road, looking back at the village diminishing beneath us as we wandered across Kirk Dale and through the fields to Magpie. The rain from the previous night's storms was still on the grass and a cold wind was cutting across the plateau. All over this Derbyshire limestone upland, there are the mounds that mark the burial sites of the first metalworkers here, while the path to the mine goes through a maze of drystone walls created by centuries of enclosure. It has the effect of making you conscious of walking through a landscape where Man has worked for a very long time.

The Peak Park have had the good sense and taste to resist any pressure to turn the old workings at Magpie into a visitor centre, complete with toilets, tea rooms and gift shop, although considerable pressure has been put on them over the years to do just this. At one time, plans that included a massive car park and information centre and the conversion of the mine manager's office and blacksmith's shop into a retail outlet, were put forward and, thankfully, were rejected. Now the only access is on foot, which is as it should be. The mine workings stand skeletal and ruinous, and if you go there on a bleak winter's day, when the wind whistles round the gaunt windings and sobs through the empty engine house, you will get something that no interpretative centre or planners' grand scheme can ever give you, a real sense of the past and the transience of all human pride and desire.

The Magpie is said to be haunted, of course, like all deserted mines. The ghosts of this mine are believed to be the spirits of long-dead miners from the Great Redsoil Mine (whose shaft stood where the reconstructed horse gin now stands) who were murdered by Magpie miners in 1833 during a dispute over mineral rights. While working a neighbouring seam, they were smoked to death 420 feet below ground by burning sulphur fumes, introduced into the Great Redsoil levels from adjoining Magpie workings. At Derby Crown Court, the Magpie miners pleaded defence of the mine and were acquitted, but

Sunset behind the old workings at Magpie Mine

the ghosts of the murdered men are said to roam the shafts and workings still, and it is believed that if you stand on the old shaft top, by the rusting winding-gear, you can hear their voices calling through the rocky galleries far below. The report of the ghostly sightings at the head of this chapter was written by one of a party exploring the mine in 1946.

In 1839, the mine fell into the hands of John Taylor, a mine manager with mineral interests all over England and as far afield as Mexico. It was he who brought fourteen Cornishmen north to Sheldon to introduce Cornish methods of extraction into Derbyshire. The engine house, round chimney and powder house they built explain the very Cornish style of the mine which looks as though it should be on the edge of Bodmin Moor rather than a Derbyshire orefield.

We left the mine and cut through the fields to Sheldon where another field path took us to Deep Dale. The walk down the dale is a gem, dropping through limestone pasture and woodland to terminate in a steep-sided gorge overhung with ferns and mosses that is a sort of miniature Lud's Church. Demon's Dell is its local name, and when excavations were carried out there, urn burials, containing the cremated ashes of the dead and dating from the Beaker Period some 2,500 years BC, were discovered. It has a tremendous atmosphere and to many locals it is still a place to be avoided.

From Demon's Dell we dropped down to cross the road and take the path through Monsal Dale which follows the course of the River Wye by broadleafed trees and below the Iron Age fort of Fin Cop and lowering rock outcrop of Hob's House.

'Hob' is often taken to mean goblin or devil and ties in neatly with the Demon's Dell, since this part of Monsal Dale is full of legends, some of which may go back as far as the Celtic and pre-Celtic peoples that came to the area. One of the giants that lived in Demon's Dell is said to have been turned to stone by the gods for attempting to rape a beautiful shepherdess. His name was Hulac Warren and the Warren

Stone stands half in the river close to the road. A local rhyme runs:

> The piper of Shacklow,
> The fiddler of Finn
> The old woman of Demon's Dale,
> Calls them all in

The fiddler is the same rapacious giant, Hulac, who lived, so legend has it, at Fin Cop. Hob is yet another guise in which the Green Man appears; Hob, Puck, Robin Goodfellow and Robin Hood are all one and the same, and his houses, graves, beds, caves and strides are found everywhere.

We followed the river – where earlier that year I had come on bunch after bunch of marsh marigolds at the water's edge – and on by a tumbling weir to the viaduct. John Ruskin, the Victorian artist and writer, so detested the viaduct and the visual effect it had on the dale, that he wrote a famous blast against its proposers which now declares itself boldly on a plaque on the viaduct. The bridge served the London Midland line which was pushed through in spite of opposition by both the Dukes of Devonshire and Rutland (for whom special stations were constructed), and when it was opened in 1863 Ruskin wrote:

'. . . once upon a time as divine as the vale of Tempe; you might have seen the gods there morning and evening Apollo and all the sweet muses of the light – walking in fair procession on the lawns of it, and to and fro among the pinnacles of its crags . . . but the valley is gone and the Gods with it, and now every fool in Bakewell can be in Buxton in half an hour and every fool in Buxton; which you think a lucrative process of exchange – you Fools everywhere.'

As somebody who campaigned to keep the Settle–Carlisle line open, I can see how people look at the viaduct today and think Ruskin himself a fool. Yet Ruskin had and still, I think, has a point. Imagine the valley without the viaduct if you can. Wouldn't it perhaps be just that little bit wilder, feral, natural, whatever you like to call it? Every

The viaduct in Monsal Dale

When we hew or delve:
After-comers cannot guess the beauty been.
Gerard Manley Hopkins: 'Binsey Poplars'

Now there are no steam trains rushing people to London, just strollers and ramblers toddling along to Cressbrook and beyond. The dead railway has found a new life as a walking and cycling route and the embankments that once carried crack expresses to London are now part of a long-distance path, the Monsal Trail, which we followed now to Cressbrook Mill.

As we rolled along, the day warmed up a little and Eddie began looking forward to his lunch. On my advice we hadn't packed any sandwiches or flask. Walking in the White Peak is hardly a wilderness experience and you're rarely more than shouting distance from a village of some size with a pub or café.

'We'll eat at Litton,' I told him. 'There's a pub there called the Red Lion.'

Cressbrook Mill, once a great proud collection of buildings, is a sad ruin now and the scene of some dispute between the Peak Park Board and its owner. For years there has been talk of its renovation but nothing has been done and it is all but falling down. It stands on the site of an earlier Arkwright mill and, like Litton Mill further west, it used the abundant water-power of the River Wye to drive its machinery. We dropped down from the Monsal Trail to the bridge and weir at Cressbrook and followed the river path along the wonderfully named and lovely Water Cum Jolly Dale, where moorhens and mallard were shunting and fussing about in the shallows, to Litton Mill and Miller's Dale.

Both Litton Mill and Cressbrook Mill 'employed', if that is the correct word, orphans sent by parishes loath to provide for them. This suited these isolated mills which, during a time of boom, found the orphans a ready source of cheap labour. The way they were treated in

The River Wye in Monsal Dale

little bit, however small, that is destroyed or changed, is another bit of the world lost. No matter what the developers say, the wilderness and wet is best left as it is, even though some people would even try and tell you that golf courses, executive Tudor villages and theme parks enhance the landscape and that the M6 through the Lune Valley is a beautiful bit of motorway. Gerard Manley Hopkins had it about right when he wrote:

O if we but knew what we do
When we delve or hew –
Hack and rack the growing green
Since country is so tender . . .
. . . even where we mean
To mend her we end her,

Walkers on the Monsal Trail through Water Cum Jolly Dale

The sad ruin of Cressbrook Mill

the two mills contrasts incredibly. Cressbrook Mill was run at the turn of the nineteenth century by William Newton, 'the Minstrel of the Peak', a carpenter-poet who had worked in the mill (then owned by Strutt and Arkwright) for fourteen hours a day until it burnt down. Literary friends clubbed together and collected enough money to buy him a partnership in the new mill that was built in its place. Eventually he became the sole owner and by all accounts treated his two to three hundred apprentices well, making sure that they were well fed and well housed in his turreted 'Apprentices House', and that they had some free time for recreation.

At Litton Mill, the owner, Elias Needham, treated the children abysmally, overworking them, beating them and starving them until, it is recorded, they were so hungry that they stole food from the pigs in the mill yard. So many died and were buried in Tideswell churchyard, that Needham himself began to worry that people might object and began burying the dead children outside the parish. Walt Unsworth's excellent novel for young people, *The Devil's Mill*, tells the story vividly.

Almost anything an apprentice did could be held against him as a 'crime' and he was savagely punished or fined, or more often than not, both. Worst crime of all was to be slow or slipshod over the work itself and the punishment for this was to have a large iron weight tied on each wrist so that every movement was ten times more laborious. Thus encumbered the poor apprentice had to keep up with the rapid machines or suffer further punishment.

Litton Mill has had a sordid past and looks set to have a sordid future if the developers get their way. There are plans to turn the mill into a massive timeshare and leisure complex, complete with disco and swimming pool, saunas and jacuzzis and lord knows what else. Just what Miller's Dale and a National Park needs. I've never understood the mentality behind mass developments like this, that transport the town to the country and destroy the very reason for

Sheepwash Bridge, Ashford-in-the-Water

The parish church in Ashford

Beyond Millersdale we took the path through Tideswell Dale, a lovely quiet dale, peaceful and woody, that took us eventually to Litton. Here we discovered not only that the pub was shut but that the village was like a wild west ghost town. I expected saloon doors to creak and tumbleweed to come rolling down the street.

'Piggin' 'eck, Tommy,' said an incredulous Eddie. My friend is a man with a great command of the more robust and Anglo-Saxon side of the dictionary who, for some unexplained reason, has, in recent years, decided to re-christen me. 'It's piggin' well shut, Tommy!' he whispered, fearful of breaking the silence. 'The whole village is piggin' well closed. Not a dog on the street. Everybody here has been spirited away by aliens in flying saucers and, what's worse, I'm starving and thirsty and you promised me a pint and a ploughman's!' His bottom lip curled. I remembered that he had been like this when his candy floss blew off the stick at Skegness. I was just wondering whether we could kill a sheep and roast it when we were literally saved by the bell, a shop door bell that tinkled somewhere not far away. We turned in its direction and saw, through the grey afternoon, the lights of the village shop. Two old ladies were almost crushed in the rush, and the woman who ran the shop made us a cup of tea and heated up two meat-and-potato pies for us in her micro-wave. We ate them outside, sitting on the guard dog's kennel, while the two old ladies said they recognised me and accused me of being Jasper Connolly.

'This is living, Tommy,' said Eddie, gravy dribbling down his chin, shortly before a splinter from the kennel roof caused him to change his mind and roundly curse Litton and its meat-and-potato pies to Hell.

The way from Litton to Cressbrook Dale passes by a quiltwork of small stone-walled fields, over good green meadows and down by a steep path through the woods to the valley and the mill. From there, we took the road to Monsal Head where, I promised Eddie, the pub

going out into the hills in the first place. I suppose the only reason is greed and we just have to accept that developers on the whole are people who look at green valleys and think not how beautiful they are, but how many building plots they can be divided up into. If they weren't so destructive of all that is wild and natural, you'd have to feel sorry for them.

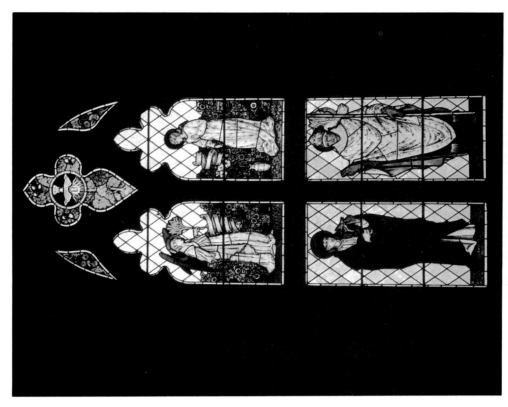

William Morris window in Ashford church

would definitely be open. It wasn't, but we found an ice cream van left behind by a retreating wave of summer visitors, still perched at the head of the dale like flotsam on a rock, and still open. So I bought him an ice cream from a shivering ice cream man who muttered that it was too cold and that he was going to close and we were just in time. When the ice cream hit the tea and meat-and-potato pie, the resulting noises were interesting but not pretty.

The footpath that is shown on the map as leading to the Monsal Trail didn't, and there were signs telling us that it was closed, so we walked to Little Longstone, a quiet village, quieter than Litton, where the village pump and old red telephone box looked interesting enough for a photograph. From there a pleasant and easy stroll of a mile and a bit brought us back to Ashford in the Water.

Ashford is a lovely village. Its Sheepwash Bridge over the river, where willows drape into the water like something from a Pre-Raphaelite painting and where obliging ducks pose in the foreground as though placed there by the English Tourist Board, must be the subject of thousands of photographs. Sheepwash Bridge is an old packhorse bridge and as many as three hundred horses passed over it each week in the 1600s. It has a side gate and fold in it through which sheep were, and still are, driven to be washed in the river.

Ashford also has one of the most interesting of the White Peak's churches, with stained glass windows by William Morris and Burne-Jones, a table of the local coloured Ashford Marble (a pigmented limestone found in black and other colours), and four 'virgins' crants', garlands of gloves and dried flowers that were carried at the funerals of unmarried girls. It is a lovely village, although I expect the people who live here get a bit fed up with the crowds that descend on the place on Bank Holidays. It was quiet enough when we were there. The pub and shops were closed and nobody was about, again.

'Those aliens have been busy, Tommy,' said Eddie, so I took him into Bakewell which was open – just.

Eyam and the Gritstone Edges

The Hottest day that I ever felt in my life. This day, much against my will, I did in Drury Lane see two or three houses marked with a red cross upon the doors, and 'Lord, have mercy on us', writ there: this was a sad sight to me.

Samuel Pepys: Diary, 1665

IF YOU WALK ROUND Eyam now on a sunny spring afternoon, when rooks are screeching in the high trees and primroses are bunched and clotted beneath the tall stones in the churchyard, you'd be forgiven for seeing it as a quaint, peaceful, almost 'chocolate box' Derbyshire village. It hides a sad past, however. In the year 1665, about the beginning of September, a journeyman tailor from London came to lodge in Eyam, with a box of old clothes which he was going to alter and re-sell. Finding that the clothes were damp, he hung them before the fire to dry, having no reason to know that the clothes had hidden in their seams and tucks, fleas from the rats of the London streets and that those fleas carried in their blood the plague that was raging in the city.

The parish register for the 7 September reads: 'Buried George Viccars.' The tailor who innocently introduced the plague to Eyam was the first in what was to be a savage roll of death. The man Viccars had lodged with died a fortnight later, followed by two neighbours in the next four days. By the first week in October, four more had died and the villagers, seeing the 'plague spots' blossoming on the chests of the victims like roses on a wall, realised that the plague was upon them. Twenty-three people died in October but only seven in November and the villagers began to hope that the cold weather

would destroy the pestilence completely, since it was known to flourish best in the hottest and driest months.

The winter was severe, with roads blocked and houses plastered with snow and great icicles hung from the eaves of the cottages, yet still nine were taken in December, five in the first month of the New Year and eight in February. Spring came and the May blossom hung heavy on the trees, but, with its coming, the plague intensified and even today in the village, it is thought to be unlucky to carry May blossom into a house for 'the smell of the Great Plague of London remains in the flower'. The rector, William Mompesson, counselled the people of the village to put themselves into voluntary quarantine. Locked in its own world, the village buried its dead, including Katherine, the wife of Mompesson himself. The outside world made contact only at outlying spots on Eyam Moor and on the hill above Stoney Middleton where coins were left in vinegar-filled holes in a boulder that still stands there today, the vinegar it was thought would destroy any traces of the plague left on the money.

Before the plague burnt itself out in 1666, the village had become a charnel house. From a total of 350 villagers, 260 were dead. In those times when people knew so little about the causes of disease, it must have been truly terrifying to have watched your family and friends

[78]

The plague cottages in Eyam

taken one after the other by the plague and to have had no hope of curing or combating it. The village was ravaged, whole families were destroyed, those that dragged the corpses off for burial succumbing themselves a few days later. The half-dead buried the dead and today, around the village and the moors about, you can find the graves of some of its victims. The Lydgate Graves, round the corner from Eyam's excellent little tea shop, contain two graves, while out of the village on the edge of the moor are the Riley Graves. A walled enclosure surrounds a handful of tombs where the Talbot family, father and two sons and two daughters were buried by the mother and wife who had nursed them. All had died within eight days. It is the most moving of places, lonely and bleak, with an air of bravely-suffered but relentless tragedy.

Not all the stories of the plague are as sad or harrowing. A carter from Bubnell was instructed to carry a load of timber from the Chatsworth Estate to Eyam. His friends warned him against the plague but still he went, determined to drop his load some way out of the village. There was nobody close by to help him unload the cart, so he did it himself, working on through a heavy drizzle that soaked him through and through. The next day he went down with a heavy chill, the symptoms of which are not dissimilar to the onset of plague. He

was put under strict quarantine by the rest of the villagers, with a watchman appointed to shoot him if he tried to come out of his house. The Duke of Devonshire, of the nearby Chatsworth estate, heard this story and instructed his own physician to treat the man. The carter stood on one side of the River Derwent while the doctor stood on the other and, carrying out what must be one of the strangest of medical examinations as doctor and patient shouted to each other across the broad waters. The doctor came to the conclusion that the man was only suffering from a chill and released him from quarantine.

The village is a quiet place now. Its church has a Saxon cross, an impressive sundial, and a number of interesting tombs (including a cricketer's gravestone, complete with bat and wickets), as well as a fine stained glass window built to commemorate the plague. There are two good pubs in the village: one, the Miner's Arms, is said to be one of the most haunted inns in the Peak District. Eyam Tea Rooms serves cakes and tea and sandwiches and, when I was last there, was giving out a little printed map and description of the village in exchange for a contribution to church funds.

A good, though fairly extensive walk from Eyam leads from the village and drops down to the River Derwent by Stoney Middleton,

The circular enclosure around the Riley Graves

The Riley Graves: note the great quarrying scar beyond

Eyam village: the manor and the old stocks

Sundial on Eyam church

climbing to the Edges of Baslow, Curbar and Froggatt and coming back by Eyam Moor. Eddie and I walked that way one summer Saturday, leaving the village by the Lydgate and following the field path by the Boundary Stone with its coin holes, to Stoney Middleton. This village has one of the most pleasing churches I have ever seen. Unusual in being octagonal in shape, it was built in 1759 and has an interesting stained glass window and a fine, nineteenth-century open timber roof. Nikolaus Pevsner calls it, 'A rarity, if not a visually very exciting one.' I disagree. It might not have the arches and the tombs of Ashford or Youlgreave but I was impressed by the clean lines and the lightness of the whole structure as well as by its unusual shape.

Close by the church is a bath-house standing over thermal springs that may have been used by the Romans, while on the main road is a toll-house that, like the chapel, is also octagonal, although now it is an octagonal chip shop. The village itself is much cleaner than I remember it being when I came here in the sixties with some climbing mates. Then, there always seemed to be a thick shroud of smoke hanging about the place: now, without having been gentrified, it certainly seems a lot cleaner and healthier. The valley above is scarred by quarrying and fluorspar mining, but the heart of the village looks unchanged from the photographs taken of it in Victorian times, with its narrow main street and overhanging cliffs. One of these cliffs was christened Lover's Leap after a girl called Hannah Badderley, who was crossed in love and who launched herself into oblivion from it in 1762. Luckily for her, the fashionable, bell-tent-like skirt she was wearing, spread like a parachute and slowed her fall. It caught on some brambles and she hung there for a while before dropping off and rolling down into a saw-pit relatively unharmed. I hope she went back and kicked the bloke concerned and married somebody else to live happily ever after, or joined a women's awareness group and sailed the Atlantic single-handed.

The walk from Stoney Middleton to Baslow by the river is an

Wellington's Cross on Baslow Edge, erected to commemorate the victor of Waterloo

The octagonal roof of Stoney Middleton church

exquisite (no other word for it) ramble along a tree-hung river path, the pleasure of which was undiminished by the number of caravan parks we passed, or by Eddie moaning about being thirsty. I tried to tell him that the old Arkwright Mill at Calver, which we were passing at the time, had been used as the setting for the prison in the television series *Colditz*, but he was unimpressed.

At Baslow we stopped for a cup of tea at the little tea rooms opposite the church and began to argue over how far we'd come. I said three miles and Eddie said five. We asked the young girl who was serving how far it was from Eyam to here.

'Where's here?' she asked.

'Piggin' 'eck, Tommy, even she's lost!' mumbled Eddie, his gruntle totally dis.

Baslow has a prosperous air to it, with several large granges on its outskirts. As you enter the village, you are immediately aware that you have left the limestone behind for the honey-yellow of the millstone grit. We crossed the busy road to the church where we had a quarter of an hour to look round before a wedding arrived. Weddings upset Eddie so I wanted to get him well out of the way before the bride arrived. There is a dog whip in the church which was used, in the days when farmers brought their dogs to service with them, for breaking up the fights in case their noise drowned out the congregation's snoring. In the porch is an old grave slab, thought to be Saxon, and some lead taken from the church roof, on which the plumbers of ages past have made tracings of the soles of their boots, pointed toes and all. It always gives me a jolt when I see something like those footprints and realise that the hands that scratched those thin lines in the lead are long dead and yet are speaking still across the hundreds of years between.

There's a gradual climb from the village to Baslow Edge that passes Lady Wall Well and, looking across from the lane, as you near its termination at the open country, you can see the Chatsworth estate,

with its grand house and the flume of its Emperor Fountain rising above the trees. On the Edge stands Wellington's Cross, erected to commemorate the victor of Waterloo, and further northwards is the Eagle Stone, a great rock boulder said to turn round each morning at cock-crow; it was also said that the young men of Baslow had to climb it before they could get married. It looked an interesting boulder but I had the wrong boots on and Eddie claimed a headache, so we left it to a young boy who was being helped up by his dad.

'He's too young to get married,' muttered Eddie, but I ignored him.

The Edge at Baslow marks the end of the limestone and the beginning of the great gritstone edges that dominate the Derwent Valley from here to Stanage and the views across the Derwent are

The Eagle Stone, said to turn round each morning at cock-crow

stunning. It's hard at times to realise that you are only four or five miles from the outskirts of Sheffield, although the number of climbers scrambling on the Edge calling each other 'love' and 'youth' and 'me duck' would tell you that you're not a million miles away from either Sheffield, Chesterfield or Derby. I once got a telling-off from a raving feminist for calling her 'love' when I swear I wasn't trying to be in any way condescending. Telling her that men in Sheffield call each other 'love' did nothing at all to soothe her and I left with a flea in my ear. Some battles come unasked for and you cannot win.

Men and boys were flying radio-controlled gliders from the edges and, all over, people of every age and sex, clad in the dayglo spandex of today's 'rock athletes', were scrabbling across the slabs and grooves and pillars. It's easy to see why, with such good gritstone so close, Sheffield and Derby have produced some of the best climbers in the world. Though, in a non-chauvinist way, I must point out that both Joe Brown and Don Whillans, the grandfathers of modern climbing, came from my own town of Manchester.

The Edge walk is glorious and well-used, rightly so. It would take millions of feet over as many years to cause any serious damage to the hard gritstone here and the edges from Baslow to Stanage have long been the lungs of countless city dwellers who've used them for fresh air and sport. Much of the land is now owned by the Peak National Park and has open access.

We dropped down from Froggatt Edge to Grindleford by Hay Wood, a dense, leafy delight with streams and paths threading through it. Grindleford was closed, even though it was a Saturday afternoon and so we trudged up the hill towards Eyam Moor, dying for a brew and, as it had started to rain, sweating up in our cagoules. There is a perfectly good way that leads from Grindleford through Sherriff Wood to the moor's edge but it is private and there are signs everywhere telling you just that, so we slogged through the rain for one and a half miles along a boring piece of road to the moor, and let me tell you, there is no rain wetter than the rain that falls on you at the end of a day's walking when you're plodding along a tarmac road. At the moor, further signs told us not to stray from the path and to go this way and not that.

The rain stopped as we followed the path through the heather. The remains of a stone circle stand on the moor at Wet Withens but there is no access to it and the trudge along the road had made me too grumpy to go and look for it, so instead I kept an eye out for the moonwort which is supposed to be plentiful around here, but couldn't find any. Of the plant, Culpepper writes that it is 'a herb which will open locks and unshoe such horses as tread upon it. This some laugh to scorn, and these no small fools neither; but country people that I know call it Unshoe the Horse.'

It felt like a long slog across Eyam Moor via Ladywash Mine to Eyam Edge, but as we dropped down through the trees to the village, I consoled Eddie with the thought of a pint in the Miner's Arms and that cheered him greatly. It was that witching hour between afternoon closing and evening opening so the pub was of course closed. Eddie just looked at me and muttered something about it being a shame the plague had died out.

Eddie on Frogatt Edge: the end of the limestone and the beginning of the great gritstone mass called the Dark Peak

The Dark Peak

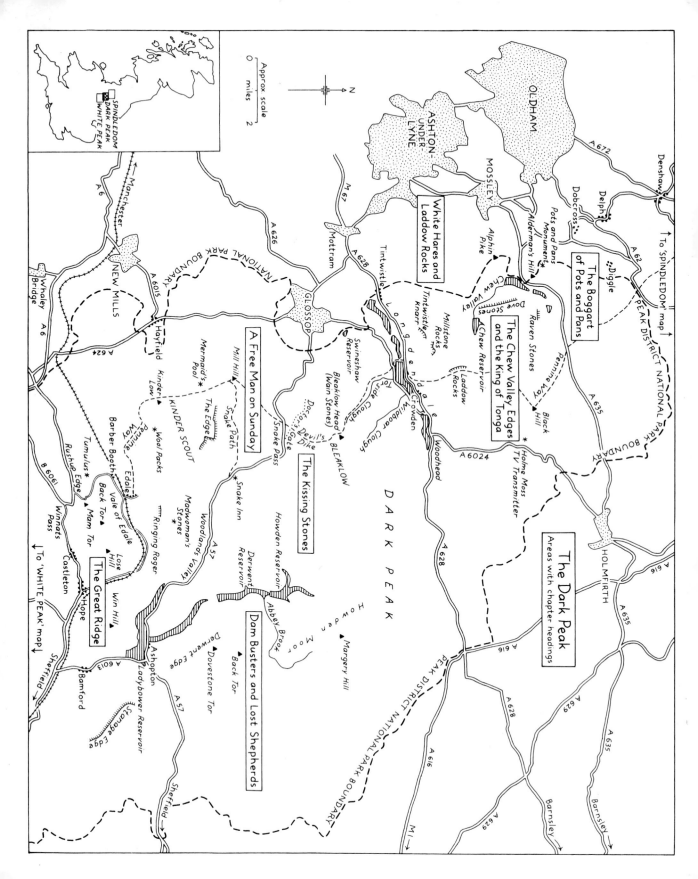

Millstone Grit – a prologue

All night the dripping lights
streak the leaden petals of the hills;
lorries loaded with shoddy or stone
scream like insomniac birds
by the peat's stinking breath,
the clowns' mask of lit pubs.
The moors are quiet as bone
alert with pleasure seekers.

Glyn Hughes: 'Above Oldham'

GRITSTONE, BLACK REEFS OF IT, like a sea gone solid. Kinder's bulk is fringed with it and Bleaklow's morass has safe islands of it and, after days of rain, ramblers look glumly from the stones' sanctuary at the sea of chocolate glue that surrounds them. At Standedge, Laddow and the Dove and Raven Stones of Saddleworth's Chew Valley, it stands frozen in vertical waves, a climber's paradise. Elsewhere it has been split and hammered and piled into the drystone walls that march across the hills, and has been dressed and mortared up into the walls of farmhouse, mill and town hall, chapel and reservoir. It has been carved into Roman pavements, packhorse causeys, horse troughs, cobbles, gravestones, tombs, stone crosses and fonts and before that, by the Celts, into the powerful, staring stone heads that were tossed as offerings into wells and springs.

The Christians took these stone heads and hung them on the walls of their churches where they were called 'gargoyles'. Like horseshoes and mistletoe, they remain as symbols remote from their past when the head was worshipped by the Celts as the dwelling place of the soul. Then real heads were hung above a chieftain's door, or placed in niches in the wall as signs of his power. Still the heads remain and in some places they are still being made and left out on the moor by people who seem to practise the old ways.

In Yorkshire, the land of the Brigantes who had adorned Stanwick fort with the real article, stone heads seem to have been invested with special properties in local superstition until this century. Twentieth-century stone heads have been carved in a style little different from that employed two

[91]

Typical aspects of the Dark Peak: the gritstone mass of the Hern Stones, and (right) stone horse troughs at Dobcross

millennia ago, and have turned up built into walls of houses and barns, to the confusion of the antiquaries.

Lloyd Laing: *Celtic Britain*

The land of the gritstone uplands is a wet boggy land; the underlying stone cups the water like a bowl and the peat holds it sponge-like so that even in the driest summers there are parts where the moor is a quaking bog which, as you walk innocently onto it, tilts and kilters like a fairground ride. With their oceans of peat, in the driving rain and cold of winter, or when grey skies are dumping snow on the land, whiting them out in seconds, the moors can be fierce and murderous. But in spring and summer you can have days when the sky seems filled with a light that trembles and shakes, and hot baking days when

even the larks are too tired to get up and sing; then the savage black ocean of Kinder is still and the dour, sour hump of Black Hill tamed to a dusty mound.

In a sense all boundaries are artificial; all lines, lines merely in the mind. But it could be said, with some truth, that by leaving Black Hill and crossing the Holmfirth to Oldham road at Saddleworth Moor, you leave the broad open moorland of the Dark Peak behind and cross into Spindledom with its crowded industrial valleys. So this third of the book concentrates on that belt of peat and gritstone moorland which lies between Mam Tor in the south and Pots and Pans in the north, ending, neatly, if a little nonsensically, at that point where the two giants, Alder and Alph threw boulders and insults at each other across Chew Valley.

The local stone seen in more attractive circumstances: Dobcross

The Dark Peak is gritstone, hacked through by ice when glaciers made the great valleys; its summit is a peat-mantled tableland where it can snow for seventy days out of 365, and where the rainfall can be more than five feet in the year. More than six inches has been known to fall in a couple of hours, and when that happens, the bogs are quaking pools and the becks can turn treacherous with flash floods scouring the cloughs, tearing everything down as they go.

It is sour, the soil here, acid and sodden. On the moor's edges, hawthorn, rowan and broom grip wherever they can, ferns fringe the tumbling waterfalls that bring the water down from the hills while, on the tops, little else but heather, moss and bent, and the occasional hardy wildflower manage to survive. Grouse chuckle from under the heather squealing 'Gawark gawark!!' when you disturb them, which

Looking down to Crowden from Laddow on a typically murky day

some people hear as 'Go back! Go back!!' but then some people would.

Sheep are the main crop here and they have long been overstocked on the hills, in some places they have gnawed them down to the bone. Rough wild fell sheep. I remember them as a boy, made grubby and grey by the chimneys of industrial Manchester; cleaner now that the mills are all dead and gone, they stare at you through the mist, lolloping off as you climb towards them. In winter they will follow you through the snow, a gang of woolly mobsters looking for food, not distinguishing between your rucksack and the nitrate bag, full of feed nuts, that the farmer lugs off his tractor.

It is wild walking country for, over all those miles between Edale and Black Hill, there is hardly a house, and the featureless moors roll on as far as you can see. When the cloud is down and driving rain lashes across the heights, it is a hard place to be out alone and unprotected.

To ramblers, peat is foul stuff, stinking black and slutchy and miserable underfoot, yet peat bogs are eco-systems on their own. For upwards of seven thousand years the bogs have been forming, their surface a home to the specialised plants that thrive on an acid rich, wet soil. Sphagnum mosses hold the bog water like sponge, and the insectivorous sundew and butterwort add their bright colours to the lime-green of the sphagnum. Cottongrass, known as 'bog-baby warning' in some local folk-lore, is a sure sign that the land beneath is very wet indeed. Bog orchid, a tiny, rare, and easily missed plant, can be found on these heights, but only where the conditions are exactly right. Left alone, peat, the rot of thousands of years, vegetation-packed and sodden and so airless that it will never turn to mulch or slime, will become instead a fuel you can cut in semi-solid bricks. Parts of the bogs are so sterile that some of the mosses that grow on their surface were used for dressing wounds in the First World War.

The bogs attract curlews, plovers and snipe for their insect life and you'll even find the occasional heron stalking frogs amongst the reeds of the open pools. Mountain hares, white in winter and fawn in summer, leap amongst the rocks; foxes are common, and somewhere, it is thought, a wild panther or two has been seen.

What homesteads there are cling to the edge of the moor or huddle in the valley. It is not kindly land and the routes across the tops were ways for men to cross as quickly as possible the wilderness that gathered round them. Early travellers speak of terrors here and, although the people are friendly in the main, they can still affront strangers, especially those from the south.

Much of the land of the rural millstone grit is having a hard time of it now. The hill farms on the sour peatlands are even harder to maintain than those on the limestone, and farmer after farmer is being forced to sell up, and meadows and intake land are taken by other farms as they turn to ranching and Euro grants in an attempt to stay in business. The old houses are either sold as holiday lets or, if they're remote and isolated, they are often left to fall down after their roofs have been stripped of the valuable York-stone roofing flags. Old Man Winter soon gets in with his frosty claws, and buckles and swells the walls until they crumble and fall; then the kestrel nests in the ruined chimney and

Bog cotton on Saddleworth Moor

cupboard doors swing in the wind that rattles the broken window pane. From Mam Tor to Saddleworth Moor and beyond, the gritstone uplands roll, wild and rough on the best of days, savage and demanding on the worst of them, but great walking country.

The Great Ridge

'The man who was never lost never went very far'
G. H. B. Ward, Q in *GHB Ward*: Ann Holt

L IKE THE DRAGON'S BACK of Chrome Hill, the Ridge stands between the last gritstone of the Dark Peak and the limestone of the White like some luckless monster or 'wurm' turned into shales and stone. It is the last shake in the tail of the great gritstone beast of Kinder, and that last shake has shattered it into humps of scales and shales that slither off it to the dales below. Lying beneath the tail, where the limestone begins, is Castleton while, on the gritstone side, is the hamlet of Edale and at both head and tail of the worm are twin carbuncles of chieftains' tombs on Lose Hill and Rushup.

One cloudless summer morning, I left Edale early and strode out on the road to Hope, looking for the path to Lose Hill. It was Saturday and Edale was crowded with walkers, day trippers and bikers. There was some sort of meet or rally going on and bikers from all over the north had swooped on Edale that weekend; great hairy men in leathers and Ray-ban sunglasses with their leather-sheathed ladies were rolling in on huge roaring machines, all chrome and hot oil, looking like a band of Visigoths. They got off their bikes and, instead of laying waste to the village, went into the café, asked politely for bacon sandwiches and cups of tea and sat down outside in the sun to talk about springs and where was the best place to get your forks re-chromed.

I walked along the road, by hedgerows thick with purple vetch and foxgloves. Men were out early before the morning's cool was burnt away, strimming their lawns, while women knelt in sun bonnets, weeding. It was one of those mornings when the smell of bacon still lingers faintly in the air and everybody and her husband is out in the garden generally doing something.

Such a morning it is when love
leans through geranium windows
and calls with a cockerel's tongue.

When red-haired girls scamper like roses
over the rain-green grass
and the sun drips honey.

When all men smell good,
and the cheeks of girls
are as baked bread to the mouth.

As bread and beanflowers
the touch of their lips
and their white teeth sweeter than cucumbers.

Laurie Lee: 'Day of These Days'

View down to Edale, the bulk of Kinder beyond

Walkers on Back Tor

Not far out of Edale is a row of cottages and a closed-down cotton mill and, just beyond, a lane leads from the road to Backtor Farm where I saw that they were advertising teas and ice cream and other temptations. I lashed myself to the mast and passed on by, knowing that if I'd stopped there I'd have stayed all day. As I climbed onwards, Edale fell below me and I could see, amongst the trees, the cottages and mill chimney and in the distance, Ringing Roger and the bulk of Kinder. Sweat rolled off me in the airless heat and recently barbered sheep stared as I climbed past them, lugging my twenty-odd pounds of cameras and rucksack up the hill.

I could see walkers up ahead of me, already on the ridge, silhouetted against the deep blue cloudless sky. Three of them stood on the summit of Back Tor looking out over the land. Back Tor, like a mini Mam Tor, has an impressive, shattered face with grit slabs outjutting. It's an imposing piece of hill and from it you can see the whole of the valley below, with dots of farms and green clots of trees and hedges.

Turning around, I could see out over to Kinder, clear away to the Derwent Edge, Win Hill, down to Castleton and the cement works, and along the ridge to Mam Tor and Rushup Edge, the way I would eventually go. There were dozens of people trailing up and down the ridge, as far as I could see. In winter I've been up here in the snow and had it virtually to myself. Now, the schools having broken up for summer, there were family groups and youth club groups and whatever.

Writers often complain that there are too many people on the hills, and although I'll admit that I often prefer to be alone on a moor rather than following a crocodile of Gortex-clad ramblers, the hills are there for everyone. There are people who feel that if you find somewhere good you should keep it to yourself, but that seems a kind of a dog-in-the-manger, begrudger attitude to me. There's enough room for all of us.

From Back Tor I headed east to Lose Hill, or as it's now known, 'Ward's Piece'. G.H.B. Ward was a Sheffield rambler, a great character and a lifelong fighter for the right to roam. Born in 1876, he left school at thirteen to work as an errand lad. Like many men and women of his time, he educated himself to such a high standard that he had more than a working knowledge of botany, geology, local history and Spanish which he spoke fluently. His politics could be described as broadly socialist, although he had no time, particularly in his later life, for politicians and hated the extremes of both left and right with equal ferocity.

In 1901 Ward helped to form the Sheffield Clarion Ramblers, the first working-class rambling club in the country. It was also mixed, which in itself was unusual. The club produced a programme, four pages long, with rambles, tea-places, notes on interesting things along the way and two quotations from Wordsworth; this was the beginnings of what was later to become the *Clarion Handbook*. It all sounds faintly folksy and Victorian now, and I suppose a lot of people would label it quaint, and yawn, but having been involved with people like Tom Stephenson and Stephen Morton, the last of that great old bunch of fighters and ramblers, I realised very early on that though their bodies had seen the best of their days, their minds were cut-throat sharp and that it was these men and women who had spent a lifetime fighting for freedoms that we now tend to take so much for granted.

Ward saw city life then as dehumanising and squalid, and he wrote constantly and at length on what he saw as the spiritual power of landscape. 'This cankering world will never consume your soul if you can only find and realise what beauties there are to be seen, what new life-wine to be drunk, what unsullied happiness awaits you, outside this grimy city – an ugly picture in a glorious frame.'

Even in his seventies, he walked lesser mortals to a standstill and all his life he was the scourge of bad gamekeepers and Water Board officials. For ten years he was under a court injunction not to trespass

Edale and the Kinder Ridge from Mam Tor

on Kinder Scout, although unofficially he did, and on one famous occasion a keeper who tried to hit him was ducked in a beck, several times. Lose Hill was bought by Sheffield's rambling community and named after him in 1945. At the presentation ceremony, Ward said that he'd never been a landowner before and handed the hill over to the National Trust to belong to the nation for all time.

An Iron Age chieftain has lain buried on this summit for two thousand years. Now as Ward's Piece, it commemorates a warrior of another kind. There's a direction finder here and little else, and feet have almost scrubbed its crown quite bare. As I arrived on the summit, a party of schoolchildren in spandex cycling shorts, mutant ninja thingy hats, tee-shirts and designer trainers, were clambering all

The same scene but in summer

over the place, and I'm quite certain Bert Ward would have approved.

I sat for a time in the sun and took a few pictures of walkers heading down to the valley and para-gliders leaping off the far away Win Hill. Local legend has it that Win Hill and Lose Hill were named after the winners and the losers of a great battle, when the Saxon King Edwin of Mercia marched against Cicholm, King of Wessex. They met and did battle in the Hope Valley; Edwin, the victor, camped on what was later to be known as Win Hill and his opponent on Lose Hill. I've got to admit it seems a bit unlikely to me, but there you go.

The hill was getting a bit crowded so I turned back the way I had come, past Back Tor and along by Hollins Cross to Mam Tor, rambling along under a searing sun with a heat haze rising from the

Walkers leaving Mam Tor for the valley

Families on Mam Tor

valley floor. The earthworks of Mam Tor showed up clearly in the sunlight. It must have been an almost impregnable site in the days when it was a manned Iron Age fort. Some people believe that 'Mam' relates to the earth mother and means exactly what 'mam' means today, the Tor being therefore 'Mother Mountain'. There was a fortified village here, three sides of it ramparts and walls, the fourth, the sheer face of the Shivering Mountain itself. When frost has poked fingers of ice into its face, the whole mountain trembles and flakes and massive earth slides and shale slips crash to the valley below. One such landslip took out the road to Castleton not so long ago and since then the Winnats Pass has been the only way in and out from this side.

When I first went to Mam Tor, I thought that, like some of the promontory forts in Ireland, it may have served as a defence only in times of war when women, children and cattle would be herded inside the ramparts while the men gave battle before the walls. But it seems that the Iron Age in this area of north Derbyshire was a lawless and troublesome time and that Mam Tor was a fortified village of a hundred or so houses contained within substantial ramparts, high enough, at 1700ft above sea level, to look down on all the land around it. Like Ingleborough in the Yorkshire Dales, it was a Brigante settlement and the earthworks which now look so insignificant, would, at the time, have been substantial. Traces of the hut circles can still be seen, particularly on the eastern side, and are the last remnants of a large community who once lived up here, ever on the watch for raiders and marauders.

Imagining what the life of the Iron Age peoples was like is difficult. The landscape itself has changed entirely for, at that time, the valley bottoms would still have been the marshy and densely-wooded haunt of wolves and wild boars, and only on the ridges would a man have had a clear view of the surrounding terrain. Barrows and beacon hills, henges and settlements would have been cleared islands, rising above an ocean of trees, but from the forests raiders could have poured at any

moment. Great pitched battles with thousands of warriors were less likely than constant skirmishes. It is probably more realistic to imagine a band of raiders, working at speed and on horseback, suddenly attacking a village, taking cattle, women and valuables, then making off as fast as they came, melting into the forests, whooping and singing. The raiders would have been tribesmen whose crops had failed perhaps, or whose women or cattle had died or proved barren. They could also have been wandering robber bands who, with their small tented camps would travel quickly, raiding and moving on.

The view from the Mother Mountain today shows not a sea of trees but a patchwork land of counterpane, with Castleton shimmering in the haze and the stumps of Baslow Cement Works to the right. And now there were families taking the sun and lying all over the summit

The tree on Rushup Edge

looking dark and thunderous. By the track is a tree, buffeted so constantly by the wind that it has grown crooked, as though it has been softened in a forge and then hammered into shape, and a little further on, at the high point of the ridge, is another tumulus to balance that on Lose Hill. The graves of these old kings or tribal chiefs must have possessed a great significance; looking out over the land below, they would have been as symbolic then as the Vatican, the White House or the Houses of Parliament are today. You find such graves all over the Pennines, from Wild Boar Fell in the north of the Yorkshire Dales, to here in the south, relics of an intriguing, but unfathomable past.

The Peak District Footpath Preservation Society managed to reclaim the old way from Barber Booth to Castleton in 1939 and a plaque at the end of the ridge, where the ridge path meets the bridleway, commemorates this. A couple were sitting here, taking a breather, and we waved to each other as I passed and began the long descent to Barber Booth.

The sky was darkening now to that shade of indigo that just precedes summer storms, an oily purple-green that brings a strange almost luminous glow to the land, making the hedges and grass of the meadows burn almost with a green fire. Great drops of rain were making splashes the size of soup plates in the dust on the road as I hurried along towards Edale but the expected storm never came and by the time I reached the Rambler Inn the clouds were breaking again and slashes of sunlight were moving along the flanks of Kinder.

where so much blood was spilt as battle and death cries tore the air all those years ago.

I left the summit and set off towards Rushup Edge, dropping down to the saddle where the road to Edale crosses the ridge, and, as I began climbing again, a bank of cloud moved over the land from the west,

A Free Man on Sunday

For an hour on Sunday mornings it looks like Bank Holiday in the Manchester stations, except that families do not go to Blackpool for Whit-week in shorts. South countrymen gasp to look at it.

Patrick Monkhouse: *On Foot in North Wales and the Peak*

WHEN I WAS A SMALL BOY, the name Kinder Scout held a magic that few other places possessed. It was hard and sometimes dangerous country, we all knew that. According to our mythology, lots of people had died there, and it was easy to get lost in its maze of bogs, particularly in winter. It was the first really hard hill-walking I did when, as second of the Fox Patrol 108th Manchester Scout Troop, I slogged across it in a pitiless rainstorm, wearing an old army cape and a pair of boots that had been handed down to me by an eccentric relation. We got lost at the top of Crowden and wandered round for hours, sinking in bogs up to our thighs and finding ourselves turning up at the same marker stone over and again. The rain came from every direction, down, sideways and upside down and all of us got so wet and frozen we ended up with colds that kept us off school for days. Not bad for June. The boots expired a few months later on a hot summer's day on the flanks of Penyghent in the Yorkshire Dales, where they were buried on the spot in a peat bog with full military honours. So far as I know, they're still there.

It was a wonder they didn't die that day up on Kinder and join the legion of lost soles up there because its sticky peat groughs have claimed many a boot and shoe. The groughs, some of them up to fifteen feet deep, are what make Kinder so terrifying. Even walking across them on a compass bearing can be totally disorientating as you descend their slimy slopes, jump the gurgling stream at the bottom and scramble up the other side to find that you've skewed several points away from your set direction. *Don't go anywhere on Kinder in any sort of weather without a map and compass. There's a lot of peat and a lot of sharp edges to fall off.*

Kinder Scout means 'water over the edge' according to one book I read and comes from the Old English *Cindur Scwd*. Another book claims that Kinder means 'hill' and Scout comes from *scutti* meaning 'crag' in Old Norse. I don't know any Old Norse but that does make more sense – the name would then mean 'hill of crags', which seems fitting enough. Scout, as in Thievely Scout above Cliviger near Burnley, is not an uncommon name for the rock outcrops of these northern valleys but Kinder meaning 'water over the edge' seems a bit prosaic for something as grand as this twenty-square-mile plateau.

But of course Kinder is something more than all of that, more than the sum of its parts. To many people, its name alone has a symbolism as strong as a flag or a religious shrine, for Kinder was the scene of one of the greatest mass-trespasses of all time and though many people feel that politically it achieved little at the time, morally and emotionally it was a powerful rallying force and still is today.

Its leaders went to prison for their conviction that the common people, having been robbed of the uplands by the Enclosures, still had a right to roam in freedom on the uncultivated moors. The story of the struggle for access in this country that brought about the Kinder Trespass is long and far too complex to be dealt with in any depth in a book of this kind, but it is something that concerns me deeply enough for me to try and sketch it out in the next few paragraphs. I do tend to go on a bit so those of you who know the story already or who suspect that I might be tub-thumping can skip the next bit.

The first application for free access to all uncultivated uplands in the British Isles was made by the Bryce Commission in 1884 and the first mass-trespass took place on Winter Hill near Bolton in 1896 when a landowner tried to close down rights of way that had been enjoyed for hundreds of years across a recently created grouse shoot and ten thousand people 'trespassed' on the moor. Therefore, the Kinder mass-trespass could be said to have had both a precedent, and to have had a legal parliamentary parallel. Much of the uplands of Britain were, until the nineteenth century, of little interest to landowners since they were often the poorest and most barren types of land – mountains, crags, heather-moor and peat bog. None but the poorest farmers lived there. Packhorse routes and paths crossed them or skirted their edges and, until the Enclosures, they were open common land, free to all.

Then, in Victoria's reign, thanks to the Widow at Windsor herself, it became fashionable for men (and women) to go onto the heathery hills to shoot little birds, and the fate of the moors was sealed. This attitude towards land that sees it as a playground for the sport of the rich dates from Norman times when the King and his knights created their deer forests and chases, and when a man could be castrated and blinded for stealing the King's Royal Venison. From their enclosure in the years of Victoria, the grouse moors of northern England, were jealously guarded, and walkers were regularly turned back from open moors, in many cases being threatened with guns or beaten with sticks. Ironically, this closure of the uplands coincided with the explosion of rambling as a leisure pastime amongst a working class that was increasingly finding life in the industrial cities unbearable.

Benny Rothman: *The 1932 Kinder Trespass*

> 1932 was a grim year in Britain. Unemployment had reached peak proportions and particularly hard hit were the big industrial areas of Lancashire and Yorkshire. Manchester, Salford, Sheffield and the dozens of smaller towns and villages in the counties were deserts of bricks, mortar and cobblestones. Living conditions were desperately bad with bug-ridden and verminous houses. Not many had gardens, there were few trees, shrubs or flowers in the soul-destroying waste. The only way to enjoy a little fresh air and sunshine was to escape into the countryside. Even though the public parks existed in towns, these were no substitute for the real thing.

So in the 1930s, thousands of young people poured out of the northern industrial cities on special trains to walk in the hills. Derbyshire was particularly popular because of its beauty and because of its proximity to the great cities. They came in their droves to walk around Dovedale and the Winnats Pass, Millersdale and Mam Tor. But although they came to Edale, and although there were footpaths round its base, the great massif of Kinder was forbidden land. Its owner in the thirties was James Watts, a cotton magnate from Manchester, whose beautifully designed city warehouse and offices is now a hotel. Watts did allow hikers on to Kinder, but only if they wrote in for a permit – and then only four or so were given for each weekend.

By 1932 things were beginning to reach boiling point in the walking world. The Access to Mountains Bill that the Ramblers Association had lobbied for so fiercely was getting nowhere slowly. Although America, as a result of the work of a Scot called John Muir, had been the first country in the world to create a National Park with the designation of Yellowstone as such in 1872, although the colonies of the Empire such as Canada and New Zealand had them, although most countries in Europe had them and although even the Free State of Ireland had just designated land in Killarney as Ireland's first National Park, Britain had nary a one, such was the jealousy and suspicion amongst its landowners and political overlords.

The actual Kinder Trespass was sparked off by an incident at Easter 1932 when a group of ramblers from London, who were guests of the British Workers' Sports Federation, were prevented from getting on to Bleaklow by a group of gamekeepers who abused and threatened them at Yellow Slacks. After the incident, ramblers from Sheffield, Manchester, Salford and Stockport decided to hold a mass trespass onto Kinder Scout, choosing Kinder as the symbolic site for the trespass because it was the largest area of prohibited land without a single footpath across it.

They publicised their intent to trespass on Kinder on Sunday 24 April and, on the Sunday appointed, Benny Rothman, one of the young organisers of the mass-trespass, arrived at Hayfield on his bicycle. It was lucky that he decided to pedal from Manchester because the police were looking for him at both Hayfield Station and Manchester's London Road Station with warrants for his arrest. Hundreds of ramblers were already there and, when Benny arrived,

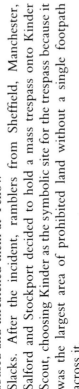

The plaque commemorating the Mass Trespass of 1932

blers cheered loudly and, after another address, turned and walked back to Hayfield, an orderly, singing and laughing crowd. In Hayfield, the police and the keepers were waiting for them and Benny Rothman and four others were arrested and taken to the Hayfield lock-up, where a rambler called Anderson who had been involved in a fracas with a keeper was already incarcerated. All the ramblers were young men aged from nineteen to twenty-three years old.

At the Derby Assizes, before a Grand Jury of two brigadier generals, three colonels, two majors, three captains, two aldermen and assorted country gentlemen, they were given sentences ranging from four to six months for unlawful assembly and breach of the peace while Anderson was charged with grievous bodily harm. One

they made their way to a disused quarry where, after a few brief speeches they set off towards Kinder with the police, who had by then arrived in some numbers, trailing behind them. Half way up William Clough, the four hundred or so ramblers, laughing and singing, turned at a given signal and began the scramble up towards the plateau's edge. At this point, a group of twenty to thirty gamekeepers arrived and threatened the trespassers with sticks.

There is some doubt as to how far onto Kinder the Manchester party got, but there is no doubt that they did trespass onto the forbidden lands where they met a group of ramblers from Sheffield who had come up the Snake Path to meet them. The ramof the defendants was given an extra month because he was also found guilty of selling the *Daily Worker* and all six of them were taken to serve their sentences in Leicester Jail.

Opinions on the effectiveness of the protest vary. Many of the people striving for access at the time, including the official Manchester Ramblers' Federation, felt that it was a retrograde step, although even Tom Stephenson, no great fan of the trespass says: 'To my mind that was nonsense. The story of the way in which Arthur Creech Jones's Access to Mountains Bill of 1939 was butchered in Parliament is sufficient indication of how little hope of access legislation there was at that time.'

What it probably did, more than anything else, was focus the public's attention on an injustice they may perhaps not even have been aware of and papers such as the liberal *Manchester Guardian* reported the case in full. Morally it pointed to a great imbalance in both the law that kept men and women from mountains which had once been free for all to roam upon, and in the machinery that could be brought to bear upon those who transgressed that law. As a letter writer to the *Guardian* pointed out, had the trespass been a Varsity Rag the defendants would have got off with a fine and a severe wigging.

Emotionally, as a piece of direct action that has near relations in the Tonypandy Riots and the Jarrow Hunger March, the Kinder Trespass served, and still serves, as a symbol of resistance and protest. The song *The Manchester Rambler*, written by Ewan McColl, the seventeen-year-old press officer on the trespass, is still the ramblers' anthem and a fine song it is too.

But things have changed little, and even as I sit here on this fine summer morning typing this chapter, Benny Rothman, now in his eightieth year, is trespassing, with other ramblers, on the moors near Holmfirth where access of a couple of hundred yards that would connect a bridleway to the Pennine Way is forbidden. In the same area, at Ramsden Clough, walkers have been threatened by game-keepers with guns on land that once belonged to the Yorkshire Water Board, now Yorkshire Water Inc; it is leased off to one of the country's major breweries who use it as a grouse moor for the entertainment of foreign visitors. La Lutte Continua!

Kinder is now free for all to roam upon, having been bought for the nation by the National Trust and although many of the ways up on to Kinder are getting very worn, it is still a magnificent plateau ('hill' is too misleading a word to use about a land mass that has no summit) and the round of Kinder from Edale is one of the best days out you'll ever have. Edale, thankfully, is on the Manchester to Sheffield main line so that it is possible to get there by train which many people do and, on a Saturday and Sunday in particular, the trains are all well packed. Edale itself is a bonny little hamlet with a camp-site, a youth hostel, two good pubs and some fine tea rooms and it is, of course, the starting point for the Pennine Way.

Jacob's Ladder is my favourite way on to Kinder from Edale. The Pennine Way route is badly worn now and needs a respite although, as Tom Stephenson once pointed out, the fact that a path is worn just means it is being used, and scars caused by footpath erosion are nothing when compared to the ravages of quarrying or the tracks gouged through the hills for deer stalking, forestry vehicles or the military. Jacob's Ladder is named (according to one story) after a 'jagger' or packhorse man called Jacob, who used to leave his animals slowly zigzagging their way up the packhorse route while he scram-bled directly up the Ladder so that he'd have time to sit and enjoy his pipe before they caught him up.

It's a good way onto the plateau although steep enough in its final half-mile to be a good hard pull. I walked it a few years ago with my mate Tony, one late autumn day when there was a damp chill in the air and clearing rain clouds were moving eastward. The wind that was following them looked as though it would keep any foul weather on

Looking north from the top of Jacob's Ladder

The half-man shapes of the Wool Packs

the move so we left Edale and followed the path towards Barber Booth and the Ladder. Booth is an old word meaning a walled enclosure and comes from the days when stock was brought in each night to protect it from wolves and rustlers. We passed Crowden Brook, another way up onto the plateau that I've used often before, and climbed up to Kinder Low from where we could see clear across to Stockport, its high-rise blocks shining in the sun.

A couple of years before I had walked the Crowden Brook path, climbing steadily into a low mist and, once on the Edge, I'd walked on a compass bearing all day. It was eerie wandering through that featureless peat moonscape and then suddenly coming on the huddled, half-man shapes of the Wool Packs in the mist. The Wool Packs are just one of the gritstone formations on Kinder that have been given

fanciful names over the years, in this case because they are said to resemble bales of wool. Other names for them are 'Whipsnade' and the 'Mushroom Garden' while some of the stones have individual names like the Moat Stone and the Pagoda. Coming at them in the mist they looked more like something out of Walt Disney's *Fantasia* and I half expected them to start dancing to Tchaikovsky but, as I've explained before, I have a funny sort of brain and am prone to such things.

The official Pennine Way route goes directly across the wilderness of Kinder and can be reasonable walking after a drought (I once crossed it kicking up dust all the way from Kinder Gates to Grindsbrook) although even then climbing up and down the twelve- to fifteen-foot gullies or 'groughs', can be a bit of a bind. After a period of good rain, however, it's like walking through a maze made of

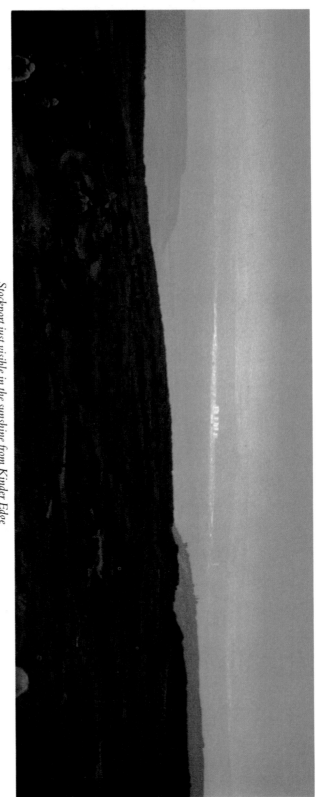

Stockport just visible in the sunshine from Kinder Edge

chocolate-coloured porridge and once in those groughs you can wander round for hours. All extremely good fun and entirely laudable if you're a masochist, but to be avoided by any with a claim to normality.

We walked the Edge to Kinder Downfall, with few people about even though it was a Sunday, and stopped there for a brew. The Downfall is where the River Kinder drops over The Edge, and its rocky gully provides both good scrambling and shelter. When there's a good deal of water flowing and a strong wind is blowing from the south, the spray from the Downfall is blown so high that people reckon you can see it from Stockport, which is a terrible thought – to be stuck in Stockport and able to see Kinder. In winter, the Downfall is a wonderful sight, thick organ pipes of ice piled one behind another hang from the lip to the rocks far below. And that's one of the best times to see Kinder, on a day of good hard frost with a dense blue sky and a warming sun, when the bogs are frozen solid and you can crack along the plateau without sinking up to your oxters in black goo.

The wind had dropped and the sun had begun to warm the day as we walked from the Downfall to Mill Hill. It's an easy stretch of walking and as we travelled the edge we could see coloured dots far below us that were walkers coming up the Pennine Way from the Snake Pass. The route crosses Featherbed Moss (one of the many so named in these Dark Peaks) and I remember that crossing it when I

Two of Kinder's gritstone outcrops: the Boxing Gloves, and (right) what looks like a row of heads

walked the Pennine Way was a nightmare. Even after a long dry spring, the Moss was a sodden mass of peat with broad deep gulleys that my little legs only just managed to leap. After that, kicking across the dusty wilderness of Kinder through Kinder Gates and on was a doddle.

I have often walked on to Kinder from Hayfield and, coming that way, you pass close to the Mermaid's Pool which, like the Doxey Pool on The Roaches has a naiad or water sprite hidden in its depths. In certain lights it can evoke a powerful atmosphere and local legend has it that the pool is connected directly to the Atlantic and that its waters are so salty that no fish can live in them. It certainly is supposed to contain a lot of salts but these have probably been leached out of the peak high above. Mrs Henry Ward used the legend of the mermaid's pool in her novel *David Grieve*, and a poet, Henry Kirke, wrote a

ballad which depicted the mermaid as a siren who lures shepherd boys into the pool where they expire from trying to breathe the water. It was claimed that anyone who saw the mermaid on Easter Eve would either be gifted with eternal life or would drop dead on the spot. Aaron Ashton, a retired soldier of Hayfield who died in 1835, came to the pool every Easter Eve and although he never saw the mermaid once he lived to be 104, which must go to show something – possibly that chasing mermaids helps you live longer.

Tony and I stopped at the Boxing Gloves – another of Kinder's famous gritstone outcroppings – and looked down at a line of walkers on the Snake Path making their way up Ashop Clough. Until recent years, it was the only permitted footpath anywhere near Kinder and runs from the Snake Inn to Hayfield via William Clough and was created after the efforts of the Peak District and Northern Counties

The valley below the summit of Kinder; the white dot is the Snake Inn

Looking towards Farebrook Naze from the Snake Pass

Footpaths Preservation Society who appealed for £1,000 to put forward their case that the Snake Path was an ancient right of way. The landowners did their best to thwart the case but eventually, after long and wearying discussions and negotiations, they reached agreement in 1897 and what had once been a right of way became a right of way again.

The walk along this part of The Edge is one of the great pleasures of the round of Kinder. The path crosses the impressive gully at Fair Brook and goes on by the stones at Seal Edge. Below is Seal Flats and the Woodlands Valley with the white speck of the Snake Inn. The inn was built in 1821 as a coaching inn where horses could be changed on the Manchester to Sheffield turnpike and the name comes from the coat of arms of the Cavendish family who owned much of the land hereabouts, their emblem being a snake.

Following the Edge round, we came to Madwoman's Stones from where you can see clear across to Derwent Edge and Howden Reservoir. Nobody knows why the stones are so called but you can't help but suspect some sad tale being associated with them. The Druid's Stone close at hand has a few small indentations on its top that have led some people to believe that they were for collecting blood while others say that they are possibly just water-worn depressions. I tend to keep an open mind when anything in these northern hills is attributed to druids.

The light was going by the time we had followed the Edge path clear round to Ringing Roger and the top of Golden Clough and, although we'd originally intended to carry on and follow Grindsbrook Clough back down to Edale, we turned instead and followed the zig-zag path below the 'Echoing Rocks' as Ringing Roger is sometimes called (Roger is an anglicisation of *roche* the French for rock). The views from the Echoing Rocks across the Edale Valley over to Mam Tor and the Great Ridge are well worth a stop and we just had

time to take it all in before we made our way through the gathering dusk to Edale.

I remember once dropping down Grindsbrook Clough and meeting two of the strangest characters I've ever seen in the hills, and I swear on my grandmother's donkey, that every word of this is true. It was late on a summer's afternoon and I had walked alone from Crowden across Bleaklow and Kinder. I was just a few hundred yards from Edale when I saw coming towards me what at first I thought were two piles of scrap metal and jumble. I shook my head, thinking it was the heat of the day that had got to me, or that all the jumping up and down in the peat groughs had done permanent damage to my imagine gland, but there they were, still coming very slowly towards me, labouring up the path, two heaps of gear the like I have never seen before or since. When I drew alongside them, I saw that it was two men, dressed identically.

I stopped to talk to them and found out that they were father and son. It was half past five in the afternoon and they were just setting off on the Pennine Way. They were carrying old Blacks' rucksacks circa 1949, around which were clustered an assortment of various sizes of billycans, a stove, a tent, a small shovel, any number of ex-army water bottles, a tin first-aid box, whistles, compasses, a large frying pan, what at first I thought was another frying pan but was in fact a ukulele-banjo, and some short coils of climbing rope. Both father and son wore tweed jackets and cavalry twill trousers, collar and tie. They said goodbye and wandered off into the heat haze, their thumb-sticks pounding the hard-baked earth in rhythm and, from amidst the clutter, an old transistor radio blared out, Brian Johnstone's smooth as cricket-turf voice, telling me that England was taking yet another pounding from the West Indies at Lords.

It was a most bizarre meeting. I hope they made it to Kirk Yetholm but I've got to say, in my heart of hearts, I doubt it.

Dam Busters and Lost Shepherds

*Through streets by shops and inns
eels inch and patrolling pike
lunge from their dens amongst gargoyles.
Chrysalids burrow in roof tiles
and chubb and bream mouth the moss
that furs the flooded ingle, while,
in the forge's cave an old roach
nuzzles at the slime-filled hearth.
Carp loom through bell towers,
mouthing lichen on dull clappers,
men walling on far fells hear them out-ring,
swung, by the lake's slow undertow tugged.*

From 'Drowned Cities' by the author

ON THE GREAT WATERSHEDS of Bleaklow and Harden Moor, the drizzle falls gently, dripping from the fringes of heather, bent and fern above the peaty pools, gathering and running over the gritstone, trickling and pooling and flowing into the groughs, the trickles becoming rills, the rills becoming becks, the becks rolling down from gritstone and peat, draining the sodden sponge bulk of the wilderness above. The valleys of Derwent, Alport and Westend drain Bleaklow while, from Derwent Edge, the cloughs carry the rushing water; and all of this white gold falls down into the great man-made lakes of Derwent and Howden. At the end of the last century, the bowl of lovely land below Bleaklow and Derwent Edge was peaceful and lush, its two villages of Derwent and Ashopton untroubled. But by 1945, the villages, their churches, houses and schools and, more importantly, their communities, had all gone and the valley had been drowned.

The dams at Howden and Derwent were built by the Derwent Valley Water Board to supply water in bulk for the cities of Derby, Nottingham, Leicester and Sheffield. Begun in 1901, Howden was finished in 1912 and Derwent in 1916. Like the railways, those other great Victorian and Edwardian feats of engineering, the dam works employed hundreds of masons, engineers, carpenters, smiths and navvies. At one time, there were more than 900 people living in a

Ladybower Reservoir

The mock castles at the dam of Howden Reservoir

temporary village called Birchinlee, half way up the road to the west of Howden Reservoir. Here the navvies lived with their families; they had a shop, hospital, village school and chapel. A third reservoir, Ladybower, was begun in May 1935 and completed in 1945, and used a staggering amount of materials – 100,000 tons of concrete, 100,000 tons of puddle clay and a million tons of earth. There was tremendous opposition both locally and nationally, and there are some who believe still that the reservoir, which destroyed the villages of Derwent and Ashopton and flooded the lovely Woodlands Valley, should never have been built. People grieved in particular at the destruction of the church at Derwent and the generations of the dead that had to be exhumed and re-interred at Bamford.

During the Second World War, Derwent Reservoir was used by the crews of RAF 617 Squadron as a practice site for what were later to be called 'The Dambuster Raids' on the Mohn and Eider dams in Germany. The famous film, with its even more famous march, was shot using the same dams. The Ladybower pub nearby has on its signboard a picture of a Lancaster Bomber and, on special occasions, a lone Lancaster makes a flight over the dam in memory of the men who died on the raids.

There has been a certain amount of regimented softwood planting on the flanks of the hills above Howden and Derwent Reservoirs but, that apart, the reservoirs have created man-made lakes that seem to blend with the landscape. If harmony between industrial man and nature is ever possible, then here, to some extent, it is achieved, particularly at Howden Dam where the stone curtain of the barrage is flanked by two mock castles, while all around its banks, the forests gather. At least the Edwardians tried.

The land above the dams is the gathering ground, peat moorland that blankets the wilds of Bleaklow and rolls in from the east over Howden Moor to end in the gritstone crags of Derwent Edge. Walk the Edge on a blue cold day in April, when a cut-throat wind skittles

small bunched clouds across the sky like tumbled white hares and sends sun and shadow ragbag over the land all the way across to Bleaklow and Kinder, and you'll have a day of days.

One such Sunday, belted up, and rucksack filled with sandwiches and a couple of cans of diet something or other, Pat and I left the Ladybower Reservoir at Ashopton and climbed up past a few well-built stone houses and through the edge of a small wood onto the fell. Our way up was by a trough gouged from the moor's edge, I would guess, by quarrymen. You find these old ditches all over the Pennines, wherever a good seam of rock out-crops. Quarrymen working small faces dragged their stone down off the tops on wooden sledges and, over the years, their daily passing scored the face of the land. Now that the quarries are gone and the ditches overgrown, they make a good way up up onto the tops, sheltered from the wind for a while. A lark, in spite of the buffeting wind, somehow rose straight in the whirling air and carolled its bubbling song above us as we climbed the last few yards to the Edge. The great thing about edge walks is that, like ridge walks, all the hard work is done at the beginning, and your reward is a toddle along the tops with the world spread below you.

'Tor' – from the OE *torr* (rock, rocky peak) – a word that is little used outside Derbyshire and Dartmoor, is here used to describe the rocky, wind-carved outcrops that are found all along the Edge. Along Derwent Edge outcrop are found the gritstone teeth of White Tor, Dovestone Tor and Back Tor, and between the first two lurks what somebody once called the 'lonely sentinel' of the Salt Cellar – although I've got to say that if I had a salt cellar like that in the house, I'd throw it out.

At Back Tor, the massive rocks, house-high, have been gnawed and battered by the wind and rain into massive rounded blocks and slabs. One rock, just below the main outcrop looks from one angle like the Mekon, the famous villain and arch-enemy of Dan Dare, the 'Pilot of the Future' hero of the *Eagle*. We found a spot out of the wind below the Mekon Stone and sat in its sun-trap for a while, watching parties of walkers coming over the moor. Close to Sheffield and Manchester, these hills

Pat climbing up on to Derwent Edge

attract thousands of walkers each weekend and have always prompted me to ask the question 'If our cities are all that good, why do so many people get out of them at the first chance they get?'

From Back Tor, where a carving in the rocks below the summit trig point reads 'Mary and Jack engaged here March 5 1933', a path leads out to a mound of stones and a round direction marker on a hump called Lost Lad. Here, one spring day in the sixteenth century, a shepherd found the body of a young boy, the only son of a widow woman of Derwent. During the previous winter, so local folk-lore tells us, the village was blocked by a snow-storm that lasted for days and the people were unable to get out to tend their flocks. When the storm subsided, the boy fought his way through the drifts encircling the village, and with his sheepdog he set out up the fell to bring down whatever sheep he could find. A blizzard blew up while he was out and, unable to find his way back, he wandered for hours lost on the moors. Lying down by the stones for shelter, he took a rock and scratched a message on a boulder before crawling beneath it. Eventually the cold took him and he died there at 1,700 feet. The pathetic sign scratched on the boulder led the shepherd the following spring to what was left of the boy's body. 'Lost Lad', the sign read, just two pitiful words, but they said it all. Ever since then, it is said, every shepherd passing this way has placed a stone

Walkers making their way to White Tor

Pat on the Salt Cellar, Derwent Edge

on the boulder, which is why there is such a massive pile there today.

We rambled along from Lost Lad, following the path down to Sheepfold Clough, looking for a place to eat our sandwiches out of the wind, a spot where the sun could warm us, and close by a brook so we could have a drink. Under Berristers Tor, a path runs parallel to Abbey Brook and we followed it for some way, the brook too far below us to be of any use, until we met the stream and ford at Cogman Clough. There, in another little suntrap, we sprawled and listened to one of the greatest sounds in the world, the noise of a moorland stream, grumbling and muttering over its rocky bed, counterpoint to the song of a lark high above. Those two sounds, and the smell of peat and heather, are things I can conjure up in my mind's eye almost at a wish and are probably what has saved me from going mad on long tours on the road, living out of a suitcase and looking out of the window of some anonymous hotel, wondering where the hell I am.

I once woke up in a big hotel somewhere, in a featureless bedroom, with the same trouser press, the same kettle and brewing facilities, the same television and the same washed out print of some minor French Depressionist and I didn't have an earthly where I was. I looked out of the window; there was an office block and a street with a McDonald's, a Marks and Sparks, a Top Shop, and all the other stores you find in every town centre in Britain, so much is our element of choice. By now I was panicking. I rang down to reception to ask where I was.

'Room 507,' she said.

'Yes, but what town?'

'Are you serious?'

'Never been more serious in my life.'

'Middlesbrough,' she said. Now there's nothing wrong with Middlesbrough – but it ain't a heather moor.

Pat and I followed Abbey Brook down to the dam at Howden, with its massive castellated walls, and sat for a while by the grassy woodland path that leads to Derwent Dam. One summer's day not long ago, I walked the Edge to Lost Lad, but instead of dropping down by Abbey Brook, had carried on to Margery Hill, coming off the Edge by Little Cut and following the path to the valley bottom and Slippery Stones. There is an old packhorse bridge here that once stood in Derwent village, where it carried the old track from Derwent to Glossop. The Water Board had plans to demolish it but it was scheduled under the Ancient Monuments Act of 1931, so they had to take it to pieces, stone by stone, numbering each one. The cost of removal and re-erection was reckoned at £1,000, towards which the Water Board contributed £50. Eventually the money was raised and the bridge re-built where you can see it now. Once across the bridge, there is a walk back to the Derwent dam that in mid-week is fairly quiet; just before the footpath meets the road at King's Tree are the stepping stones at Linch Clough.

There were farms all along this valley once that were abandoned after the flooding, on the grounds of pollution. One of them, Ronksley Farm, stood just up from the stepping stones; Joseph Tagg was born there in 1867. Joe Tagg was one of the best known sheep-farmers and sheepdog-trainers in the South Pennines. He was a champion trialist and bred, trained and sold dogs all his life; many of the dogs that are winning trials today are great-grandpups of dogs bred by Joe.

In 1953 Joe was eighty-six and was becoming confused and forgetful. On a cold December day, he set off with his dog, Tip, and wandered up into the Westend valley as the light was fading and a cold night coming in. He was never seen alive again. People think that perhaps he was wandering back to the fells of his youth or perhaps he was going up to fetch down sheep he remembered from sixty years ago. Nobody will ever know what drove him up onto the fell. He was found fifteen weeks later at the end of March on Ridgewalk Moor,

An outcrop on Derwent Edge which looks just like the Mekon

more than 1500 feet up. Tip, his faithful bitch, emaciated and so weak she was close to death, had remained beside him all that time. Rescue teams had come close but none close enough, so Tip had stayed with her master. She survived the ordeal and, when she eventually died, she was buried up on the moors above Derwent. A memorial plaque telling her story stands near the wall of the dam.

We sat for ages beside the lake in sunshine that, for a cold April day, was proving almost summer like. Eventually we had to go and hauling on the packs containing the wet weather gear and survival blankets and fibre-piles and mittens and balaclavas we had taken just in case, we sweated our way down the dale. They were selling giant ice creams at Jubilee Cottage and I reckoned we'd earned one after the day we'd had, so I asked Pat if she would buy us some. I never have any money because I'm always forgetting to go to the hole in the wall that gives you money. Sometimes she finds this amusing, other times she reminds me that the only people who consistently go round without money are Royalty and lunatics. I know which group she thinks I belong to.

The Kissing Stones
or The World's Worst Paper Round

Bleaklow Stones ring in a gritty wind, ringing rochers,
fluting the columns of air, vox humana, their great pipe
booms over the Devil's Dyke.

    Above the smoky towns

where sweating apprentices and millgirls walked
the free man's Sunday under keepers' stares, his dust
now blows, dust from a Salford street, and two stones,
bulge, bouldered faces, angle-eyed, two Celtic heads,
twin worlds of life and death. Our voices on the wind,
the murmurings of lark and singing lips,
in these stones seem to meet and, singing, kiss.

    'Bleaklow Stones' by the author, in memoriam Ewan MacColl

B LEAKLOW. The name can make strong men shudder and children weep, for like Black Hill further north, Bleaklow can have its moods and on a sad day, when grey flannel clouds spew water upon you and the peat moors suck you down into their nightmarish groughs, then you can feel like a piece of human meat in a very wet sandwich. Tempers get high, morale and language get low and you wonder what the Lady Chatterley you're doing up here when sensible people are still abed or are devouring the Sunday comics over the smoked salmon, scrambled egg and Buck's Fizz. Still, Bleaklow exists to impress. It is a hulk of a moor, with shoulders of gritstone, and a

good way on to it is to walk in by the Roman road that climbs from Glossop up to the Devil's Dike. I've climbed Bleaklow dozens of times and in every variety of weather except really good.

Eddie and I walked Bleaklow on a late Indian summer's day that promised to be fine in Glossop but changed its mind as we climbed Doctor's Gate. Like Kinder, Doctor's Gate was forbidden to ramblers and was the scene of struggle and trespass. Now it is open for all comers and for most of its length runs along the remains of the old Roman road that took legionnaires over the bleak moor from Glossop to Sheffield. W. A. Poucher in his book, *The Peak and Pennines*, says:

The Roman road at Doctor's Gate

'This sinister mountain should never be explored by the lone climber, even in clear weather, and his only safe wandering should always be in clear sight of the traffic passing over the Snake.'

It isn't quite as bad as that, although I've had times up here when you couldn't see a worm at your feet, never mind a Snake half a mile away. When the mist comes down, or in white-out conditions, it can be bad, and a map and compass can be the only things between you and a pair of Gortex wings and a week's free harp lessons.

It was warm, even though it was still early in the morning when we left Glossop by the side of the old church and, taking the footpath out by the big factory on the outskirts of the town, hit open country just as a local gun club were shooting clay pigeons in a field nearby.

'They're actually clay ramblers and they're just practising,' said ever-cheerful Eddie, although I didn't find it all that funny since two walkers had been shot that summer by grouse-shooters firing across a public footpath near Torside Castle.

Glossop, by the way, is said to mean 'the valley of the staring men' from the Old English 'hop' meaning valley and 'glott', a nickname meaning starer, related to the modern English gloat. One explanation for the name could be nothing to do with the people of Glossop at all, but could relate to the many stone heads that have been found here and in parts of Longdendale as part of what seems to have been the strongest stone head cult in the north, dating from Celtic times, and which may even still be carried on today. All the stone heads have strange staring eyes, hence the name – 'valley of the staring men' – oh well, it's only a theory.

We took the path that runs by Shelf Brook as it flows under Shire Hill and climbed slowly along Doctor's Gate with the morning getting warmer. 'Gate' doesn't mean a door or entrance, it simply means 'path' or 'way', as in Salter's Gate or Limmer's Gate, and Doctor's Gate is just one stretch of a Roman road that ran from what the Romans knew as 'Austerlands' (now called Castleshaw), near

Two of the stone heads at Glossop: note the strange staring eyes

Scout Head above Oldham; it came round by Mossley and Mottram to Glossop, the 'Melandra' of the Romans. From Melandra, it went by the Doctor's Gate to a marching camp at Anvio near Hope, then on by Bamford and Stanage to Sheffield. An inscribed stone found at Melandra indicates that the fort there was manned, like that at Knott Mill in Mancunium, by a cohort of Frisians, from what is now Germany. What they thought of these uplands with their forests and moors, their peat hags, groughs and swamps can only be guessed at.

We climbed slowly up what is left of the old road under Coldhar-

bour Moor towards the nicely-named Birchen Orchard Clough and Urchin Clough. 'Clough' is an old Lancashire word meaning 'gully' or 'small valley', and usually refers to a cut in a hillside with a beck running down it. 'Cloughs' are found in the Lancashire gritstone, 'denes', on the White Rose side of the hill. Doctor's Gate and Devil's Dike, the long trench it meets on the moor top, have a number of myths attached to them.

The Gate is said to be named after a Doctor Talbot, illegitimate son of the Earl of Shrewsbury, who was vicar of Glossop from 1494 to

Walkers in the Devil's Dike

1550 and who used the path frequently, travelling this way on horseback to visit friends in Hope and Castleton. It seems a bit of a prosaic reason for calling something Doctor's Gate and I much prefer another piece of local folk-lore that tells of an apothecary or quack doctor who sold his soul to the devil and, when Old Nick came to claim him, set off on horseback towards Glossop with Old Nick in hot pursuit. Old Nick almost had him when the 'doctor', reaching the deep ditch that is now called Devil's Dike, set his horse to leap it. Since the Dike had a beck running down it, and since the Devil, like all vampires, zombies, ghouls and buggaloos, is unable to cross running water, Old Nick was left on the other side, cursing and hitting himself on the head with his forked tail while the doctor got clean away. Fable and romance apart, the real history of the dyke is not known and some historians feel it may simply mark a Saxon territorial boundary.

For the last few hundred yards of its way, Doctor's Gate is still paved, although much of it is now no more than a rough worn track. We followed it up the gentle pull above Rose Clough, the great walls of Shelf Stones and the deep gully of White Clough away to our left. Shelf Stones are an impressive outcrop at the head of a thousand-foot sweep to the valley bottom. Reaching the top of the Gate, we came by the paved way onto the moor where the track meets with the Pennine Way at a place named on the map as Old Woman.

'This place is called Old Woman,' I told Eddie.

'Sh' int' ere, any road, Tommy,' was all he said as he trudged off to follow the Pennine Way along Devil's Dike and the peat hag maze to Bleaklow. In poor weather, it is here that a compass and map come in very handy, for the moor is a fairly featureless bog. Attempts have been made to plant poles as a guide, although most of them, I'm glad to say, have fallen down or seem to be leading anywhere but where you want to go. The best thing is to ignore them and to look for Hern Clough where a good dry path leads by the beck to the Hern Stones.

The Pennine Way is very eroded here and various trials are being carried out to establish some sort of a path. The Romans and the packhorse-way builders floated their tracks on bales of wool; nowadays we use plastic floating rafts with hard-core surfaces. It seems to have worked in parts but I'm not sure whether the best solution wouldn't be to dig down to the gritstone since natural erosion has done just this along parts of the Dike in any case. Perhaps, left alone, the passage of feet would gouge out something like a track in any case. Too much path-making urbanises a landscape and, just as sticking car parks everywhere simply encourages more cars, so creating artificial footpaths creates more problems. If footpaths get really bad then only the most determined will use them and the very difficulty of a landscape will have a self-limiting effect.

On the subject of waymarking I've got to say that I'm agin it. I don't mind footpath indicators telling you where you leave a road, and the occasional daub of yellow paint to get you round a farmyard, but beyond that waymarkers and cairns and posts turn the wilderness into an urban park. If waymarkers, why not stairs and bannisters and signs telling us we are approaching a 'photo opportunity' like they do in America?

Accuse me of elitism and I'll take it as an accolade. I learned how to get around (and get lost) in the hills the hard way and I think that serving that apprenticeship helped me to understand the nature of the game and to respect the wilderness. 'Things easy got are little thought of,' my Irish grandmother used to say, and turning the wilderness into yet another consumer experience will make us all the poorer. I can do no better than to quote Patrick Monkhouse, the *Guardian* writer and author of two of the best walking books ever written on the subject who, sixty years ago, wrote: 'Walking on mountains seems to me a highly individualised sport and one which repays apprenticeship.' There is I think a danger of over-organising and over-simplifying it.

We trudged along the Devil's Dike, then through the peat bogs on a north-east bearing to Hern Clough and the beck, then continued by the Hern Stones towards Bleaklow Head. 'Hern' I presume is something to do with Herne the Hunter, one of the Green Man figures that crops up in history, myth and literature. As I mentioned earlier in this book, he is the Corn Spirit whose head is literally cut off by the mower each year at harvest, but who miraculously comes back to life again each spring. The leaping in the traditional English Morris Dance is said to represent the Corn Spirit coming back to life and the long-sword tradition of the Morris Dance with its plaited swords, its 'beheading' and 'resurrection' are other echoes. Even the Easter Pace Egg play, with 'dead' St. George being brought back to life by the quack doctor, can be seen as a drama that has come down to us from the first peoples in these islands. Death and Resurrection, Good Friday and Easter, there is a pattern running through them all.

Various images of the Green Man appear all over Britain, often carved on pew ends or misericords in churches. A head peering through thick thorny branches, he is the very spirit of the world, 'the force that through the green fuse drives the flower' as Dylan Thomas says. In his manifestation as Herne, he is a Horned God, the Cernunos of the Celts, and of course also appears as Hob, Jack in the Green and since he had horns, he readily became transformed into the horned devil of Christianity. The Hern Stones and Devil's Dike and the stone heads that have been discovered in great numbers in Glossop and Longdendale may have had strong connections. When the new religion supplanted the old and tried to turn the people away from their old beliefs, many of the gods and rituals went underground and maypoles and November bonfires, hobby horses and mistletoe, lucky horse-shoes and well-dressing go back before any St Bede or St Patrick.

Thinking about it at the time, it felt strange to be walking over a wild part of a moor named after one of the old gods. But that's one of the things I love about walking and maps, the feeling that the land is multi-layered and that, beneath your feet, the scratches and scribbles of history and the hand of man lie upon each other, skin on skin.

Language gives some clues and place names, others, while maps are like books in which, with patience, you can riddle out more than you first see on the page. What at first sight looks like a pulp airport novel turns out to be something good like *Ulysses*. I came across a lovely word a couple of years ago, 'palimpsest'; it means a manuscript that has traces of layers of text, each layer scraped off and written over, but never quite obliterated. It was done to save parchment when parchment was difficult to get hold of, but it meant that you could always trace the other writings faintly under the new. That is the way I view a landscape, as a palimpsest of meanings and people, map upon map, shadow upon shadow.

So my amateur-inspired guess leads me to believe that, if Hern Clough and Bleaklow are so named, they must have been a place of some religious significance to the tribes who lived here. 'Low' as in Arbor Low, means a hill-top burial mound and 'bleak' means dark or black. Bleak as it can be, it is a very special place and a place of some mystery and magic to the thousands of ramblers who come here from the industrial cities of Lancashire and Yorkshire. To one rambler in particular it had a very deep and special significance and I want now to tell you a small story.

I was in Ireland recently, walking around Kerry's beautiful Dingle peninsula, and one lovely June evening I rolled into O'Flaherty's Bar in Dingle town, a pub famous all over the world for the quality of its Irish traditional music. There's rarely a night in O'Flaherty's when musicians of quality don't gather for the *sessiún*. I wandered in, bought a pint of Black Mischief and stood awhile listening to some fiddlers and a box player ripping into a set of reels.

They reckon that if you stay in Dingle town long enough, you will meet everybody you've ever known, and there, coming back from the bar with a pint of Guinness in her hand, was Peggy Seeger, the widow of Ewan MacColl. Ewan, Salford born and bred, was one of the most powerful personalities behind the British Folk Song Revival. He was a

Walkers contemplating the morass of peat hags near the Kissing Stones on Bleaklow

great singer, songwriter, playwright and political agitator, press officer to the Workers' Sports Federation on the occasion of the Mass-Trespass and author of the walker's anthem, *The Manchester Rambler*. He was also a co-founder, with Joan Littlewood, of Theatre Workshop and originator with Peggy of that wonderful BBC series that won the Prix Italia, *The Radio Ballads*.

Not long before he died, I was lucky enough to work with Peggy and Ewan in concert at T.U.C. House, Manchester, now the Museum of Working Class History. He seemed in very good form, if a little tired, and sang beautifully. One recently written song struck me most forcefully as beautiful and dignified, a heartfelt goodbye to everything and everyone he had known and he sang it passionately. He must have known that night he was saying goodbye. It is called 'The Joy of Living'.

Near the Kissing Stones

> Take me to some high place
> Of heather, rock and ling.
> Scatter my dust and ashes
> Feed me to the wind.
> So that I will be
> Part of all you see,
> The air you are breathing.
> I'll be part of the curlew's cry
> And the soaring hawk,
> The blue milkwort
> And the sundew hung with diamonds.
> I'll be riding the gentle wind
> That blows through your hair,
> Reminding you of how we shared
> In the joy of living.

From Ewan MacColl: *Journeyman*

Ewan had died not long before and Peggy told me how the whole family had taken his ashes and several bottles of good Malt and had climbed Bleaklow on a rough old day to scatter his remains about the stones. So if you climb Bleaklow now, think a while of that brave man. Don't pray for him; someone as confirmed an atheist as Ewan wouldn't thank you for prayers. Think instead of some of the great songs he wrote, think of his struggle for working-class culture, and think of how, right until his death, he fought for the rights of people everywhere to freedom, justice and peace, those three most used and most abused words.

The day turned decidedly humpty as we reached the Wain Stones, the Kissing Stones as most people more properly call them. The sun had vanished in thick cloud and the promising summer's day had turned sour and chilly. I've been here in the midst of winter and standing at the Wain Stones in icy mists, it's easy to understand why so many homecoming aircraft were wrecked here during the Second World War as they made for their bases. Lost in low cloud, they slammed

Sunset behind the Kissing Stones

into the peat bogs of Bleaklow and Kinder, some of their crews surviving, though many, of course, were lost. Yards from where we stood, a Lancaster Bomber, a C-47 Skytrain and a Superfortress had crashed in bad weather and the bleak expanse of Kinder is peppered with wrecked aircraft.

In fact, the story of the Mountain Rescue Service really began in this area in 1942 with the work of 'Doc' Crichton and the men of 28 Maintenance Unit who were based at Buxton. As far as the Air Ministry was concerned, they didn't exist, but drawing together a band of volunteers who were prepared to be on call-out, and by 'winning' a jeep, a rocket gun, walkie-talkie sets and various other bits of equipment, they were able to get together a squad that would turn out, often after a day's work, struggle through the night to locate and save downed airmen, and then be back on duty the following morning. Eventually, by the end of 1943, after 571 airmen had died on high ground, the Ministry was convinced, and in January 1944 the Mountain Rescue Service was officially formed.

The rain that had been threatening for the last half-hour finally arrived and by way of variety decided to fall sideways. I pointed out to Eddie the two stones that, when viewed from the right angle, look as though they're kissing. 'The Pennine Way is 270 miles long,' I said, 'and this is the only bit of sex you get.' Eddie just grunted something about not being surprised it was the only sex you'd get up here if the weather was this bad all the time.

We sat in the shelter of the stones to eat our butties and opened the flask of hot tea. We hadn't been sitting for more than a few minutes before we saw, coming slowly through the murk and peat bogs before us, a lone cyclist on a mountain bike. He huffed his way up to us through the mist, slowed to a halt in the peat and leant on his handlebars, waiting for his breath to arrive. The rain stopped coming sideways and fell as a light drizzle instead. The cyclist had a large bag slung over his shoulder.

'You've got one hell of a paper round,' chirped Eddie wittily. The man said something about sex and travel, then implied that Eddie's mother and father were not married and their son was not likely to be in MENSA, and finally pedalled off into the grey and brown.

'I think it destroys cyclists' sense of humour,' said Eddie.

'What does?' I asked. 'The weather?'

'No. Their little legs going round and round all the time. It must stop the blood going to whatever part of the brain the sense of humour is in.'

Faced with such a gem of anatomical insight I remained silent, packed the things away and went behind a rock for a pee so he couldn't see me laughing.

We followed the Pennine Way north for a short distance before cutting off towards Torside Castle. For years I thought that the castle was an old Iron Age fort and was prepared at this juncture to wax my lyricals and go on at length about Iron Age men and peat bogs, wolves and wild boar, but in fact it's only a landslip like that at Alport Castle, close to the Snake Road on the edge of the Bleaklow massif, which is a shame since the Ordnance Survey have just put it on their map of antiquities of the British Isles. Ah well, I suppose somebody will write a thesis on it some day.

At Torside, the weather changed yet again. The mist and murk blew away, the sun came out, larks started drying their feathers and beating their chests and the whole land bloomed with a soft late summer glow. It has been pointed out to me that most of my walks end up with either something about a pub or a café or some sentence about the sun going down and the landscape turning golden. Well, I can't help it if that's the way it happens, and it did. It was a lovely walk back to Glossop over open moorland through an afternoon made pure gold by a late September sun under a bowl of blue, and the grass was springy under our feet and when we got to Glossop we had a pint – and that was lovely and golden too.

White Hares and Laddow Rocks

I've seen the white hare in the heather
And the curlew fly high overhead
And sooner than part from these mountains I love
I think I would rather be dead

Ewan MacColl: *The Manchester Rambler*

THE LONGDENDALE VALLEY has been sadly abused by industry. Reservoirs and railways, pylons and the Manchester—Sheffield road over Woodhead march through its length so that at bottom it is a scarred mess. But above, both to the north and south, are some of the best hills in the Pennines, and some of the quietest of places where you can often wander all day and not see a soul. It has some of the best and wildest walking in the Pennines as well as some good rock climbing at Laddow and exciting scrambles such as the route up on to Bleaklow by Wildboar Clough. For much of its length, it is devoid of villages, pubs or cafés and it is probably for that reason that it's not so well known or frequented.

Its capital is Tintwistle and close by, along the road towards Manchester, lies Mottram in Longdendale where the painter L.S. Lowry spent much of his life. He didn't paint much in the way of rural landscapes; he didn't like it or understand it, he told people, and those he did paint are quite depressing and dreary. He hated Mottram and the house he lived in but couldn't be bothered to move since he was convinced that anywhere else would probably be as bad. He painted one moorland landscape that is as miserable as anything you can imagine and, having been stuck on the moors in the wet and the mist on more than a few occasions, the painting seems to me to be very truthful but ultimately very glum. I mean, we all know that Life can be like that but but we tend to shrug our shoulders and get on with it.

Mottram has one of the most outstanding churches in the area, St Michael's, called by many 'the Cathedral of East Cheshire'. Much of it dates from the fifteenth century although it stands on the site of an earlier thirteenth-century building. Old churches dedicated to St Michael always have a special significance, since (as my mother never tired of telling me) it was St Michael who drove Lucifer and his devils out of Paradise and down into the depths of Pandemonium. Since the area has such a strong link still with the 'old religion', it's a half-reasonable assumption that Michael was invoked by the church to keep the servants of Lucifer at bay.

Within the church are two chapels to the Hollingworth and Staveley families while near the north-east corner of the church is an admonition to body snatchers:

Sun setting behind St Michael's church, Longdendale

To wretches who pursue this barbarous trade
Your carcases in turn may be convey'd
Like his, to some unfeeling surgeon's room
Nor can they justly meet a better doom.

Another carving records the fecundity but not the stud fee of a parishioner who was 'father, grandfather and great-grandfather to 147 persons' – it must be something to do with the water. St Michael's also has the largest collection of stone heads I have ever seen, every window corner, down spout and corbel is cut and fashioned into a grotesque head, some basic and Celtic in style, others strangely twisted and threatening.

Mottram has the air of a village under siege, for not more than spitting distance from the old stones of the church, a motorway comes to a truncated halt, pointing out through Mottram to Longdendale and Sheffield, cutting clear across the National Park. The road haulage lobby have been pushing for this cross-Pennine motorway link between Manchester and Sheffield for years and although opposition has so far meant that the six-lane highway ends like a sliced-off concrete river just west of Mottram, the unending pressure for the world to be made a safer and easier place for motor cars has caused the plans to become a sickening reality again.

There's a well-hidden car park at Crowden and a youth hostel where many Pennine Wayfarers stay after the long slog across Kinder and Bleaklow in order to gird their loins before that hump of despair called Black Hill. As far as facilities go in Longdendale, the youth hostel is about it and there's not a pub or café between Tintwistle and the pubs by Thurlestone Moor. Thirty years ago, there was a pub here called the George and Dragon, but Manchester Corporation Water Board closed it down and demolished it on the grounds of health, much as the privatised water companies are now trying to close access to many of the moors round here on the same grounds. Apparently

St Michael's church

the railway and road that pass by the reservoirs, and the sheep that pee and crap and then die and rot in the feeder streams cause no problems, but walkers on the moors do. Strange, isn't it?

It's hard to believe now looking at Longdendale that at one time it was so thickly wooded that a squirrel could travel from Tintwistle to Woodhead (obvious name) without touching the ground. I want to know who followed the squirrel all that way to check whether the story was true or not.

There's a fine walk that goes from Tintwistle along Longdendale, up by Laddow Rocks and over into Chew Valley from where a high path curves back, bringing you eventually to the village. Pat and I took that way one weekday morning, leaving the village by Arnfield Reservoir and the path that leads to Tintwistle Low Moor. 'Wistle' means village and Oswaldtwistle and Tintwistle mean the village of

Lad's Leap at the head of Coombes Clough

Oswald and the village of Tin Tin, at least according to my daughters.

It was a cold March day with little wind stirring and a chill in the air as we climbed the moorland path. The sky was veiled with thin grey cloud which gave the day that soft milky light you often get in these northern hills. The earth lay dead and still, and beneath us the moorland grasses were brown and sodden and dead-looking. The path became more distinct as we reached the edge of Tintwistle Knarr where springs ran across the path from the moss above. There were traces of old quarries all around and below us was a huge face sliced out of the gritstone bedrock of the fell. We stopped and looked across Longdendale to Wildboar Clough and Torside Clough. North of Tintwistle lies Boar Flat and above that still Swineshaw Moor.

This area must have been a good place for wild pig at one time and men of the Iron Age and Saxon times would have roamed these hills when they were largely forests, hunting the boar. Now of course they're all gone and the only bores and boars are in the pubs because, as well as the two-legged sort, there's a pub not so far away that advertises wild boar on its menu. The mind boggles at the thought of 'Wild Boar and Chips in the basket'. I don't think the landlord goes out with his spear tracking it and then lugging it back to the deep fryer slung across his shoulders; apparently somebody is breeding wild boar and so successfully that they are talking of turning them loose for hunting. God knows, it's bad enough with bulls and Water Board officials on the warpath, without three hundredweight of pork sausages with razor blades for nasal hair chasing you up a tree – and try finding a tree here anyway!

Beyond the old quarry we started to climb towards Millstone Rocks and suddenly, ahead of us in the rocks and grass, I saw a moving white shape bounding over the gritstone blocks and heather; it was something I'd seen several times on this particular stretch of the fell, a white hare. For a moment it paused on the skyline, sniffing the air for danger signals, then it was off again. Three times on that climb we saw white

The Chew Valley seen from the Laddow Rocks

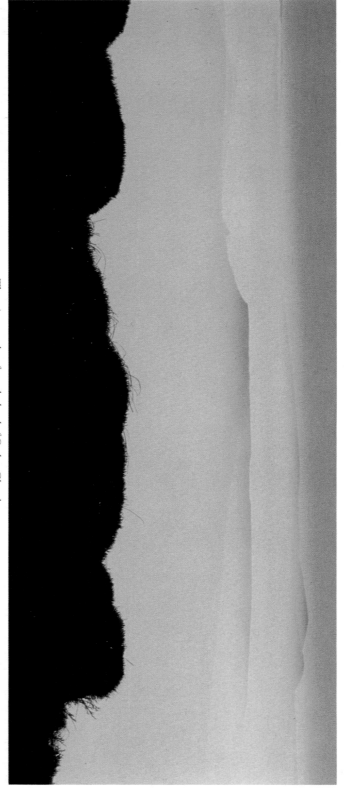

The gritstone edges from the head of Ogden Clough

hares on the moor. They were introduced here from Scotland during Victoria's reign and are now native. Their coats turn from drab brown to a beautiful pure white at the onset of winter and only change back again with the warm days of spring. Like all hares, they live above ground, sleeping and rearing their young in a 'form' instead of digging burrows as rabbits do. When I lived in Ribblesdale, an old farmer told me that if you start a hare, it will run off in a wide circle, always returning to the same place. I must have stood for hours in the rain one day after surprising a hare but it never came back;

it was probably hiding behind a tree, giggling as I got wet and cold.

Lad's Leap at the head of Coombes Clough is a narrow, deep ravine that is better skirted than leaped and it's no wonder there are Lad's Graves and Lost Lads all over the place if this is what they got up to. I can't help wondering whether 'Lad' in some cases, as at Lad Law and Laddow, might not be a corruption of Ludd, itself a form of Lug, the old God of the Celts.

We contoured round from the ravine rather than drop down to the Pennine Way and met it again below Rakes Rocks. The sun was

Near Ogden Clough: autumn is a good time to be up here

making the occasional sortie through the clouds but the day had become much colder with a wind which had more than a hint of north in it. The valley beneath us was dead and cold looking, but even so there were climbers on Laddow; a father with his young son top-roping the Pillar and making it look easy and a group of three women on the Cobbler making that look even easier.

We sat and watched them while we had our tea and then, feeling the cold beginning to bite, we set off from Laddow Rocks towards Chew Valley by Laddow Moss. The best way across this particular bit of land is to follow the brooks that drain the moss, following the path to the watershed and coming by what at times is a path and at times a waterway down to the reservoir at Chew. From there, instead of following the track down to Dove Stones, you keep to the contours, taking the path above Wilderness Gully where the views over to the Dove Stones and Alderman Hill are superb. It's easy walking along the edge and even though the day was grey and dull it was still a

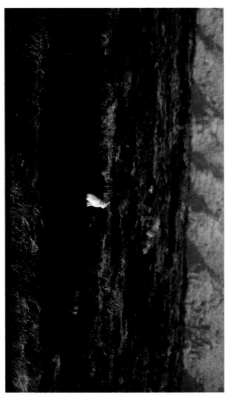

The real white hare and (right) what I thought was a hare

splendid walk along the rim. From the head of Wilderness Gully you must take a compass bearing to find your way over the moor. A maze of sheep tracks and peat bogs awaits you and it's easy to get disorientated and then lost.

We walked off on a bearing and crossed the moor to see, ahead of us, what looked like the silhouette of a hare but was in reality a heap of stones. Beyond, in the far distance, Howden and the Derwent Edge were smeared into pastel shades by mist, the few peaks looking like an archipelago above a pale peach sea. We dropped down from the moor and followed the path by Ogden Clough to Arnfield Lane where, as the last of the afternoon light faded, we passed a car with its windows steamed up. Even through the fug, and without looking very hard, we could see that there were two people in it who had no clothes on.

'They must be very poor,' I said, wondering how they could afford a car if they couldn't afford clothes, but Pat just looked at me sideways in a funny way she has.

The Chew Valley Edges and The King of Tonga

Peat naked and unashamed. Nature fashioned it, but for once has no suggestion for clothing it. Nothing can grow in this acid waste. There is no roothold in this sea of ooze. . . . It is not a place to visit unaccompanied, especially after prolonged rainy weather, because of the risk of becoming trapped or even entombed in the seepage hollows, where the wet peat closes over and grips submerged legs like a vice.

A. Wainwright: *Pennine Way Companion*

MILLSTONE GRIT in shattered cliffs, dark and hard and out-thrust, peering down like an overhung brow at the smoking towns clustered in the valleys. All this and more is gritstone country. Grit weathering in the fierce weather, and grit in the speech and the faces of the people.

Cotton towns and woollen towns spindle out along valleys that run like the gaps between the giant fingers of the moors; it is a land where larks bubble in summer, and where sheep-killing and man-killing snows sweep in during winter; it is a land of dialect, where people call a spade a shovel and where they can be as close-bunched as a fist. Purple prose maybe, but it suits the purple heather-skinned ridges and hills.

Pots and Pans Monument stand on one side of the Oldham to Holmfirth road, Chew Valley and Indian Head on the other, and the round of the gritstone edges from Dove Stone Reservoir and back by Birchen Clough is a walk and a half. One afternoon in September, judging that I'd just enough daylight time to get onto the edge and back before night fell, I walked from the reservoir to take the Water Board track towards Chew Reservoir and the tops. There was a bite in the air that was winter showing its gums if not its teeth, and a hard

wind was screaming up the valley. I'd spent weeks pinned in hotel rooms and on trains and planes, and knew that if I didn't get out I'd end up talking to the walls. So I packed a rucksack with some waterproofs and a flask and left to try and catch the coat tails of the day. I planned to follow the track up to Chew Reservoir and then work my way along the edge to the Raven Stones and come down by Holme Clough.

When the reservoirs were built in this valley, a tramway was built to take materials up to the highest of the reservoirs at Chew Head. The tramway has gone now but its bed has become a good track that makes an easy start to a walk that, in good weather, can be continued over as far as Black Hill, that fearsome, soggy treacle lump so hated by Pennine Way walkers. From Black Hill, the way back is difficult since there is no open access and most of the way you'll be tramping over open moor but, on a long summer day, it's a great outing and the walk down to the valley by Holme Clough is pleasant, though a bit hairy at its bottom end, if you'll pardon the description.

I've walked Black Hill many times in all kinds of weather. It is a dreary and, at times, lonesome and threatening place, but you should be safe enough if you remember that there are escape routes to the east following Holme Moss TV aerial (if you can see it) or north-north-east to Issue Clough and a lane that will lead you to safety. On this latter route, you will be trespassing for a few hundred yards, but only a fool would deny you the right to do that for safety's sake.

According to Wainwright, Black Hill, at 1908 feet, is the highest land in Cheshire although, according to my map, it now lies in Greater Manchester North Euro Const. which even to a Mancunian sounds much less interesting than Cheshire, but it is an intriguing place nonetheless. Years ago they found in the peat pudding of its summit the timber legs of the Ramsden Great Theodolite that were left behind during the triangular survey of the country, begun in 1784. The survey was carried out by soldiers of the Royal Engineers under the command of the Royal Ordnance, so on the Ordnance Survey maps, even up to a few years ago, Black Hill was known as Soldier's Lump.

The path on to Black Hill from the head of Chew Reservoir winds its way through peak and gritstone, following a beck for much of its way to Laddow Moss and meeting the Pennine Way near Laddow Rocks. From there the path is quite easy to distinguish until the Big Black Lump itself is reached, when it's every man for himself. One rainy day when I arrived at Black Hill, the surrounding peat was a filthy lagoon of sloppy and hungry goo, with the trig point and concrete base at its heart being the only safe haven for any walkers daft enough to be out that day. Clustered round it, peering out glumly through the rain at the peat they had to cross to get to anything remotely like solid ground, were half a dozen Scouts and their leader. I remember reading in the Scouting Law, or whatever it was they gave me when I first joined myself, that 'A scout whistles and smiles under all difficulties.' They weren't whistling and they weren't smiling.

That day I cut over to the A635 by the Pennine Way and walked back by the road for a while, before jumping a wall and dropping down to the path by Greenfield Reservoir, wet and not whistling much myself.

Memorial cross on Chew Valley edge

On this particular autumn day, however, with only a short afternoon ahead of me, I followed the line of the old tramway from Dove Stone Reservoir along the sheer-sided valley to Chew Reservoir. The hard wind had turned into a gale by the time I reached the head of the tramway and it was whipping the peaty waters into waves under a sky that was ever more dark and ugly. At the reservoir wall I turned west to follow the edge path to Dish Stone Rocks, a rocky lump weathered vaguely into the shape of a pile of dishes – if you have that kind of imagination. Across the steep-sided valley from the rocks stands Wilderness, and the gully where two Manchester climbers were killed in an avalanche in January 1963. It can be a wild and desperate place at times and none of these moors and gritstone outcrops should be approached with your brains in neutral.

As I walked along the edge, the day worsened and what had been fairly bumbly, non-violent clouds suddenly ganged together, got

The Dish Stone Rocks overlooking the Wilderness

The Dove Stones and the reservoir taken from the Raven Stones

The Trinacle Stone overlooking Greenfield Brook

coward's courage and became a black massif, an inverted peat bog, squeezing itself out over my head. A wind came from nowhere that was so strong you could actually lie on it, and from the edge, I looked down into a suddenly darkened valley across which a hard rain came lashing, stabbing the skin of my face and hands. It was the kind of sudden storm you can imagine King Lear railing against in the heart of that blasted landscape, and its power and majesty gladdened me so that, without realising what I was doing, I laughed out loud at the wonder and glory of it all; the suddenly black day, the raging storm and the dark mass of moor and gritstone. Anybody coming along would have thought I was as mad as old Lear himself. Then, as suddenly as it had come, the storm melted away, leaving a drenched land and a fitful sun stabbing through gaps in the breaking cloud and sweeping across the valley and water below.

I contoured round from the Dish Stone Rocks, following the edge above Bramley's Cot, a cleverly designed shooting hut with two of its walls cut into the gritstone face, and crossing a beck that had suddenly turned from a dribble into a torrent, walked towards the Dove Stones. Across the valley I could make out Bill o' Jack's Plantation where the pub once stood that was the site of the double murder, the story of which appears in the Pots and Pans' walk. The Dove Stones and Raven Stones are grit outcrops with sheer faces lurking on the lip of the moor. They're great climbing faces, but in mist or low cloud they offer no way down to the walker or scrambler and the only safe thing to do is follow down one of the cloughs, and even they can involve some scrambling. Prominent on the Dove Stone is Fox's Stone with, below it, a monument to two local climbers who were killed climbing the second Sella Tower in the Dolomites in 1972. It was on the Dove Stones and the Raven Stones that they did much of their training for the climb and the plaque was erected by their mates.

Some way in from the edge is a smoke-blackened cross that stands as memorial to another tragic death, the accidental shooting of James

Platt, MP for Oldham, who died during a grouse shoot in 1857. Keepers and beaters carried him down to his brother's shooting lodge, Ashway Gap House, but he died two days later. The Platts were textile machinery manufacturers of Oldham and their firm later became the world famous Mather and Platt. The cross and the shooting lodge were designed by George Shaw, the architect who designed St Chad's at Saddleworth. The lovely old house at Ashway Gap was a Victorian mock-Gothic castle, a landmark to many people who travelled this way. It was knocked down by the Water Authority some years ago in another act of bureaucratic senselessness. The cross has had to be repaired a couple of times, so strong are the winter winds that scour this plateau, and is supported now by rusting iron rods.

Dove Stone Reservoir

I rambled along the plateau's edge in a falling light to the Raven Stones where golden eagles nested at the end of the eighteenth century. The Trinacle Stone stands apart from the rest, overlooking Greenfield Brook and, in the poor light, the whole scene looked pretty dismal and a little hairy. If the light got any worse, finding my way off would, I knew, become a problem.

I decided to cut the walk short and drop down by Birchen Clough. It was a good scramble but it did mean my jumping from bank to bank to find the best way down. It is sheer sided in parts and does involve some scrambling and I wouldn't advise it as a way off the plateau in icy conditions. In the gathering murk, it was all I could do to find my way out and onto the track that took me safely back down to Dove Stone Reservoir.

Ironically, the light changed as I left the clough, and I saw behind me breaking clouds that were bloodied at their edges by a dropping sun, while a sliver of the rising moon curled over Alphin Pike and I couldn't help but wonder what the King of Tonga thought of the Chew Valley when he came here in 1981.

The Yeoman Hey Reservoir had just been fitted with a new wave wall to combat expected floods and the contractors responsible for the work had also done some work in Tonga. The King, over here for the Royal wedding, was invited to inspect the works and he came all the way to Oldham and beyond to the wilds of Saddleworth to do so. A plaque on the north side of the wave wall commemorates the visit of King Taua'ahau who, after being entertained by the Mayor of Oldham, laid the stone and went back home to Tonga. There is something terribly strange about a Polynesian monarch from a land of sun and flowers being commemorated on a reservoir wall in what can be the bleakest of these northern upland valleys but, as they say in Tonga, 'There's nowt so queer as folk.'

The Boggart of Pots and Pans

Saddleworth is, today, the generic name for a group of villages whose names – Dobcross, Denshaw, Diggle and Delph – when pronounced together make a musical phrase with a heavy mechanical rhythm, like a brass band tune insensitively played.

Glyn Hughes: *Millstone Grit*

H E WAS CALLED HAPPY HARRIS, he wore glasses, and was my mate as well as being the drummer in our rock-and-roll band. Our band was called the Stylos after a shoe shop in Manchester and, before you laugh, remember that the Beatles were called after something that runs under the floorboards, and U2 after a spyplane.

Happy was his nickname because he was always smiling. My nickname was Sherlock because I'd once affected a long, bent pipe which I held between my teeth, unlit for most of the time. I was fifteen going on sixteen and thought it made me look mature. The pipe cost ten and sixpence and the only tobacco I could afford after shelling out for that was a few inches of thick black twist. You have to be an old man of seventy with no teeth and a larynx of tungsten to enjoy that stuff. I took it home and, in the secrecy of the outside toilet, cut it up, shredding and rubbing it between thumb and palm, like I'd seen the old men do. I filled the bowl, but knowing well and good that my mother would have killed me if she caught me smoking (amazingly, she smoked herself – cigarettes, not a briar) I set off for a walk to smoke my first pipe.

It was a warm summer's evening and not far from our house was a hospital with a long driveway lined with trees and rhododendron bushes. I lit the pipe and puffed away like the wazzok I was; I got about half way up the hospital drive before the pavement turned into marshmallow under my feet, the world went out of focus and I broke out into a cold sweat. I spent the next half hour with my head in the rhododendron bushes waiting for the Angel of Death to come. Instead, an ambulance arrived on its way back to the hospital and asked if I needed a lift or could I make it the rest of the way by myself – which I thought at the time was ironic bordering on the hilarious, and still do.

So Sherlock and Happy, having two weeks free at the end of August and the beginning of September, left the pipe behind and took a tent, a nest of billycans, some sausages and potatoes and our sleeping bags to Victoria Station, Manchester, and got on the train to the hills feeling as free as birds.

It was a dry, fried-egg-on-pavement-hot summer's day as we left Rainy City and its smells behind. Greengate & Irwell rubber factory was vying with a brewery and a glue-works to see which could make the foulest stench but we were escaping, footloose and fancy free. We sat in the warm compartment, watching the landscape outside the window changing from mean huddled streets and factories to the suburbs and then to the open countryside of fields and moorland hills, broken only by the occasional cotton mill and village. We somehow got off at the wrong station (we had a map but we'd been too excited to look at it) and we sweated under our bulky rucksacks as we crawled along the road and climbed slowly up from Greenfield in the valley bottom to the old disused quarry beneath the Pots and Pans monument.

I went back a few years ago and how small it all looked, compared to how I remember it. To us, it was a great adventure, living rough under Pots and Pans for two weeks, climbing and walking all over Saddleworth Moor. I suppose time lends romance to everything, smooths out the rough edges, takes away the pain. I expect that during those weeks there were times when we were fed up – when it rained, when we were cold and miserable even – but I don't remember them. All I remember is a feeling of freedom, from school and exams, from parents, from everything, and in the mythology of my today-mind, the sun shone every day, all day.

We walked all over that valley and the moors above, explored farms that were ruins on the hillside, washed in the streams, swam in the reservoirs above Diggle and even had a brief romantic fling with two girls who wandered into our camp – although what they saw in a couple of wild-haired and scruffy mad-men from Manchester is beyond me. Perhaps it was the lure of the primitive.

I remember one night when Happy and I were alone (it must have been late because it was very dark) and as we sat by our camp-fire, we could see the lights of Uppermill sparking far below us. We'd just eaten beans and baked potatoes, baked in the fire, and were sitting talking quietly, when the conversation got round to ghosts and monsters, as it often does round camp-fires. Happy, as a confirmed atheist, scorned all ideas of anything other than the physical world. Nothing, he swore, existed that could not be measured by science. I think I remember pointing out to him that it was Kant who first said,

'Nihil est in intellectu quid non prius fuerit in sensu,'* and I think I remember what Happy said back, and it wasn't Latin. It was all well and good for Happy to be a Rationalist, but as a recently lapsed Roman Catholic, who'd been brought up by an Irish grandmother who believed absolutely in saints, apparitions, Old Nick, banshees, hobgoblins, stigmata, ghosts and the infallibility of the Pope, all with equal conviction, I still had the residue of old fears lurking somewhere at the back of my mind, like the scum-line on a bath. We talked about horror films we'd seen, about zombies, vampires, werewolves, ghouls and gibbets until we scared ourselves witless. Just before turning in, I pointed out to Happy that, according to the map, above us, beyond Pots and Pans, was a group of rocks called the Boggart Stones – and boggarts, as everyone knows, are demons of the worst kind, appearing at times as headless men, at others as great black dogs or bearlike creatures.

We can't have been asleep more than an hour when we both shot up in our sleeping bags.

'Did you hear that?' whispered Happy, the atheist.

I nodded, but since it was dark he couldn't see me. I tried to say 'yes' but, like Macbeth, my tongue had been velcroed to the roof of my mouth.

'There's something outside,' he croaked.

'Ssssh!' I croaked back at him.

Somebody or some *thing* out there was breathing heavily and groaning, and whatever it was was *big*, judging by the stamping and stumbling noises it was making. We lifted the side of the tent to peer out into the black night. Beyond the dying embers of the fire, four green eyes stared back at us. We shut the flap and sat rigid in the darkness. For what seemed like hours, the noises circled the tent and the night was thick with loud bangs, groans and the clatter of things

*Nothing is in the intellect which is not first of all in the senses.

'So have I!' groaned Happy, falling over the guy ropes.

There was a brief pause, then a moment of rare synchronicity that would have delighted Arthur Koestler as we handed each other each other's glasses. Once the gift of sight was returned to us, we could assess the chaos that had taken place: there were tins of food in every direction, and our store of wood was scattered all over the place.

'It was probably just a few sheep mooching about for food,' I said, forgetting my lapsed-Catholic fears now that the sun was struggling over Indian Head, filling the valley with warmth.

'Whatever did that was big and strong. And it's pinched me penknife,' said Happy. He had left his penknife out near the fire and it had disappeared. I suggested that it might have been a couple of big strong sheep who needed a penknife to get a Boy Scout out of a horse's hoof and Happy, who was from Salford where there aren't many farms, asked me – after he had stopped using a lot of bad language – if sheep were meat eaters. I told him no, and at the time I believed it, yet, years later at Stoodley Pike, a sheep pinched a lamb sandwich out of my hand and ate it in a couple of bites, so who knows. Perhaps they were were-sheep and maybe only the fact that I had a St Christopher medal round my neck had saved us from being turned into the un-dead.

The Huddersfield Canal at Uppermill

There's a lovely short walk from Uppermill onto Pots and Pans that cuts round to Alderman's Hill from where you can ramble back the way you came or cut back by the Boggart Stones to Slades Lane and the parish church. Uppermill is a well kept village with several good pubs and cafés and an excellent museum. The Huddersfield Canal passes by the museum, and on most days in the season a narrow boat runs what the Victorians used to call 'pleasure trips' up and down the cut. When our children were small, we often came to Uppermill to walk and one favourite toddle follows the canal south out of the village, cutting up by Boarshurst and Tunstead to the hill. It's quite a

being rattled and flung about. We sat for the rest of that short-long night, unable to move, daring each other to open the flap and go out into the dark to see what it was but neither of us had the Captain Oates spirit. With the dawn, the noises finally ceased and, in a sort of half-terror half-coma, we groped for our glasses in the gloom and crawled out of the tent.

'I've gone blind!' I moaned staring at the world around me, which was a uniform grey blur.

climb but Boarshurst and Tunstead are both interesting 'folds' – clusters of houses and weavers' cottages that reflect the mix of industry and farming that was the basis of life here. The oldest houses are three-storeyed with long mullioned windows to let the light in for the handloom weavers to work by. High Kinders at Boarshurst is one of the best preserved weaver's houses in the valley with a lovely single row of steps leading to a high door, a 'takin'-in' door, which gave direct access to the workshop. Many of the houses of the folds have been renovated and modernised although most of them have kept much of their character, and it's good to find that even the highest of the farms are lived in now. When Happy and Sherlock were here first, many of the far-intake farms, where the good land gives way to sour moss, were empty and on their way to ruin; now there seems to be a good-sized community up on the hill.

The monument at Pots and Pans was built to commemorate the dead of the war to end all wars. Sadly, the names of the fallen of World War Two were added only a decade or so later. The stones of Pots and Pans are a jumble of soot-blackened gritstones, some of them twelve feet high, and the tops of the largest are weathered down into bowl-shaped depressions. According to local legend they are sacrificial stones, the site of druidic ceremonies, and the hollows were used to collect the victim's blood. Other sources say they are simply weather-worn holes, yet locals still believe that the water in them has a magical ability that will help to heal sore eyes.

I think the holes in the Pots and Pans stones seem too round and too deep to have been caused by natural erosion, and two of them seem to have been linked by a cut runnel; so, although there is no proof of human sacrifice, they may have been hollowed out so that offerings of beer and bread could be placed in them. Strangely, the last time I climbed Pots and Pans on a hot August afternoon, I found bread scattered in the water of the largest bowl in the stones, and somebody must have climbed up to put it there. Like Stoodley Pike, the Pots and

Weavers' cottages at High Boarshurst

Pans monument stands on what was once the holy ground of an early people, modern monoliths on hills remembered in race-memory as very important places.

Alderman's Hill is an impressive peak and from it you look down on Dove Stone Reservoir and over to Indian Head above Chew Valley. Local folk-lore tells us that a giant called Alder once lived on this hill, while on the opposite side of the valley on the Raven Stones, lived the giant, Alphin. They were great friends until they quarrelled over a water nymph called Rimmon who lived near the waters of Chew Brook. Alphin won her favours and she became his wife. In a fit of mad jealousy Alder began flinging rocks across the valley at Alphin. Battle royal commenced and the two giants hurled massive boulders at each other for seven days and nights after which Alphin

Offerings floating in the bowl of the stones near the Pots and Pans monument

was slain. Alder was about to claim Rimmon as his, when she drowned herself in a deep pool and lies buried now, with Alphin, below the peak to the south which bears his name, Alphin Pike. Exactly the same legend clings to Loch Annascaul on Kerry's Dingle Peninsula where the great hero Cuchulain engaged a giant in battle to save the virtue of a maiden called Scaul. Facing each other across the loch, they hurled boulders at each other for nine days and nights. Cuchulain was struck by a boulder the size of a house and let out a howl and Scaul, thinking he was dead, threw herself into the lake, which is now named after her. The common heritage of these two tales in Celtic mythology is obvious and I think it's interesting that a version of the legend should have remained up here in a remote Pennine valley.

From Alderman's Hill, I usually follow the footpath to the road near Upperwood House and then cut back across the moor to the Boggart Stones. Boggarts were mischievous, sometimes bad, spirits and seem to have been found mainly in the Pennines. (You don't hear, for example, of 'The Boggart of Kensington Gore' or the 'Mornington Crescent Boggart'). Sometimes they assumed the shape of a black dog and then they were thought to be evil; but more often than not, they appeared as sprites or poltergeists or mischievous little men. 'Boggart' is thought to come from the German *Bar-gheist*, meaning 'bear ghost', which would fit in with the black dog theory. Boggart Hole Clough near Manchester was the haunt of a famous Boggart, as were Healey Dell and Crime Lake, and on the slopes of Yorkshire's Ingleborough is a Roaring Boggart Hole – what was a Lancashire Boggart doing in Yorkshire? So perhaps the night visitor to our tent was the Boggart of Pots and Pans, you never know.

Close by Upperwood House was the old Moorcock Inn, demolished in 1937 by the water authority. It was here in the first week of April 1832, that a notorious and very gory murder took place. The pub was then known as 'Bill o' Jacks' – 'the pub belonging to

Saddleworth church from across the valley

The memorial tablet at Saddleworth church

Jack's son Bill'. In 1832, 'Bill o' Jacks' was owned by William Bradbury and his son, Thomas, and on that dread night in April, 'person or persons unknown' entered the inn and took them both apart with an axe. The motive was thought to be robbery, but little was taken and, such was the bloody nature of the murder, the Manchester newspapers reported, that 'the floor was covered with blood as if it was a butcher's slaughter house'.

The murder attracted thousands of ghouls and gawkers, *thirty thousand* on the Sunday following alone, but the crime was never solved although there were many suspects, amongst them the Burn-platters. Part gypsies, part tramps, they were wild people who lived rough on the moors earning a living by cutting rushes and weaving them into baskets.

North of the Boggart Stones at Featherbed Moss (yes, yet another of them!) you can see on your left a broad, flattish hump leading into the distance, covered in bog cotton and flanked by ditches. This is a famine road, stretching off across the moor leading nowhere. Built during the days of the Cotton Famine to give work to starving weavers, it was a way of giving charity without seeming to give it. The Samuel Smiles school of famine relief. I've stood on that famine road numerous times and it never fails to move me. Marked on the map simply as a pair of parallel drains, it is a memorial to the labour of who knows how many workless hands and how much dark suffering and misery.

The moss itself can be a nightmare after weeks of rain and A. Wainwright's *Pennine Way Companion* is worth quoting on the subject: 'There is a good Lancashire word that well describes the conglomerate ooze and mud and mire of Featherbed Moss. The word is sLUTCH. Say it slowly, with feeling, and you have the sound of a boot extricating itself from the filthy stuff.'

In good weather, I often follow the Pennine Way over the moss to where it meets the Oldham—Huddersfield road at Standedge, a road originally driven across these moors by Blind Jack Metcalf, the first of the great road engineers. Then I follow the road a little way to the footpath that cuts off to Diggle Edge, and either scrabble up to Big Rough and follow the lane back, or work my way by the footpath to Running Hill Head. But, if the weather looks as though it could turn nasty, I cut off down Slade's Lane and head back by Saddleworth's parish church. Coming that way one recent summer's day, I managed to find the caretaker working in a little stone-mason's shed near the pub and he opened up the church for me. (Isn't it tragic how so many churches are locked now because of vandals and thieves?) It is a gem of a church and its size indicates how large the congregation must once have been, when this part of Saddleworth was more important than either Uppermill or Greenfield. There's some good Victorian stained glass and a monumental plaque to a local soldier who rose through the ranks to become an officer, only to be killed at Corunna, but most interesting of all is a small outbuilding with an inscribed stone tablet set in the wall in memory of George Ogden and James Taylor, church wardens, with the date 1824 and the legend 'know thyself'. Above it a stone head has been carved into the apex of the roof, not a Celtic head nor a Green Man but something in between; a face covered in hair, a wild man perhaps, but a strange pagan head nonetheless to find in a Christian place.

Ignored by many walkers as too industrial perhaps, or too close to Oldham, the hills of Saddleworth are shot through with mystery and legend. It's a fascinating place, go there in good weather but go there in foul weather too and feel the primitive force of those wild moors. But if you're coming off the moor when light is falling, then watch out for the Boggart! And if you see it, ask it if it's got Happy's penknife.

Stained glass in Saddleworth church

Sunset over Saddleworth Moor: Stoodley Pike in the far distance

Spindledom

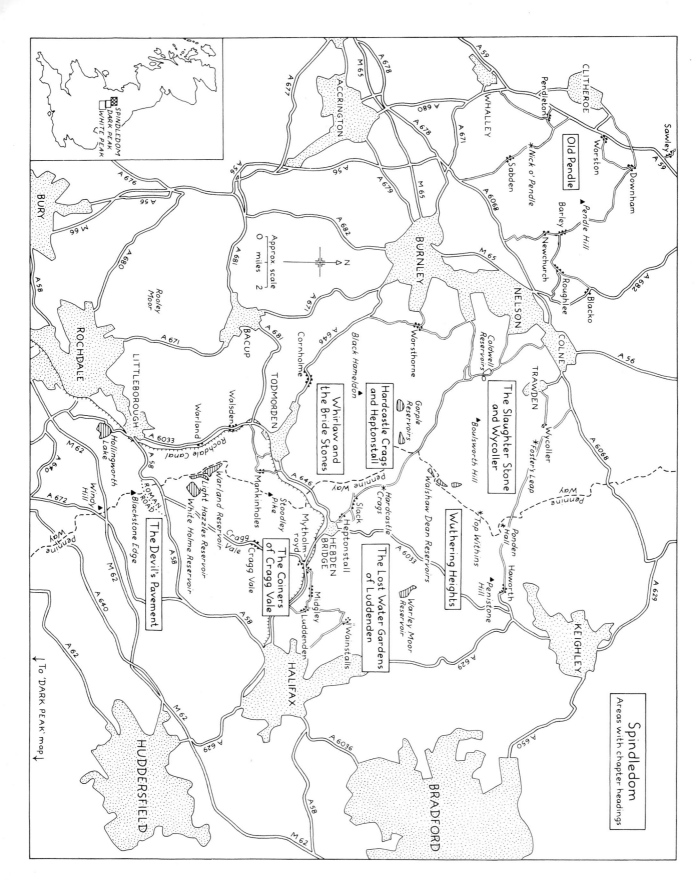

The Smoke-blackened Rocks – a prologue

Work we can not, starve we must
We dare not beg for bread,
God of the hungry hear our prayer
We wish that we were dead.

Anon – from the time of the Cotton Famine

S O MUCH OF MY CHILDHOOD seems to have been spent in these hills that when I came to write this book I shied away from some of the most obvious titles for this section. 'Brontë Country' would have been an insult to the rest of the population; 'South Pennines' it says on the map, but then so are Kinder and Bleaklow and they're in the largely non-industrial Dark Peak; 'Spindledom' was a word that came to me over and again, because this is the heart and soul, ribcage and belly of the Industrial Revolution. It was here that the first real machines and the first great mills were built and where the first mass enslavement of men, women and children took place. Never mind that it was the water power of Cromford that brought about the development of the water frame, it was in this cluster of valleys around Rochdale, Oldham and Halifax that the real revolution happened, the revolution that destroyed the cottage industry and turned a mediaeval village called Manchester into the second city in the kingdom within a century.

At one time, 17% of the cotton spindles in the whole world were twirling in Oldham. Cotton came to Lancashire raw and, with its plentiful water power (and later coal and steam), and its humid climate ideal for fine spinning, Lancashire spun and wove and bleached and dyed the cotton and sent it back again, shipping it out of Liverpool to dress and clothe the world. Then Manchester got tired of paying Liverpool to handle its cargo and built the 'Big Ditch', the Manchester Ship Canal, that brought the ships sailing into Salford, for which Liverpool has never forgiven it. The Manchester Cotton Exchange, in its main dealing hall, boasted the largest room in the world and you can still see the closing prices in that great marble cavern, marked up high just as they were the minute trading stopped; Egyptian Raw – Fifteen Shillings; American Fine – Twelve and sixpence.

Blake had visions of Christ walking again the green hills above those dark Satanic factories. He knew that these great mills, lit at night like liners riding above the valley bottoms, their many windows

[159]

sending out light into the dark, were hell-ships, and for twelve and thirteen hours every day, the wage-slaves of Spindledom laboured in what Blake called their –

> cruel Works
> Of many wheels . . . wheel without wheel, with cogs tyrannic
> Moving by compulsion with each other . . .

'These houses are not fit for people to live in,' said a factory inspector to a mill-owner of the row of mean cottages built for his employees.

'T' mill's fer 'em to live in, houses are nobbut fer sleepin' in,' was the answer he got.

Still, there is a strange kind of beauty in the buildings. Palaces of King Cotton where generations laboured. Yet wage-slaves though they were, the millworkers read and thought and agitated. The spirit of dissent that had blossomed in Methodism and its many splinters such as Rechabitism and Primitivism meant that the people of Spindledom cultivated a strength and an independence that, it could be claimed, has never fully died out. It was this spirit that meant that the Lancashire cotton operatives were prepared to starve to support President Lincoln and the northern states of America in their war against slavery. The blockade of the South stopped the flow of cotton to Lancashire, but the millworkers didn't waver in their support and, in the heart of Manchester now, there is a statue of Abraham Lincoln erected by the people of America in gratitude to the cotton operatives of Lancashire and the sacrifice they made. And sacrifice the Cotton Famine truly was, for the hardships and deprivation were severe; hundreds of thousands went hungry and the chimneys of the mills stood smokeless for months.

There were attempts to provide other 'employments' rather than give money to the starving cotton workers and see them become 'feckless' (a phrase used by Queen Victoria when she, and others, expressed a similar fear during the Irish Potato Famine). Follies were built and great pikes and towers erected on the moors that looked out over the silent valleys and smokeless chimneys. Roads were built: some of them, like the stone paths above Mankinholes, and on Rooley Moor near Rochdale, are still used by walkers; others, like that on Saddleworth Moor, lead nowhere, 'famine roads', going out across the moor, leading from nothing to nothing and now only visible as faint broad imprints amongst the peat and shivering bog cotton.

As a boy, I worked in some of the mills during the school holidays and remember how the landscape around Oldham, Burnley, Bolton and Rochdale was peppered with them. Titanic, four-square and, in the main, red-brick, they dominated the mean streets and the valleys with their great engine houses and the high towers of their chimneys. One foggy day, riding on my bike in the hills near Rochdale, I cycled up on to the moor edge and, suddenly leaving the fog behind, saw the valley spread out below me, the gathered fog rolling in swelling waves between the walls of hills like a yellow-grey sea and, nearly thirty years ago now, I wrote this poem.

MILLS IN THE FOG

Along the autumn valley that chillblown, chillbrown day,
fog meshed and wove about the mills, until
it took the bottom windows in its grasp
and spun out spars and twists of amber light.

Then, mills cast off and loomed above the mist,
like tall ships tugging at their moorings. One
by one the gas lamps bloomed and hissed to life,
became puffballs of fiery orange steam and soon

only the tallest windows cast their lights,
fine trembling warps into the weft of fog,

With the death of the working landscape, the walkers and fishermen take over

and mills sailed off across oceans of dank mist
as hidden lorries snarled and lumbered past.

Worlds trembled in the leaf-hung drops of fog,
and the wet breath of the darkness took the day.

Today the mills are almost all gone. Immigrants from Pakistan now stand at the loom face, just as the starving Irish and dispossessed hill people came once, but even they cannot stop the death rattle in Old King Cotton's throat, and with him are going his cousins, King Wool, King Fustian and King Corduroy. I lament the passing of the trades and crafts, because with them go the jobs and the communities. I lament the passing of the pride in a job well done but, having been a wage-slave once over, and having found little nobility in the position itself, I cannot lament the passing of the factories and the dreadful grind of the work.

In Lancashire it was cotton, in Yorkshire wool, and if you look at that belt of country bounded by Halifax, Leeds and Bradford in the north and Manchester, Rochdale and Oldham in the south, you'll see the hills standing like havens above dark gorges and crowded denes. It's not a pretty country. For too long, its drystone walls have been blackened by the sour breath of a million chimneys, and 'brasting' (bursting) clouds and hard winters have scoured out the hills and the valleys. Deserted farms edge the moss and lurk above the cloughs, carious and fallen, while above them still, the gritstone crags and pikes look down on the valley below.

For beneath the tops are the valleys, the dales and 'denes', of Todmorden, Luddenden, Crimsworth Dene and Calderdale, clustered with mills and forges, dye-works and bleaching-works and the houses snaking along the valley. In some places, the sides of the valleys run so close together that they become gorges with barely room for the canals, roads and railways that thread their way through

Along the Rochdale Canal

them. Yet even there the mills and factories stand squarely by the river while, up the steep valley sides, flues stretch to stubby chimneys that posture like standing stones amidst the bracken.

Yet it has a rare and powerful beauty in all its seasons. In spring, the new flowers bring their flags of hope back to the waiting land, and larks, those tiny flecks on the sky bursting with song, carol over the bog cotton – how, I always ask myself, can something so small make a noise so loud and sweet? And even amongst the ruins and the waste the green is fighting its way back, and through the cinders and the rusting chains and wheels, the fireweed pushes its way; rosebay willowherb, the plant that, when I was a child, covered over the scars in the cities made by Hitler's bombs. Strangest of all, by broken factory gates and weed-clogged mill lodges I have seen the delicate flower of the Himalayan balsam, a migrant here from the jungles of India and Nepal: children like to hold its seed pods and feel them explode with the heat of their hands.

In autumn, the bracken, in the softening sun, is rust-red and the flying bent is a pale gold, so that the moors can seem to be washed with a gentle fire. In summer, becks gabble as you lie beside them on the gritstone, baking in the heat, and in winter, the teeth of snow-bellied gales gnaw at the ridges of stone on the moss and bite through your clothes as you trudge head-down towards the fires of home.

This is a land I know in my bones, a land of chapels and mills, of millstone grit and smoke-blackened crags, and it's a land I have walked and cycled through since I was small, and there's been more than a few times when it has tugged very strongly at my sleeve.

I once spent some time working in a cotton mill in Manchester. Every morning I queued with all the other wage-slaves for the bus that would take me into work. I earned five pounds and some shillings for a five-and-a-half-day week. On a certain delicious August morning, I sniffed the promise of a wonderful day in the air. I had my sandwiches in my pocket, a little tin with tea and sugar for my brew, and a small bottle of milk. The heat was already melting the pitch between the cobbles and, above, a clear blue sky spread over the rooftops and the warren of red-brick streets. The bus came and, as we shuffled forward to get on, I suddenly had a vision of the hours I would spend that day in that dark noisy mill, only breaking for lunch; an hour of freedom, just time to have our tea and sandwiches, and kick a tennis ball around the millyard. I put one hand on the platform bar, thought 'Stuff it', crossed the road and got a bus going in the opposite direction, empty except for a few mothers with trolleys going to the nursery, and kids going to school.

I stayed on the bus until Rochdale where I took another bus to Littleborough and then set off walking, without a map or compass, to

A green lane in the mist near Whirlaw

Blackstone Edge, asking my way as I went. I climbed the Roman road to the crags and walked all day in the hot sun, eating my sandwiches by the side of a moorland beck instead of in the millyard, washing them down with chill water instead of stewed tea. The larks above scolded me for a truancy and freedom that never tasted better. Below, through the heat haze, I could see Hollingworth Lake and beyond, the shimmering mirage of industrial Lancashire, the Heartland.

East of Blackstone Edge, beyond the motorway, are the Dinner Stones where you'll find a plaque to Amon Wrigley. Wrigley was what I suppose you might call a 'folk poet'. He was self-educated, an 'autodidact'. Like many another weaver poet, he taught himself all he knew, studying after work, learning to express himself, not in the language of the University man, with its Latinate phrases and learned

Geese about to enjoy the Rochdale Canal

sounds, but in the language of the people around him. This tradition of folk poetry still hasn't died in the North, where scraps and bits of dialect verse appear from time to time in the local newspapers and in small collections. It's got a lot to do with the richness of the local speech – someone who talks a lot will be told, 'If tha'd any more mouth tha'd 'ave no face to wash' and anybody ugly is said to have a face 'like a bag of spanners'. The humour, unlike the climate, is dry and straightfaced. Tales, of course, are told, over pints or cups of tea or at street corners and many of them used to be called Tacklers' Tales. Tacklers were the men who came round to 'fettle' the looms when they broke down or set them up ready for weaving. They were skilled men but, perhaps because of their powerful position within the mill they were scorned by the rest of the workforce and a whole folklore grew up around them. An old friend, the late Paul Graney, weaver, folk-song collector and fighter in the Spanish Civil War, told me many a tacklers' tale in the sixties. One of them tells of two tacklers, Teddy and Jimmy, who are having a wash after work.

'Jimmy, tha's kept thy cap on!'

'Aye, that's so ah know where me face ends.'

Another tells of a tackler fishing in the canal with his little boy. Nearby are two other fishermen, with their sons. The rods whip forward and the floats settle on the water and all three men nod at each other. An hour passes and no one speaks. Then the quiet ends.

'What's thy little lad called?' asked one fisherman.

'I called him George 'cos he were born on St George's Day,' was the reply. 'Why, what's thy nipper called?'

'David – I called 'm that because 'ee were born on St David's Day.'

The third tackler, who had been listening to all this started reeling his line in and, turning to his little lad, said, 'Come on, our Pancake, we're gooin' 'ome.'

Weavers Square, Heptonstall

There's a great deal of fine walking country in Spindledom, both on the tops where the moor and boglands stretch to the sky, and below where cobbled pack-lanes lead from village to village and go by chapels and farms, deans and crags up onto the moor's edge. But always you are conscious that, although the air now is fresh and clean and the water in the becks as cool and as sweet as you could wish, the rocks about are still smoke-blackened and will be for another hundred years.

The Devil's Pavement

Well, I think that Defoe was a bit of a Wet Nellie because I've been up on Blackstone Edge in all sorts of weathers and have never found it that bad, although I must admit there was one, just one, winter's day on the Edge, when the wind was blowing sheep inside out and the snow was coming upside down, that I did think I must be mad to be there. I cowered in the cracks between the ice-mantled rocks as the fiercest wind-storm I have ever been in ranted all round me for an hour. I was pinned down, unable to put my head above the level of my hiding hole, never mind stand.

When it finally dropped a little, I scooted off the Edge as fast as my legs and the drifting snow would allow. On my way down, I met an army team carrying an injured soldier down the old causeway. They looked at me as though I were a ghost or madman, appearing through the whirling snow. And I suppose, to be fair to Defoe, there was no mountain rescue about at that time, so that if he had gone missing,

he'd have stayed missing and we'd never have heard of Robinson Crusoe. On the other hand, he might have been saved and gone on to write a follow up to Robinson Crusoe called 'Albert Fothergill and the Yeti'. But such fancies are just the product of my fevered brain, I beg you to ignore them.

I've walked Blackstone Edge and the Roman road onto the Pennine Way so many times I've never bothered to count. It's an easy walk with the added advantage that, since the Pennine Way follows an edge path above the valley, you can drop off at several points along the way, and come back by the towpath of the Rochdale Canal, so that you can make as long or as short a day of it as you like.

From Littleborough, a few miles north-east of Rochdale, I usually follow the A58 to just out of the town, and then take one of the many paths that lead to the bottom of the Roman road at Lydgate. You could even walk to the Roman road from Hollingworth Lake Country Park if

Blackstone Edge in snow

Fearsome weather on Blackstone Edge

you like. Built originally as a feeder for the Rochdale Canal, the lake became a pleasure resort in the mid 1800s when it was known as Th' Wevver's Sayport (the Weaver's Seaport). There were swings and roundabouts, one of which was a huge, steam-powered affair, side-shows offered bearded ladies, boxing booths and sword swallowers. You could have your picture taken by the new daguerreotype or be ferried across to the 'Cheshire side' and watch Captain Webb training for his cross-channel swim in the 'coldest waters in England'. Now the amusement park has gone apart from a few kiddy rides, and the lake is much more sedate with waymarked walks, water-fowl and sailing boats.

Eddie and I set out from Littleborough one morning at the end of a long Indian summer and walked from the road across the canal and along the lane to Whittaker. It's a nice start to a day with some interesting old stone-built houses along the way. One had a red phone box in the garden which appeared to be used as a tool shed; it was guarded, on the day we were there, by some ducks that barked. Eddie said they were dogs with feathers on but I thought they were just ducks with laryngitis. We got a bit lost for a while by walking off the end of the South Pennine map (always a daft thing to do) and ended up walking too far east. We noticed this at the point when Eddie's toupee got ripped off by the slipstream of a juggernaut on the M62 but, following the Harding Patent Foolproof Map Error Correction System – 'if in doubt go back a bit until you know where you are' – we came at length to the foot of the Roman road.

Celia Fiennes, that noted woman traveller, came this way in 1698 and noted in her journal:

Then I came to Blackstone Edge, noted all over England for a dismal high precipice and steep in the ascent and descent on Either End; it's a very moorish ground all about and Even just at the top, tho' so high, that you travel on a Causey yet is very troublesome as its a moist ground soe as is usual on these hills; they stagnate the aire and hold mist and raines almost perpetually.

The 'Causey' above Todmorden

The 'causey' she spoke of was of course the Roman road. 'Causey' is a local word and often refers to packhorse trails, the motorways of pre-canal England. To the west near Whitworth is a track called on the map 'Long Causeway', and above the Todmorden Valley another 'Long Causeway' leads to Burnley. The packhorse ways were the main routes by which goods travelled the country in the eighteenth century; coal, salt, wool, iron, lime for the farmers' fields and peat for the fires. All the staples of life were carried on the backs of strong, specially bred horses. Train after train of up to forty horses would cross these moors, the lead horse fitted with a tree of bells to warn other pack trains they were coming, and to lead the way in bad weather. The numerous inns dotted all over the Pennines called The Packhorse are testimony to the importance of the trade.

The Roman road below Blackstone Edge

The closest I came to imagining what life was like in those days was recently when, trekking through the Nepal Himalaya on the route in to Annapurna base camp, we met endless pony trains making their way over the mountains, coming and going from Tibet with loads of salt, hides and finished goods. As I lay in my sleeping bag in the morning, dawn would rise with a total silence that was soon broken by cocks crowing, women lighting fires and calling to children and then, as the light flooded into the valley, I would hear the first sounds of the pony trains, their bells jangling, and men whooping and mushing them on up the trail towards us, a noise that went on all day. It must have been exactly what a village in the Pennines would have sounded like two hundred years ago.

Now, as an amateur historian of no note at all, I'm not going to cross

fountain pens with greater worthies who have variously declared the road below Blackstone Edge to be a Roman road, a seventeenth-century packhorse road, a quarry track or a landing site for UFOs but, in my humble opinion, it probably is a Roman road since it's too wide to be a metalled packhorse road and if it were a coaching and carters' road, it would have had two lines of worn slabs running its length instead of just one. It is certainly on the line of what is almost certainly an ancient pre-Roman and Roman trackway, and the well-worn groove in the centre of the way is as likely to have been scored out by horses' hooves as anything. So there you go, I now sit back and await the angry letters from UFO'ers, Crop-Circletes and New-Age Leyliners.

The old name for the 'causey' is the 'dhoul's pavement', dhoul being an old North Country word for devil. It seems that anything country people found hard to explain they blamed on Old Nick: Devil's Dyke on Bleaklow, the Devil's Arrows at Boroughbridge and the Devil's Bridge at Kirkby Lonsdale are just a few of the things laid in Old Nick's lap – and of course 'dhoul' is just another word for Hob, Puck or Robin Goodfellow.

The Aiggin Stone is an ancient marker standing at an important crossing place of major trans-Pennine routes, where the old roads from Rochdale to Halifax and from Oldham and Delph to Burnley meet. It lay prone on the earth for a number of years, after having been knocked down, and it was only raised up and placed back in its hole a few years ago; seven feet long, much of it is buried in the peat and only three feet or so, smoke-blackened and marked with a cross, is now showing. There were once mounting blocks close by the Aiggin Stone, and it must have been a busy little spot in years long gone, something akin to the café on the M1 at Watford Gap.

Looking back after your climb up the Roman road, you can see Hollingworth Lake and the edges of industrial Lancashire and you're welcome to them. I'm deeply interested in the industrial history of the North, but I still find the thought of the destruction of those beautiful valleys and the enslavement of millions of people ultimately depressing. I once wrote a song in which I tried to express something of the feelings I had for the moorland-factory, free man–wage-slave antithesis. Called *A Small High Window*, it was written about a boy I met when I was working in an iron foundry in Manchester. I was employed by a firm contracted to scale the boilers, he was an apprentice steelworker. We were roughly the same age and had similar interests in cycling and walking. We would sit together at dinner time and eat our sandwiches, perched on casings and boxes of waste steel in the silent factory, the great steel hammers quiet while maintenance work was being carried out. Small birds, symbols of freedom, would fly in through the broken window panes high in the foundry wall to eat the crumbs that we threw for them and to drink from the puddles on the floor. Then they would fly out through the broken window. At the end of the contract, I moved on to another job somewhere else, but I often wonder what happened to him.

There's a small high window where the sun comes in
And it falls and makes a rainbow in the puddles on the floor
There's a small bird singing in the broken pane
And how I wish, oh how I wish that I were free
Free as that bird out on the moor.

The author: 'A Small High Window'

The nude, giant girls on Blackstone Edge

From the Aiggin Stone, Eddie and I walked south and climbed onto Blackstone Edge to scramble on the rocks and look down on the landscape below. There were sails on Hollingworth Lake and the late summer morning was already skinned with a haze that was softening colours and distances. We sat for a little while before retracing our steps back along the Pennine Way, heading north into Darkest Yorkshire. I've been told that somewhere on the rocks of the Edge, below the trig point, is something called 'Robin Hood's Bed' but we failed to find it. Eddie said that a bed would stick out like a sore thumb

in all these rocks. I told him that Robin Hood's Bed *was* a rock. 'Oh!' was all he said.

The Pennine Way north of Blackstone Edge follows another packhorse route alongside one of the reservoir drains for a while, before crossing the main road from Rochdale to Halifax. There's an old packman's inn called The White House at the crossing, but by a

The Aiggin Stone on Blackstone Edge, marking an important crossing-place of trans-Pennine pack-routes

great feat of self-denial, we managed not to be waylaid. Past the pub, the Pennine Way goes on to Light Hazzles and Warland Reservoirs and here the hand of Man is heavy on the moors. The artificial lakes are walled with blackened cut-and-dressed stone and, by them, massive pylons cross the bogs and millstone grit, striding off into the far distance, mile on mile of them. They remind me of a lovely poem by Stephen Spender, 'The Pylons'.

The secret of these hills was stone, and cottages
Of that stone made,
And crumbling roads
That turned on sudden hidden villages.

Now over these small hills, they have built the concrete
That trails black wire;
Pylons, those pillars
Bare like nude, giant girls that have no secret.

The valley with its gilt and evening look
And the green chestnut
Of customary root,
Are mocked dry like the parched bed of a brook.

But far above and far as sight endures
Like whips of anger
With lightning's danger
There runs the quick perspective of the future.

This dwarfs our emerald country by its trek
So tall with prophecy:
Dreaming of cities
Where often clouds shall lean their swan-white necks.

'Do you think they look like nude girls?' I asked Eddie.

'Most of the girls I know are less than seventy feet high and have got a bit more meat on them,' his unpoetic soul uttered forth.

I've walked this path dozens of times but one time I remember in particular. I was just coming to the end of my journey along the Pennine Way which I'd travelled north to south because I wanted the sun on my face rather than my back, and also because, psychologically, it felt as though I was walking home. I'd walked from Ponden Hall on a very hot day and was aiming for the motorway at Windy Hill, where I was hoping to hitch a lift to my bed for the night. I remember those few miles of crushed gritstone walking as being the hardest of the whole day. Every step felt as though the soles of my feet were being smacked with hot mallets and it was an incredible relief later when my steaming feet crossed the soft peat above Blackstone Edge and Slippery Moss to Lad's Grave. Lad's Grave stands above the M62 and the last time I was there a large cross stood on the mound. Who or what the Lad was I've not been able to find out, but what with this one, Lad's Leap above Longdendale, and Lost Lad on Derwent Edge, the Pennines must have been an unhealthy place for 'lads' to be.

Eddie and I sat by a reservoir wall now for our 'baggin' or 'snap'. The reservoirs, unlike most of the other artificial lakes of the Pennines, were not built by a civic water board, but by the Rochdale Canal Company as feeders for their canal system. The three reservoirs here, Warland, Light Hazzels and White Holme, were all built solely for the canal which opened in 1804, well before any thoughts of public health and civic water and are still in Rochdale Canal Company's hands.

We left the Pennine Way at Warland and cut down towards the Cat Stones. The Way continues to Stoodley Pike by Withens Gate and crosses the Calderdale Way near the Te Deum stone. On long summer days, I've carried this walk on to the Pike returning by the canal, but this time we'd dawdled and rambled around too much to push much further, so we followed a sheep track down off the hill. The grass that covers the rough grazing land here has an oily purple head in summer, but in autumn and winter it dries to a yellowy white and then the winds of winter tear it and scatter it across the bogs, hence its local name of 'flying bent'? Beyond Warland, the bent gives way to thick belts of purple heather.

The Cat Stones are a jumble of rock outcroppings but nothing as definite as an edge, and we walked by them with the afternoon sun gilding the valley with the spire of Walsden church in the far distance, smoky and soft in the haze. We dropped steeply to a tumble-down house that somebody seems to be in the process of renovating and past a cluster of farm buildings where the footpath disappeared, as footpaths always seems to do near farm buildings. I've decided that the cows must eat them.

There were savage-looking ducks barking beyond an iron gate (do all the ducks in the hills have laryngitis?) and Eddie and I eyed them with caution. Un-muzzled ducks can make a mess of your achilles tendon and Eddie, in particular, as first overweight bat in our village cricket team, had his career in leather and willow to consider. Luckily

a farmer appeared, obviously alerted by the barking of the ducks and showed us the footpath. We stopped to have a bit of a crack with him and he invited us in for a cup of tea and a slice of cake made by his wife. I don't know where this reputation for aggression and cussedness that farmers seem to get comes from; perhaps it's the lowland farmers who get the rest a bad name. Most of the hill farmers I know are friendly enough and, with the exception of one psychopath in Upper Wharfedale, I've never had a run in with one yet.

Once on the canal towpath, it was an easy four miles back to Littleborough. There were a few fishermen staring at their floats and jammy-faced kids out from school, playing pooh sticks. The canal is being slowly brought back into use now. New road bridges are being put in where, at one time, it ran through choked and

A lock and its keeper's cottage on Rochdale Canal

stinking culverts. The locks are being repaired and it looks as though, at some time in the future, it may all be opened up again. The biggest obstacle to opening it up all the way through to Manchester seems to be the M62. When the motorway was built, the canal was culverted under the new road through a drain, a demeaning end for something that had once been such a grand piece of engineering.

The Rochdale Canal Act was passed in April 1794 and though many of the other canals of the time had been built to 7ft-narrow-boat standard, the Rochdale was built to take wider 14ft boats. That meant it could run craft through from the Bridgewater to the Calder and Hebble Navigation. The speed with which it was built, across very difficult terrain, was impressive even by today's standards. By August 1798 the route was open from Todmorden to Sowerby Bridge, cutting through deep rock masses and riding high above the Summit Pass. Finally opened in 1804, it was the first trans-Pennine canal and justified its promoters' claims that it was the first canal that would 'complete communications between the German Ocean and the Irish Channel by the nearest practical course' and that it would carry from the towns of the north-west 'nearly all the whole of their manufactures which are exported to all parts of the known world'.

The canal was thirty-three miles long and at its highest point stood 600ft above sea level. From Sowerby Bridge, it rose 315ft to the Summit, then dropped an incredible 500ft to Manchester. There were ninety-two locks between Sowerby Bridge and the junction with the Bridgewater Canal, where there is now a good pub called The Duke's Ninety-Two.

We reached Littleborough along the re-cobbled towpath, just as the pubs were opening and there's no better way of replacing all that salt and liquid you have sweated out than with two pints of best.

As we lifted the glasses to our lips, Eddie looked at the landlord and said, 'You look like an intelligent man.' The landlord nodded and then he and I waited while Eddie wiped the foam off his moustache, and then asked, 'Well, can you tell me, why would Robin Hood sleep on a rock?'

The Coiners of Cragg Vale

From Hull, Hell and Halifax
Good Lord deliver me.

Anon. Felon's prayer

THE DEEP DENES BELOW THE CRAGS of the Hebden Bridge area of the West Riding were lawless places until quite recently. It has much to do with the wild nature of these windy moorland acres and even more to do with the nature of the people. It is still a place where you'll find dissent, and the kind of craggy cussedness that ridicules convention and cocks a snoot at authority at every chance. Whether the blood here still runs thick with the iron of Celt and Anglo-Saxon I don't know, but there is certainly something different about the place and its natives. You can still come across them in some of the more far-flung farms of the Pennines, bearded men and silent women who wait for you to speak first so they can size you up, in case you're from yet another Ministry of This and That, some busybody come to complicate their lives still further. A bit of illegal pig-killing still goes on up there, and there are people who know how to lift a pheasant or two, or make a drop of moonshine – I know this for a fact, because I've drunk some of the stuff. But at least you don't get hanged, drawn and quartered for moonshining like you did for coining, and in the secret fastness of Cragg Vale near Mytholmroyd, two hundred years ago, they coined in a very big way.

Coining or 'clipping' is a form of counterfeiting that uses metal cut from the edges of legal tender to make new forged coins. The edges of guineas or other gold coins were clipped with a pair of heavy shears and then the edges were milled with a file until they looked passable. The metal clippings taken from them were melted and cast as blanks upon which the head and tail of the new coin were stamped with a die.

The ringleader of the coiners was a blacksmith, David Hartley who grew to be so powerful that he was known as King David, had his own treasury and banking system, and had an army of coiners and informers who ran the dale and the moors round about as though they were lords of an independent kingdom. Hartley lived at Bell House, high on the moors to the south-west of Mytholmroyd. The house still stands today, in a wild and rugged spot at the end of a barely passable track. Then, before four-wheel drives and black-top roads, it must have seemed a desolate and lonely spot. Perhaps that was its attraction – not too good for company perhaps, but good for those who needed to be left alone and to keep a weather eye out for unwanted visitors.

David's brothers, Isaac and William, who were to become known as the Dukes of York and Edinburgh respectively to David's King-ship, also lived at Bell House, and neighbours from nearby farms at Keelham and Hill House, John Wilcock and David Greenwood, were drawn in to the King's circle.

It has to be remembered that, although coining was punishable by death, the times were desperately hard, with no welfare for people to turn to. If you were poor and fell on hard times, then you could well starve to death, so the temptation to make money by illegal means must have been great. To die of starvation or on the scaffold was a choice faced by many at the time and one horrific statistic is that, of the many thousands that died by the rope in those years, more than ninety per cent were under twenty years of age.

Although there was some outcry at the activities of the coiners, a number of the first families of Halifax soon made use of them. King David and his dukes had their own banking system that was as attractive as anything the big merchant banks in Halifax could offer. Wealthy capitalists would invest their bright guineas with the Cragg Vale Royal Family and, when they had been clipped, get their guineas back with a good few of the new-minted coins as well, a better return than if they'd invested in capital bonds.

But Hartley didn't have it all his own way. An exciseman called William Deighton, infuriated by the coiners' activities, determined to topple the Royals of Cragg Vale. He was foolish enough to raid Bell House on the word of an informer, and although he found the Hartleys busy at the forge – they had seen him coming across the moor – they were only making an iron shuttle. Deighton didn't know it, but he had just loaded the pistol that was to take his life.

Some days later, Deighton took the sworn affidavit of a paid informer who was prepared to state under oath that he had seen a Hartley coining. Armed with this evidence, Deighton met a lawyer called Robert Parker in the hall of the Old Cock in Halifax on 14 October 1770. The lawyer told him that King David was in the tap room boozing with some cronies. Stepping through into the smoke-filled room, that was lit only by a few fitful oil lamps and candles, Deighton and his two bailiffs clapped a pair of manacles on a drink-sodden and fuddled Hartley before he knew what was happening. The King was dragged off to the lock-up at the side of the Duke of Leeds Inn in Jail Lane, where the publican also acted as the gaoler, and the next day was taken in a post-chaise to Leeds where a magistrate committed him for trial at the next York Assizes.

The Hartley family was outraged by the arrest and Isaac set about raising funds that would secure not his brother's release – he was almost certain to be hanged now – but the death of his captor. Two men from the area, Matthew Normington and Robert Thomas, known to be desperate criminals with records of dreadful violence, were promised a hundred pounds for the murder of Deighton. Isaac Hartley supplied them with two blunderbusses, two pistols, powder and slugs, and the men lay in wait for Deighton for several nights. On the night of the full November moon, they saw the exciseman making his way towards his house in Halifax. There they shot him in the head and, after kicking and beating his dying body, rifled his pockets and melted into the night.

The whole country was horrified at the murder. King George III personally offered a free pardon to any informer who would give the names of the murderers, together with a hundred pounds' bounty, which was further reinforced by another hundred pounds subscribed by the tradesmen of Halifax. A man called Broadbent, who had acted as a lookout for the murderers, was arrested, and immediately informed, obviously hoping the reward would come his way. The three men were taken to York Jail and the Treasury, that had for so long ignored the activities of the Cragg Vale coiners, began a search-and-harry operation that raged over the moors and dells to the south of Halifax for months, but few new coiners were found.

The murderers were acquitted due to lack of evidence, but David Hartley, who had killed no one, was hanged in York and his body brought back to Heptonstall for burial, a distance of almost fifty miles. The cortège, with Grace, his wife, following the coffin, wound through Halifax and along the new turnpike to Luddenden Foot. Sympathetic watchers lined the route as the coffin-waggon was couple, a musician and a midwife who have chosen the isolation and privacy of this spot and have re-roofed and renovated the house whilst still managing to keep it very much as it was in King David's day.

There is a good but fairly long walk to Cragg Vale and back from Todmorden. It goes to Stoodley Pike, following the old lanes past Bell House and then drops down into Cragg Vale, coming back by the canal. One winter Sunday, with snow on the tops and the sound of church bells rolling along the valley, Pat and I left the car at Castle Street on the fringes of Todmorden, and followed the path to Mankinholes. There's any number of footpaths and tracks all over these hills, evidence of how much traffic there was here a hundred and more years ago; at Mankinholes there is a line of stone troughs where the packhorses used to drink on their way over the tops.

From the village, we took the Calderdale Way that here follows a lovely long stretch of causeway, paved and culverted for the pack trains, that snakes and curves its way up onto the edge, meeting the Pennine Way just where the breath runs out and the views crowd in. It's a stiff old climb first thing on a winter's morning and by the time we got to the edge, we were well out of breath. So we stopped for a while to get it back and then left our planned route to walk a little further on the Calderdale Way to the Te Deum stone. Here coffins were rested on their way along this old corpse road from Withens to Mankinholes. It is thought that the Te Deum stone, with its fine carving of 'Te Deum Laudamus' was carved by the same mediaeval cleric who, at Catholes where the Cliviger Valley goes from Todmorden to Burnley, carved on a boulder, 'Jesu Deus Dominus Montanum' – Jesus God Lord of the Mountains. We cut back to the edge and looked down at the valley below us, crisp and sharp in the winter morning air, a light layer of mist in the bottoms. Smoke coiled from the chimneys of the houses while spires and mill chimneys stood like misty fingers above the clustered roofs. Immediately below was

The Calderdale Way follows a long stretch of causeway

dragged up the steep cobbled brew of the Buttress, opposite the Hole in the Wall public house in Hebden Bridge, and all the way to Heptonstall churchyard to be given a hero's burial. His tomb lies there now, a few paces from the old door, and the parish register records in Latin: 1770, May 1st: David Hartley of Bell House in the township of Erringden, hanged by the neck near York for unlawfully stamping and clipping public coin.' To some people he was a wicked man, others saw him as a hero, a Robin Hood, who merely ran against the authorities of the time.

When I walked by Bell House years ago, it was empty and deserted. Passing that way recently, however, there were curtains at the windows and a new oak door. No coiners live here now but a young

Lumbutts Tower where three enormous water-wheels once drove the engines of the mill, and a scattering of farms led the eye back to Mankinholes.

Once back on the edge it was an easy ramble along a gritstone path to Stoodley Pike. The Pike was built to commemorate the Peace of Ghent and the abdication of Napoleon in 1814, and walkers on the Pennine Way reckon that you can see it coming for days as you walk towards it, yet it never gets any closer. You certainly can see it from miles away and so dominant a symbol has it become in the area that some of the tombstones in the graveyard at Mankinholes are carved in the shape of the monument while at the southern end of Hardcastle Crags a miniature Pike stands on a bluff over the dale. According to local legend, the Pike at Stoodley was erected on the site of an Iron Age burial mound. It is documented that a stone pike or mound was there long before the building of the monument and there are references to a Stoodley Pike as early as 1737 – interestingly, when the foundations for the tower were being dug in 1815, the labourers discovered a heap of bones. 'Pike' denotes a beacon hill and, like Rivington Pike, Lantern Pike and Alphin Pike, Stoodley may have also been one in the chain of warning fires that threaded the country. It was finished after the Battle of Waterloo and has twice fallen down and been re-built. Ironically, the last time it fell down was on the morning of 11 November 1918, just before peace was declared. It is 120ft high and hollow, and a dark smelly winding staircase takes you to the 'gallery', forty feet above the edge. It's an eerie and groping climb but the views from the top are worth it. One day while sitting at the base of the monument eating my 'baggin' out of the wind, a sheep pinched my sandwich out of my hand and ate it, which I thought bizarre at the time since it was a lamb sandwich.

From the Pike we followed the Pennine Way for a while before cutting off to Dick's Lane, one of the hundreds of walled green lanes that thread these hills, and from the lane end we followed an indistinct

Bell House, one-time haunt of the coiners

path to Bell House. You have no difficulty at all in imagining Hartley and the coiners there for the house is little changed with its courtyard and high walls, its mullioned windows and stone slate roof. Keelham, the next house on the lane, was also a coiner's house and we passed it on our way down to Crumber and Cragg Vale; from there we walked down by the road to Mytholmroyd and then followed the Rochdale Canal back to Hebden Bridge. It was an easy walk but at Hebden we fell amongst thieves in the shape of a tea shop and ended up getting the bus back to Todmorden as the street lights were coming on. On the way to Tod we remembered how, a few years back, we'd walked to Cragg Vale from Blackstone Edge on a scorching hot summer's day, coming back over Great Manshead Hill. There were fires burning

Tombstones at Mankinholes echo the Stoodley Pike monument seen on the gritstone edge beyond

Cragg Vale

The sun setting behind the water tower at Lambutts

The evening sun behind Stoodley Pike

everywhere, hidden under the peat, and we'd had a hell of a job to get back since every other step kicked holes in a dry black land that was glowing red and smoking underneath. It was a nightmare I never want to repeat.

Last year I walked under Stoodley Pike at the end of a long summer's evening. The sun was setting behind the water tower at Lumbutts and I was leaning on a drystone wall to steady the camera while I got a shot of the orange sky and the sheep turning brass in the dying light, when an old man with a walking stick tapped his way up to me.

'Now then,' he said. In this part of Yorkshire, 'now then' can mean anything from 'What are you doing here, you funny looking stranger' to 'Hullo, Harry, fancy a pint' – it is a form of telepathy unknown outside this area.

'Grand evening,' I replied.

'Takin' pictures then,' he said, half statement and half question but said in a way that implied that people who took photographs weren't right in the head.

'Yes, it's a lovely evening and the light's just right behind the water tower, and all the sheep and meadows are back lit.' My voice tailed off into the gathering dusk.

'Aye?' was all he said. There was a long silence. I turned to focus the camera, and he spat in the dust.

'We get some funny buggers around here.' There was another long silence while I considered whether I was included in that description.

'I were walkin past t'graveyard t'other night and I heard voices.. "Now what's that," I says to meself, "there's somebody up to no good," and I stopped to listen. It was a man and a woman I could hear, and they were in t'graveyard. I couldn't see 'em cos of t'wall but I thought to meself, "they're up to no good."

'Then t'woman said, "Can I stroke it before you put it in?" and feller said, "Aye, go on then," and I thought to meself, "they're up to no good."

'"Oooh!" she says, "it's gone stiff all ready!" Well, I thought, they're up to no good and I stood on a stone and looked over t'wall and d'you know what they were doin'?'

'No,' I said, fearing the worst.

'They were buryin' a cat—goodnight.'

And he walked off, leaving me helpless with laughter. Most of the pictures of that lovely sunset were ruined with camera-shake, and all the way home in the car I found myself bursting out laughing so that people beside me at traffic lights began tapping their heads and looking at each other knowingly.

And, if you believe nothing else in this book, I swear to you that every word of the above is true.

Whirlaw and the Bride Stones

Every day and every night
that I say the genealogy of Bride
I shall not be killed, I shall not be harried,
I shall not be put in a cell, I shall not be wounded . . .
No fire, no sun, no moon shall burn me,
no lake, no water, nor sea shall drown me

'Carmina Gadelica'. Quoted in Caitlin Mathews: *The Celtic Tradition*

W HEN I WAS IN MY MID TEENS, I read four or five books a
week, humping them home from the local library. I gobbled
rather than read them and was never without a book open – at the
kitchen table, in bed and on the school bus. I was at that stage where
ideas become as important as a good story and I had begun to read
books not just for the adventures but for the things they were trying
to say. I devoured books like a starving man and went through most
of the modern authors, English, American and European. Greene and
Huxley, Celine and Camus fed my teenage angst while Dos Passos,
Steinbeck and Kerouac encouraged my latent Bohemianism and
awoke within me a sense of a great world out there of thought and
experience that began with that first step across the threshold and the
closing of the door behind you.

At one time I almost had squatters' rights on our local lending
library. I would spend hours there after school and on Saturday
mornings, and one night I picked up a book with a strange crude
woodcut on its dust jacket, all orange and black swirls with a devil or

demon in black at its centre. It was called *The Wizard of Whirlaw* and
since it looked interesting, I stuck it on top of the pile and carried it to
the desk to be stamped by the librarian. I didn't find it an easy read, it
was too full of strange symbolism and mysticism to be easy but it
drew me in forcefully. Set in an imaginary valley in the cotton belt of
Lancashire, I knew then that its setting was somewhere close, and
later, when I found out more about its author, William Holt, I realised
just how close it was. He lived at Todmorden, a town that to this day
has its fair share of characters; and Whirlaw itself is on the hills above,
a rocky outcrop whose romantic name suggests swirling mists and
scouring winds.

Billy Holt was an amazing character, an autodidact in the true
northern tradition. He was a weaver who, while working at his loom,
taught himself languages because he wanted to read the classics in the
original, writing out the words in the dust on the loom bars. He became
an officer in the First World War, then a stuntman, the organiser of a
fleet of mobile libraries, a broadcaster, author, and a mystical visionary

painter. He pioneered the idea of holiday camps by founding one at Hardcastle Crags and he travelled round Europe on horseback, selling the books he published from panniers carried by Trigger his white horse. He discovered Trigger in the 1950s, pulling a coal cart in Todmorden. The plight of the poor animal seemed so like his own, trapped between the shafts of the cart, as he was by the narrow valley, that he bought it for five pounds and travelled all over Europe on Trigger's back, travelling more than 20,000 miles through France, Austria, Italy, Germany, Russia and the Netherlands.

He was a personal friend of H.G. Wells, Bernard Shaw, Henry Williamson and Eleanor Farjeon and had a long affair with the wife of Sir Percy Harris, the Liberal chief whip. He travelled in Russia and Spain where he covered the Revolution and the Spanish Civil War, and in India, where he met Nehru and lived with a holy man in his cave meditating with him and discussing philosophy. He was a philosopher with a taste for the mystic, 'a non-conformist who refused to conform with the non-conformists', as he described himself, and his paintings reflect his mysticism. 'Christ Overcoming Time and Space' is a powerful example of his primitive but moving style, and many of his sketches show a vision which, though crude, is dynamic, original and daring. Aged eighty, he divorced his wife and went to live in the barn that adjoined the house. Shortly after his divorce, he married the heiress to the Whitley brewery fortunes. It

Rochdale Canal near Todmorden

lasted ten years: Billy couldn't stand her dusting.

The bloody world's made from dust. We came from dust and we end in dust. Sometimes it's been very useful to me, when I used to write in it as it fell on the machines in the mill. I'm not going to get upset by a bit of dust when I've more important things to do.

Billy was cremated and his remains scattered on Whirlaw although, by all accounts, when his dust and ashes were thrown into the wind the breeze took them and blew them into the faces of the mourners. Billy would have seen the humour in that.

Billy is not untypical of the people you still find round these hills, non-conformists and anarchists who refuse to become what Billy called 'Massman'. And what can you expect of an area whose town hall is a pseudo Romano-Graeco piece of trumpery, complete with columns and frieze à la Parthenon, cotton money creating its own symbols of a brasher empire. But the last laugh is that the town hall was built on the county boundary so that it is half in Yorkshire and half in Lancashire, which may account in some way for the character of the people.

There's a superb but long walk from Todmorden that takes you up by Whirlaw to Black Hambledon, round by Gorple Reservoir and Reaps Cross and back to Tod (as locals call it) by the canal. I know it's a long walk because I took the family and some friends on it one day and I

The Bride Stones, weatherworn rocks beneath an outcropping of gritstone

The Bride Stone herself

think they came the closest they've ever been to lynching me. From the town centre, we threaded our way, heading north-west, via the walled lanes up on to the Calderdale Way. There a good path takes you by the farms of East and West Whirlaw set under the Whirlaw Stones. It's a fine green way and another part of the spider's web of packhorse routes that covers these hills.

Above the lane, and worth a diversionary visit or indeed a trip on its own, are the Bride Stones, close enough to the pub at Keb Bridge on the road above to be a pleasant evening ramble with the alehouse as a base. The Bride Stones are a group of weatherworn rocks beneath an outcropping face of millstone grit that looks down to the Todmorden Valley. One stone in particular, balloon-shaped on a narrow eroded pedestal, stands out from the others. This is the Bride Stone itself and nearby are said to be the remains of another stone called the Groom that was apparently torn down some time in the remote past by 'the country people'. 'Bride Stones' are found all over Britain; another set of Bride Stones at Bosely Cloud near Biddulph in Staffordshire seem to be part of what was once a much larger religious and burial complex, while High Bridestones, five miles south-west of Whitby, is the remains of two stone circles, one of which has a menhir seven foot high.

The Todmorden stones are natural rock formations although they may well have been used for religious purposes. They have been known as Bride Stones for some time, for this was the name by which they were known towards the end of the fifteenth century when they are mentioned in a land transaction. One explanation for the name 'Bride Stones' is that they were of religious significance and were named after 'Brid' the Celtic goddess and Earth Mother. The Bride Stone itself looks to me fairly like the Venus of Willendorf, the limestone fertility figurine found in Austria, hence the link with marriage. Interestingly, the last time that I walked to the Bride Stones I noticed something I had never seen before, what appears to be a horned head cut or scratched into one of the rocks. How recent or the house was high up, she could see passers-by – travellers, pedlars, walkers or whatever – on their way, climbing slowly the long drag up the steep hill and she would fetch them out a cup of tea just as they reached her house. A nice story.

Above Mount Cross, we followed the road for a while then set out across wild open country to Wolf Stones and Black Hambledon, following the boundary ditch that marks the line where red and white rose meet. Dug originally to mark the division of their manors by the Norman overlords who ruled the country, the ditch, a shallow channel twenty-five foot wide, can still be traced a thousand years on. There's a good view from Hoof Stones Height and it is reckoned that you can see Pendle, Ingleborough, Penyghent and even Blackpool Tower on a good day. On a bad day you can't even see your feet.

We couldn't see all that much because of the heat haze that was partly rising from the surrounding peat and partly from the boots of some of the party. We crossed the moor going by the Hare Stones to the Gorple Reservoirs to pick up the Pennine Way. It was here, a number of years ago, that one of the reservoir keepers living in the cottages nearby died when he was trapped in a blizzard only a few hundred yards from his own house door, a reminder that the moor can be a hard, hard mistress when she wants to be.

A late summer's day that had been at times wet and misty and at other times misty and wet, suddenly became sunny. The heather on the moor shone deep purple as we walked along the path towards Reaps Cross leaving behind us the Boggart Stones with, sadly, no time to visit the delicately named Pisser Hill, Pisser Clough and Pisser Rough. It's a fair way across Heptonstall Moor by the Pennine Way, but it was only after Reaps Cross that the team really started moaning and asking how much further it was. I had the map and was keeping it close to my chest in case of mutiny but they quietened down when they saw that the trail was winding down to the valley bottom to meet the canal at Charlesworth.

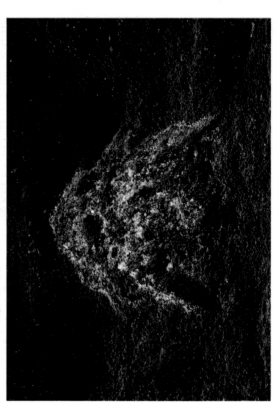

The horned head cut or scratched on to one of the Bride Stones

how old it is is anybody's guess and whether it was made by natural weathering and flaking of the rock or cut deliberately is another.

Further along the Calderdale Way, Mount Cross, a lovely stone waymarker, marks the meeting of packways to Rochdale, Halifax and Burnley above Cornholme, a village clustered in the bottom of the steep dark Cliviger Gorge. A number of years ago, when our children were very small, we were given the use of a cottage just outside the village for a short holiday, and on our way up to the tops, we passed a little house at a bend on the steep road that led to the Long Causeway. An old lady was always standing at the door of the house as we passed, and she would wave and call out to us. One night in the pub I learned that the house was named 'Tea-Pot Hall'. It was called that by the locals because the old lady always had the kettle on and, because

The trig point on Hoof Stones Height, Pendle Hill in the far distance

Frozen lock gates near Todmorden

The Rochdale Canal is still open here and work is being carried out that will, it is hoped, turn the entire length back into use; but it's a long job, and most of the filthy work of cleaning out fouled locks and clogged sluices is being done by volunteers. It makes a lovely end to the day, though, to walk back along the old canal with grumpy fishermen staring at their floats and little boys and girls on bikes charging up and down the towpath, past pools where pike lie laughing at the anglers and swans look down their noses at everybody.

Walking back along the canal, I thought again of Billy Holt and the thousands of men and women like him who, in spite of having to work a full and tiring day in the forge or factory, still managed to educate themselves, some to a very high standard. While working on the buses in Manchester, I knew an inspector who was an amateur astronomer, specialising in the study of the moon. His knowledge was so vast and detailed that he was asked to help with some of the preparatory work for the moon-shots. I know an Irishman joiner, working on building sites, who is an expert on grasses, in particular on meadow fescues. Tom Stephenson, the architect of the Pennine Way, was a calico-blockmaker who taught himself geology and won a place at London University, which he was debarred from taking because of a prison record picked up when he was jailed as a conscientious objector during the First World War. Elizabeth Gaskell describes such

The Rochdale Canal, nearly frozen over

people in *Mary Barton*, men and women from the mills of Yorkshire and Lancashire who formed themselves into debating societies and botanical societies, the latter spending their leisure hours roaming the hills collecting and observing.

There's a pub near Manchester called The Railway and Naturalist which commemorates the local amateur society and in The Ring o'Bells in Middleton, one of the first pubs I sang in as a lad, there was a collection of insects put together by the local naturalists. There were thousands of moths, butterflies and beetles, mounted and framed, drawer after drawer of them that filled the upstairs room of the pub while pictures made from butterflies and moths decorated the walls. I always thought the pictures were sad affairs and couldn't see how men who had won their few hours of freedom could capture and kill things as beautiful as butterflies just to make pictures from them.

We walked the last few miles in silence, the soft light and winds of evening moving over the surface of the canal, shaking its surface, and I led my exhausted team back into Tod just as the pubs were opening which raised a few weary grins but they started nodding off after one drink and a packet of crisps each. They all crashed out in the car on the way back home and, since I still had the map, they didn't realise that they'd walked more than twenty miles.

Hardcastle Crags and Heptonstall

The tercel's domain, gulf of air
he rounds on, a skater's heel
cutting the ice of the sky.
Out over a vale aloud with
new bombs of buds,
crisp gunshots of ferns uncoiling,
the mortars of corms, the clamorous drums of birth.
A dead king thrusts through the
ranting earth this Lazarus day,
the wind carolling his wares along the crags
and the brass-gong sun beating offertory
to the catechism of the buds.
Cauled Lazarus scrambles yet again,
rehearsing the rehearsal, thrusting, through
the husks, the swaddled cerements of the year.

The author: 'Christ at Hardcastle Crags'

HEBDEN BRIDGE IS a busy town now. Some say it's too busy and that it's been tarted up by a bunch of off-comers, others that it's been saved from dereliction and destruction by the input of new blood. I'm not going to enter into any argument other than to say (for what it's worth) that twenty years ago, when I first came here, the town looked run down and forlorn; now, antique shops notwithstanding, it again has a community that's alive and kicking. It's a good starting point for a fair number of splendid days out, and

one of my favourite short walks, winter and summer, leads out of town from the information centre, along through the narrow wooded valley of Hebden Dale to Hardcastle Crags, once described as 'the Switzerland of the Pennine Chain'. I've got to say that I've never heard anybody yodelling here yet, nor seen men in leather shorts slapping their thighs and blowing long trumpets, but the day is young. In any case, the name is also claimed by How Stean Gorge in Nidderdale. From the Crags, I usually come back by the Pennine Way

Looking down to Hebden Bridge

and Calderdale Way, or follow the field paths to Heptonstall and then drop down to Hebden Bridge. It's an easy walk, the hardest part being actually finding your way out of Hebden Bridge without getting lost. Even with the 1:25,000 series map, it's a pig, and I've led parties out of the car park in confidence at least half a dozen times, only to have them muttering behind me as, half an hour later, we have fought our way under somebody's washing line for the third or fourth time. Now there's a booklet you can buy from the information centre for ten pee that shows you how to get out of Darkest Hebden to Midgehole without some house-husband beating you to death with a rolled up copy of the *Guardian*. It's worth every pee.

On one very bad occasion, I led everybody so far astray that we found ourselves heading upstream on the south bank of Hebden Dale. I covered up my stupidity by pretending I meant to go that way and led them through Hebden Wood to the stepping stones at Hebden Hey. It was a biting cold winter's day, bright and sunny but cold enough, in the shadows of the Dale, to freeze running water. The river was high and the stepping stones were covered with a nice fat layer of ice. We all got across – in the end – but I've never heard such foul language from women in my life, and I know a lot of sailors.

The valley at Hebden Dale was created during the last Ice Age by glacial melt waters which scoured out the deep gritstone gorge, leaving the Crags and Slurring Rock as blackened outcrops. The woods are amongst the oldest in the Pennines, with oak, ash, birch, beech and rowan lining the river's banks and conifers growing thickly in the steep-sided valley, though these are not totally natural. Many of the trees were planted during the late nineteenth century by Baron Saville who wanted to improve the value of his estate and, at one time, charcoal burners worked here, chipping the bark from whole tree trunks and burning it in pits in the ground.

Hardcastle Crags and the woods of the Hebden Valley below have been a favourite day out for people from the Lancashire and Yorkshire industrial valleys for more than a hundred years. Wagonettes, horse drawn and motor driven, would come from Rochdale and Halifax, Bradford and Bury. Little boys in Norfolk jackets and little girls in smocks, their fathers in Sunday best and billycock hats, their mothers in white blouses, long skirts and buttoned up boots, look out at us from the fading sepia photographs of that remote and innocent-seeming past. Old ladies in black bombazine and gaffers haloed in whiskers sit frozen on the log seats near Gibson Mill and children with hoops stare at a dancing bear and its mustachioed keeper with his hurdy-gurdy. It was a great place for romance, for those who were paired off to come 'courtin'' and for those who weren't to go walking in the hope of 'coppin' on' or 'clicking' (as they used to call 'forming a relationship' in those days), parading up and down what cheeky little boys used to call 'the monkey run'. A little guide to the Crags published in the early years of this century tells us: 'Swans and boats glide on the ponds. Swings ply for hire and stalls display their wares. Skating rinks provide for wet days. Lectures are given and accepted on clicking, gossip, jealousy or copology etc.'

Well, the swings and roundabouts are all gone now and the valley is a quieter place, although it still gets busy with walkers and trippers on holiday weekends. In autumn, the woods are brassy and gold for those last few weeks before the greys of winter grip the land; in winter, it can be deserted, watchful and silent.

During the last forty years, there have been three attempts to flood the beautiful valley below Hardcastle Crags and, thankfully, so far, all have been defeated. Like any old wood, it smells wonderful, particularly after rain. Woods like these, old woods with water running through them, have a smell and an atmosphere that could belong nowhere else, pungently damp with the mulch of years and the green shade throbbing like a power house. Which is really what it is when you think about it, there is a fantastic amount of energy generated by a wood like this. The leaves of the trees and plants gather the warmth and light of the sun and transmute them into the power that propels an acorn bud fifty feet into the air or that unfolds tiny curls of ferns and draws them out until they're almost man high. And, in the breathing green world are an infinity of insects and birds, voles, weasels, foxes and badgers.

Compare that to the barren chipboard factories of Sitka spruce that blanket much of our uplands now. Crypts, with floors of needles that give no mulch, a featureless maze of poles with few birds but plenty of vermin, a well-managed investment for the accountant, a disaster for the landscape.

TREES

There were trees here once
thick-spread across this moor
until monks, scuttling brown
slugs across the forest floor,

staggered through the naves
of this green abbey
under the axe's weight,
gave a few snickering blows
and dissolved this clerestory of leaves
in a muttering of thunder heard across the dale.

Now blocks of spruce in regimented rows
march up the fell. Their hollow halls are still,
barren of song, their needles functional,
you might say – accountable.
New churches observant of the building regs.,
there are no corners here no
bloodstains on the stone;

no reredos of fern and underwood, no history,
just a London pension fund at prayer,
an electric fence all round –
a concentration camp
for trees.

Now across the fells' bare shoulder
the last deer scud from ghyll to ghyll
searching for the priest holes
of the relict wood.

The author

Almost hidden in the trees is Gibson Mill, an old cotton spinning factory powered by the Hebden Water. Built in 1800, it employed twenty-two people by 1833, each working a 72-hour week. They started work at 6 am and clocked off at 7.30pm, with two short breaks for breakfast and dinner.

Like all good entrepreneurs, the owner of Gibson Mill employed children since they were small enough to crawl under the machines and carry out any cleaning operations or minor repairs without having to shut down the machine and therefore lose working time. The mill was converted to steam in the 1860s, but by the early years of this century, it had ceased to operate as a mill. It has been since, amongst other things, a dance hall and an indoor roller skating rink and although it is now owned by the National Trust, they seem to be doing nothing with it at all.

Above Gibson Mill one day in late autumn, I was walking and day-dreaming by the weed-choked mill lodge when I suddenly froze at the sight of a white flash through the trees ahead of me. I parted the dying leaves and saw, caught in a wash of light, a heron fishing at the weir's edge. I must have watched it for ten minutes or more as it stalked and fished in the pool, but the moment I swung my camera

The stepping stones across Hebden Water

Autumn colours in Hebden Dale

bag round to fit on a long lens and try for a shot, it was away, its great wings powering it slowly upstream and out of sight.

From Gibson Mill, I like to carry on through the woods to the open country above the dale by the path beneath the Crags. Interesting little farms abound, and if you're thirsty at this point, you can carry on up the track until you hit the Pennine Way and the road to the Shoulder of Mutton at Blackshaw Head where they serve Tetley Bitter. A better pint does not exist – there's many as good but none better – and the landlady does lovely home-made food. The Shoulder of Mutton is a common name for pubs in the hills, and one theory is that the landlords in the old days were also butchers. If that's true, I wonder why you never see pubs called 'The Lean Lamb Chop' or 'The Pound of Lean Mince'.

From the pub, you can either follow the Pennine Way back towards Heptonstall or take the jumble of footpaths and ways by Colden Water to the village. In summer, there are lots of sunny places where you can sprawl out in the grass by the cool water in the wooded dene, and there's a lovely stone footbridge where the Calderdale Way crosses the beck beneath an overhang of trees.

Heptonstall is a fascinating village. Its name probably comes from the Anglo-Saxon *Hep*, a proper name and *tunstall* meaning 'township',

Weir on Hebden Water

death, controversy still rages about her. Many feminists claim that she was a victim and it looks as though some of the more extreme amongst them have vandalised her grave. It is tragic that violence and hatred should still fly around the grave of this woman, causing more suffering each time the grave is abused.

There are two churches in Heptonstall. The old thirteenth-century church of St Thomas à Becket is in ruins now, only the tower and external walls standing. It survived the batterings of the Civil War, the

It was the most prosperous of the villages of Calderdale, and the first village in Yorkshire to have a cloth hall where merchants would have come to bargain for the lengths of cloth, the Piece Hall at Halifax being much later. With the coming of turnpike road and steam power, Hebden Bridge took prominence as a wool centre and Heptonstall was left high and dry, which is probably why the village is so well-preserved today.

Just outside the village is the chapel at Slack. Fay Godwin has a wonderful photograph of it in the book she made with Ted Hughes, *Remains of Elmet*, and beyond the chapel is Lumb Bank where courses are held for writers, run by writers. Founded by the poet Ted Hughes and his wife, the poet, Sylvia Plath, it has a sister organisation in Devon, the Arvon Foundation. Sylvia Plath is buried at Heptonstall. She lived a troubled life and, years after her

The Quaker plaque

Sylvia Plath's grave, Heptonstall church

Corn Riots and the Luddites, only to be damaged by a terrible storm in 1847, and the new church was built soon after by public subscription. The old church, now a husk, looms above a sea of tombs, upright and reclining, the resting ground, some say, of a hundred thousand souls. Many of the gravestones have been used more than once, having been turned over and carved on the clean side when the other was filled with nanes, and there are at least two mediaeval gravestones in amongst them. It is thought that these are probably the graves of priests.

The village was Parliamentarian during the Civil War under the influence of the Fairfaxes of Halifax, and when the Earl of Newcastle's Royalist Army set up their guns on Gun Hill, the old church was covered in sheepskins to protect it from the cannonballs. The Royal-

ists attacked in the middle of a fierce storm and many of their soldiers were swept away while crossing the swollen Hebden River below the packhorse lane called The Buttress. The screams of the drowning men alerted the Roundheads in the village above, who routed the Royalists and rolled huge boulders down the hill after the retreating men, causing even more slaughter.

A stone plaque above a doorway in Northgate, depicting a man and woman holding hands, is said to commemorate the peace after the Civil War. This seems more folk-lore than fact since the carving is dated 1736, a long time after the Restoration. The figures are said to represent Henry and Elizabeth Forster, a Quaker couple who built the house, in which case the carving could certainly be said to represent peace since this is the bed-rock of the Quaker faith. In 1970, the

The ruined church, now a mere husk, at Heptonstall

One of Heptonstall's many cats

The octagonal Methodist chapel built in 1746

Quakers of Washington DC held a spring fair, when two twelve-feet high models of these stone carvings were placed one either side of the Washington interstate – a pleasing thought.

David Hartley, 'King David' of the coiners of the previous chapter, is buried close to the old church, while buried in the new church, close to the font, is a poor lad called Mark Saltonstall, hanged at Halifax in August 1783 for 'leading' the Corn Riots in the town. He was nineteen years old, more a scapegoat than a leader of the demonstrations against the crippling price of bread.

Inside the new church, at the tower end, is an amazing copy of Leonardo da Vinci's 'Last Supper'. Painted in 1905 by Gringaschi, it was commissioned by the Italian government and then hung alongside the original while that was being renovated. In 1906, the copy was bought by a Hebden Bridge man and bequeathed to the church by one of his relations. I've heard it said that local wags often tell visitors that the painting is an original, and was painted by Leonardo in payment for a bill he had run up at the Cross Inn while staying there during the Renaissance at Luddenden Foot.

An octagonal Methodist chapel was built in Heptonstall in 1746 to the design of Charles Wesley, who wanted all his preaching houses to be that shape so that the devil would not be able to find a corner in which to hide. The roof was built at Rotherham and then transported here on the backs of packhorses, escorted, for the last part of its

The grave of David Hartley, 'King of the Coiners'

journey, by hundreds of hymn-singing worshippers. It was one of the first Methodist preaching houses in the country, and, though two of its sides were lengthened to accommodate the swelling congregations, it still retains much of its original shape. Smoke-blackened now, it looks down on the valley, prim, grim and proper.

At one time, there were seven pubs in Heptonstall, an indication of how important the village was. Now there are two, the White Lion and the Cross. The Cross Inn is one of the North's great pubs where, a long long time ago, I served part of my apprenticeship on the folk scene, and where, not so long ago, two mates of mine, Big Phil and Tex, appeared one lunchtime for a pint. They had decided that both of them were out of condition and needed to do some walking. So, every weekend for a couple of months, they set off with the best intentions, only to fall by the wayside in any pub that had its doors open.

They took the train to Hebden Bridge one summer's morning and walked to Heptonstall, arriving just as the pub doors opened. Having worked up a thirst walking from the station, they decided to replace the lost salts and liquid before carrying on with their projected fifteen miles or so. A lot of hours later, as afternoon's golden light filtered through the pub's windows, the landlord computed that they'd sunk fourteen pints each and, in his dry Yorkshire voice asked, 'How many miles do you do to the gallon, lads?'

The Lost Water Gardens Of Luddenden

Mary Ellen Clark – aged 14 years
Alice Devitt – aged 12 years
Elizabeth Edwards – aged 17 years
Jane Johnson – aged 12 years
Sarah Shaw – aged 15 years
Marie Emery – aged 15 years
Anne Larrings – aged 15 years
The gravestone of the orphans of Calvert's Mill, Wainstalls

'WHERE THERE'S MUCK, THERE'S BRASS' is one of those northernisms conjured up out of the cliché-monger's store at Lud. 'at and yet there's an element of truth in it, in that the drop of a flat 'at and yet there's an element of truth in it, in that the dirt and grime of industry produced money. In some cases a great deal of money although most of it, strangely refusing to follow the Thatcher Law of Good Samaritanism, did not percolate down into the lower strata of society but stayed in the hands of those who ran the game.

A little philanthropy did spurt up here and there, but men like Titus Salt, who created Saltaire the model village, although they are often lauded as an example of the kindly capitalist, were the exception rather than any kind of rule. The industrialists were, in the main, men who saw themselves, in the old Calvinist mode, justified by their faith. They were successful through hard work and through the beneficence of the Almighty; therefore, they were twice blessed. And success in this world was seen as a sign of favour in the next.

Such a man was Captain Joseph Priestley Edwards of the Vale of Lud. Born on 29 December 1818, the son of a wealthy Halifax manufacturer, Captain Edwards became a man of some import in the affairs of Yorkshire. He was a JP, a Deputy Lieutenant of the West Riding, Lord of the Manor of Oxenhope and a Captain in the Second West Yorkshire Yeoman Cavalry. His brother, Sir Henry Edwards, Bt, was a high ranking freemason and Conservative MP for Halifax from 1847 to 1854.

Captain Edwards had an estate at Fixby Park near Huddersfield and also rented a shooting estate in Perthshire to which he travelled for his sport – before, that is, he took possession of the valley and moors above Luddenden. Like many of the manufacturing class, he was land-hungry, seeing land as a way of gaining respectability, and when the moorlands of Saltonstall were enclosed under the 1852 Warley Inclosure Act, he bought the moors from the commissioners. The moors had been used since time beyond memory for rights of turbary and grazing, and were crossed by footpaths and packhorse routes, but as far as Edwards was concerned the lands were now his by law, and the valley and the moors above it were closed to the public.

An anonymous poem written earlier, at the time of the major enclosures, jibes:

> They hang the man and flog the woman
> That steal the goose from off the common,
> But leave the greater villain loose
> That steals the common from the goose.

A few local people, mainly from Midgley, took legal action against the Captain but the Edwardses were an autocratic family, used to having their way, and they did. By dint of gamekeepers, trespass notices and freshly-tarred gates, the commons were taken from the people.

In 1853 'Colonel' Edwards (as one account promotes him) further obtained the rights to hunting, shooting and fishing at Saltonstall and the rights of the manor in the townships of Warley and Oxenhope. He also obtained the exclusive right under the Halifax Improvement Act of 1853 (his brother being MP for the town presumably would have ensured there was little opposition) of angling and shooting on the Warley Moor, Dean Head and Castle Carr Reservoirs and the right to keep a boat on each of these waters for his personal use.

Having acquired the land, all he needed now was the castle to go with it. So in 1859 he began the construction of Castle Carr, a mock Scottish pile that took thirteen years to build and that he never lived to see. Hundreds of workmen camped out on the moor's edge and thousands of tons of local stone were quarried and cut for its battlements and crenellations. Mr Ponto, Captain Edwards's gardener at Fixby Park, was called in to oversee the landscaping of the gardens and he did a magnificent job. As part compensation for giving rights to the Halifax Corporation Water Board to extract water and build

reservoirs on the land he had recently acquired, Edwards arranged for the waters from the reservoir above to be channelled through a series of cascades and aqueducts laid out with the formality of a Japanese water garden. The most impressive features were the great fountains, capable of firing a jet of water 130 feet into the air; they were said to be the second highest in Europe, topped only by the Nicholas Fountain at Chatsworth House.

By 1872 the mansion was nearing completion and contemporary accounts give the impression of a lodge typical of the new *pharos* of Woollenopolis. Built in a mixture of Norman and Elizabethan style, it had battlements, turrets and a great clock tower that sounded the curfew every night at ten o'clock. The building was wrapped round a massive courtyard and stables, with a stone gateway complete with portcullis; at its heart, central to the courtyard, was a huge stone basin cornered by four carved stone Talbot hounds, the symbol of the Edwards family. The great ballroom, the billiard room and the oak-panelled banqueting hall, together with the massive stone entrance hall and staircase, declared Castle Carr to be the country dwelling of a gentleman of some substance.

Unfortunately, before its grand design had reached fruition, the Captain was dead, killed with one of his sons in an horrific train crash that in itself is ironic, the steam and engineering that made the mill owner's family fortunes bringing about his own destruction. The Edwardses were travelling to Holyhead on 20 August 1868 aboard a packed Irish Mail en route to visit Captain Edwards's sister at her estate in County Dublin. At Flintshire Oil Refinery near Chester, their train hit two runaway wagons loaded with nearly eight tons of paraffin oil. Captain Edwards and his son were locked in their first-class compartment at the very front of the train, next to the engine. That was the custom of the day and was done for the safety of the first-class passengers, although in the end it probably killed them. Within seconds of the collision, the front three carriages of the express were covered in paraffin and were ablaze. The rear carriages were undamaged but all thirty-two first-class passengers were roasted alive, the women only distinguishable from the men by the metal hoops of their crinolines which had not melted. On the day of the Edwards' funeral, most of the shops in Halifax and Huddersfield were closed and the Calderdale Flower Festival was cancelled.

The building work at Castle Carr was completed under the supervision of another son, Lea Priestley Edwards who lived in it until 1876 when it was sold to a Mr Laycock. The estate passed eventually into the hands of the Murgatroyds, worsted spinners of Luddenden, who held it from 1895 to 1961 when the estate was sold off.

The hall itself, although it lasted longer than its builder, still stood less than a hundred years from completion to destruction. Now, only

The gate lodge of Castle Carr

Sad remnants, including the family crest, of Castle Carr

Dereliction at Castle Carr, and one lone monkey-puzzle tree

the gate lodges remain to give any idea of the splendour of this Palace of Spindledom. Dry rot and its isolated position brought about its demolition in 1962 although today it would probably have been saved. Its oak panelling and fittings, its slates and stones were sold and the house pulled down in ruins. The castle ruins and the water gardens remain, overgrown and to some extent vandalised. I stumbled across them years ago while trying to find a way up on to the moors from Luddenden.

Luddenden is a bonny little village set deep in the 'dene' with a lovely old church and churchyard and, close by, a weir where the river tumbles on its way down the valley.

I had left Luddenden with its inn – the Lord Nelson where Branwell Brontë used to meet with the members of the Luddenden Reading Club, carousing and boozing when he should have been looking after the goods trains shunting up and down the line – and followed the footpath by the cemetery to Booth, and the bottom of Jerusalem Lane, a name that gives some indication of the fervent religious devotion underlying these hills and moors. From Jerusalem, the Calderdale Way leads to the lane to Throstle Bower – 'throstle' is one of the country words for thrush, a lovely name I always think.

By the lane is an old Methodist graveyard and at its very edge a sad stone stands memorial to seven orphan girls who died while working at Calvert's Mill at Wainstalls. Seventy-two such orphan girls came from Kirkdale Industrial School in Liverpool to work at the mill. They were a cheap source of labour and, if we are to believe contemporary accounts, they must have known little other than hardship and poverty. In the school register, the mill owner is described as their Guardian.

The orphans' grave at Wainstalls

I remember a millworker telling me once that orphans were often employed in the mills because they were exceptionally cheap labour, few questions were ever asked about their welfare and the parishes responsible for their upkeep were only too glad to be rid of them. Many of the Yorkshire and Lancashire mill owners, like those in Derbyshire, mistreated the children terribly and there is at least one documented case of dead mill-orphans being buried in the mill yard under the flag stones.

On this particular day, I followed Heys Lane down from Throstle Bower past The Nunnery to the bridge where I got terribly lost and, wandering off the road, found myself in a rhododendron jungle of Himalayan proportions. I crashed around for ages, falling over roots and nettling myself all over (shorts had seemed a good idea when I set off), before stumbling out after much thrashing about and cursing into a clearing. Here I saw before me what, at first sight, looked like the remnants of a lost city that had been hidden for years in some South American jungle. Curved walls of cut stone, topped by great copings, followed the slope of the land, and cobbled aqueducts led from a massive wall down into the overgrowth below. It was strangely quiet and the whole place had the fossilised air of Miss Haversham's wedding cake.

I rambled round the old aqueducts, then struggled through more nettles and rhododendrons until I broke out into the open ground above the dams. There a further shock awaited me, the lone tower of the gatehouse of Castle Carr and everywhere the carved stones of walls and corbels. Close by was the last of Mr Ponto's monkey-puzzle trees. At the time I had no knowledge of Castle Carr and the lost water gardens so the whole place had an air of mystery and dereliction. From the castle I struck north-westwards across the moor above to High Brown Knoll, to come back down to Luddenden past the deserted worsted mill of the Murgatroyds, still mystified by the overgrown works of man in the valley below.

Later that week, whilst being interviewed on a local radio programme, I mentioned the ruins on air and a few days later got a witty letter from Ian Wright, Yorkshire Water's Headworks Supervisor and it is he I have to thank for supplying much of the background information on the castle and Edwards family.

Apparently, at the beneficence of the Murgatroyds, the great fountains were switched on once a year at Whitsuntide, and hundreds of their workers and other folk from Halifax and the environs came out in charabancs to picnic in the grounds and watch the water spouting up into the air. Water Board officials hacked a way into the jungle in the spring of 1983 and managed to turn the fountains on, and in his letter Ian Wright said there was talk of the gardens being renovated and opened again to the public. But sadly, when I passed there recently, they were as overgrown, hidden and neglected as ever; the land around and the ruins of Castle Carr are privately owned and there is no access unless you get permission from the landowner.

The water gardens of Luddenden

The neglected water gardens resemble some lost city

A jungle of undergrowth surrounds the old gardens

Wuthering Heights

No coward soul is mine
That neath the rude wind's blast doth flinch
Even though ice should stab
The very welkin yet no inch
Shall I be made to give

Emily Brontë

PEOPLE CALL IT 'Brontë Country' but it isn't, any more than the Yorkshire Dales is 'Herriot Country', Dorset is 'Hardy Country' or Huntingdonshire is 'Cromwell Country', although the Heritage Industry would have us believe it to be so.

From a literary point of view, *Wuthering Heights* is the only book that could be said to be set specifically in the Haworth area, *Jane Eyre*, *Agnes Grey*, *Villette* and *The Tenant of Wildfell Hall*, though they are without doubt *northern*, could be set in a band of country stretching anywhere from Leek to Dumfries. Therefore, if you're going to call it any kind of country at all, you should, more properly, call it after the people whose names we most often associate with these moors, 'Cathy and Heathcliff Country', although it has other claims to fame and could equally well merit the titles 'Mad Parson Grimshaw Country', or 'Dead Balloon Parachutist Country'.

The Heritage Industry with its associated gee-gaws and knick knacks (most of which seem to be made in Korea or Singapore) would turn the whole world into Disneyland given a chance. The once quiet streets of Haworth are turned into Blackpool for seven months of the year now, and people mill round in their thousands looking for consumer experiences; a triumph for the marketing people in the Bradford Tourist Office, a disaster for the village. The place is swamped with visitors and although tourism obviously provides jobs, the balance has swung so far towards exploiting whatever literary interest the place may have had that it has destroyed its essential character.

Top Withins's claim to be the inspiration for the geographical position of Wuthering Heights is dubious anyway. It is based on its isolation, its position at the end of what is now called the Brontë Way and by the two stunted trees that somehow manage to survive the withering blasts. All of which is as may be. It certainly is a wild place in winter, and even in summer you are conscious of the sky as a great bowl above you, as though there is more of it here than anywhere else in England. It is open and bare and the air is full of energy. It almost crackles around you as you look down towards Haworth on a frosty autumn day. It is certainly no place for a 'coward soul', which may be why Emily felt so kin to the wild and the wuthering.

[212]

Top Withins: no place for a 'coward soul'

People have written volumes, dozens of them, claiming to know what made three sisters turn out such a small but powerful body of writing. Scholars have assessed their work from every angle. Marxist, Feminist, Freudian, Structuralist, most of the critical schools have had a go at one time or another. I've even got a book called *The Key to the Brontë Works* which claims that Charlotte wrote them all, and I once met a bloke in a pub in Keighley who said it was all down to constipation and that, had their bowels been regular, they wouldn't have written half the stuff. But since he claimed never to read anything other than the racing pages and whatever his chips were wrapped in, I don't really know what school of English literary criticism he falls into. The Brontës' father and mother may be one part of the explanation for such a flowering of literary talent; the Celtic lines of Maria's Cornishness and Patrick's Irishness could well have been the spark that set all four of their surviving children off into their inner worlds. Patrick was an Irishman who set about destroying all that was Irish within him. Born in a one-room cabin in Co Donegal he learned his letters at a hedge school and was educated by a local schoolmaster who saw raw talent in the boy. He became a Protestant, changed his name from Prunty to Brunty then Bronte and finally Brontë and entered the Church of England as a parson. After livings at Thornton and Bradford, he came to Haworth succeeding the incumbent who had taken over from Mad Grimshaw, the Rev Mr Redhead.

Redhead had no control over the congregation (to be fair, Grimshaw must have been a hard act to follow); more of Grimshaw later) and during his first service the entire congregation walked out, clogs clattering. During his second service the village idiot was driven into church seated backwards on a donkey! Parson Brontë had no such trouble, partly perhaps because of his habit of never going anywhere without a loaded pistol in his pocket.

Emily, Charlotte, Anne and Branwell spent almost all their lives at Haworth and worked both in they travelled and although

Haworth Parsonage in the snow

England and abroad, they always returned to Haworth. Emily's own experience was that any of her family who left the parsonage either died or returned utterly changed and it is interesting that all the characters in *Wuthering Heights*, except the servants, leave the house to return changed, the only constants in this whirlpool of a book being the house and the moors around it.

The parsonage and the moors are much tamer now than they were in the Brontës' day; then the roads were foul, the drains were worse and the death toll from disease was such that there was a daily procession of corpses coming to be buried in Haworth graveyard. If you really want to know what inspired a book like *Wuthering Heights*, then go to the moor in the filthiest weather and stand there for half an hour if you can. Then come back in the summer when the sun is on the heather and it's hot enough to lie naked in the grass under a glass-clear sky and you'll get some idea of the extremes of love and hate mirrored in the elements in Emily's most powerful book.

My favourite walk from Haworth leaves the village by the lane that leads to the moors, out past the parsonage and follows the gritstone path to Withins. It is a way I've gone over and again, in all kinds of weathers, and the times I've enjoyed best were two very special days, one in high summer and the other fast in the clasp of winter. One day larks and curlew wittered away all around me as I dawdled through the heat of the day, the other an eerie silence cloaked the world as I walked by frozen waterfalls over a windless land made solid by nights of hard frost.

The walk to Withins by the Brontë Waterfall and the Brontë Bridge leads you from the Stanbury road along a pleasant path, passing houses ruined and empty (because they are on Water Board land, I presume) until, leaving the falls and bridge behind, you climb onto the edge of a heathery moor and see in the far distance the ruins of the two farms, Lower and Top Withins. It's a pleasant walk and if, as people suggest, Emily often walked this way, you can see how the wild and windy outlook from Top Withins could have given her a location for the Heights. But that seems to be where any connection ends because the house described in *Wuthering Heights* is a Tudor yeoman farmer's residence, more like Wycoller Hall might have been, or Ponden Hall perhaps. Top Withins in the best of its days was a humble, moor-

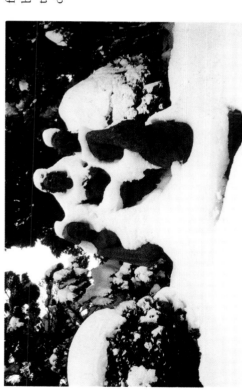

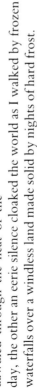

The statue to the Brontë sisters

farmer's dwelling, with laith and barns attached and with none of the fine carvings or courtyard described in the book:

> Wuthering Heights is the name of Mr Heathcliff's dwelling, 'Wuthering' being a significant provincial adjective, descriptive of the atmospheric tumult to which its station is exposed in stormy weather. Pure, bracing ventilation they must have up there at all times, indeed: one may guess the power of the north wind, blowing over the edge, by the excessive slant of a few stunted firs at the end of the house; and by a range of gaunt thorns all stretching their limbs one way, as if craving alms of the sun. Happily the architect had foresight to build it strong; the narrow windows are deeply set in the wall, and the corners defended with larger jutting stones.
>
> Before passing the threshold, I paused to admire a quantity of grotesque carving lavished over the front, and especially about the principal door, above which, among a wilderness of crumbling griffins and shameless little boys, I detected the date '1500' and the name, 'Hareton Earnshaw'.

Thrushcross Grange is described as being six miles away across open moorland. No such house exists and though Ponden Hall sans 'shameless little boys' is often seen as the model for it, it is far too humble to have been the Grange. Wycoller Hall, nine miles away, would be far more likely. I would suggest that we give Emily Brontë credit for creating a powerful and symbolic world in her own imagination, a world that drew on the real wild and wuthering moors

The path to the ruins of Lower and Top Withins

that she knew, but a world nevertheless to be found more in the mind than anywhere else. Seeking the real models for literary places is a harmless pastime, but in the end you may as well go crawling round on your hands and knees in Oxfordshire looking for Hobbit holes just because Tolkien lived there, or go climbing Catbells in the hope of meeting Mrs Tiggy Winkle.

The ruins of Top Withins have changed much in the last fifty years, a testament to the wild and savage weather they get up here. When Bill Brandt took his famous picture in 1944, bits of the roof were still intact; now only the concrete capping put there by the Brontë Society has stopped the walls tumbling down altogether. I'm not sure whether I like it half-saved or whether it wouldn't be better off left mouldering into ruins. The building looks strangely stopped, arrested in its decline back into the moor, neither one thing nor another, as though it would like either to be re-built or allowed to fall down altogether, but not suspended in this limbo-like state.

From the ruin and its few stunted trees, you can either go back to Haworth the way you came, or follow the track north to Ponden Hall via 'the Kirk' or, if you feel like a good stretch, you can take a longer route by the Pennine Way to the reservoirs of Walshaw Dean. From there, come back to Haworth via Hardcastle Crags and the beautiful Crimsworth Dean. It's a long day out, but it is a superb walk through some lovely

Lily Cove's grave in Haworth churchyard

country and, if you like solitude, you're not likely to meet many people, particularly in winter.

One day, following my usual route, I left the village and went out towards the moor by the cemetery. I'm fascinated by graveyards (put it down to the Irish in me) and there is a particularly fascinating stone in Haworth graveyard that marks the last mortal remains of poor Lily Cove, the tragic balloon parachutist. Lily a 'world renowned aeronaut' was booked to appear at the Haworth Annual Gala in June 1906 to perform her act of derring-do before a crowd of thousands. She arrived the day before and checked into the old White Lion at the top of Main Street with her employer, 'Captain' Frederick Bigmead. Some of the local worthies were scandalised that not only was she travelling unaccompanied with a man who was neither her father nor brother, but that she was rumoured to wear tights whilst performing her act and, as the press reported, she was a 'good-looking, well-proportioned young woman'. On the day of the gala, the balloon failed to ascend, due, it was asserted, to impure gases. The Captain promised that the next evening the balloon would ascend without failure so the crowds gathered again and the balloon swept into the sky without any difficulty. Somewhere near Ponden Reservoir, Lily jumped as she had done so many times before but, for reasons the inquest was unable to discover, her parachute failed to open and she

A green lane near Crimsworth Dean, Stoodley Pike in the far distance

cartwheeled to her death among the buttercup-smothered fields far below. Though Lily came from London, she was buried in Haworth, her father travelling north for the funeral dressed in a 'suit of decent black' bought at Captain Bigmead's expense.

I said goodbye to Lily, crossed the road above Stanbury Height and followed the track that contours above Lower Laithe Reservoir and Bully Trees Farm, a name that has always fascinated me. I have visions of great thick oaks or beeches towering above little alders and holly trees and shoving them out of the way to get the best bit of ground or the most sunlight.

'If you elderberries don't pick up your roots and push off, we're going to rip your leaves off!'

I dropped down to the brook and, passing by the Brontë Bridge and Falls, found that the former was being repaired by a group of volunteers. It had been smashed that summer by a 'beck-brast' or 'bog-burst' as they're variously called. This occurs when heavy rains hit the moors above and the water, filling the peaty ground like water in a balloon, suddenly bursts out and runs down in flood, tearing everything with it as it goes roaring down from the tops and into the valleys, carrying along trees, boulders, bridges, cattle and all. Patrick Brontë, father of the famous children, himself witnessed a 'horrible bog-burst' at Crow Hill in 1824 which he used as the basis for a hell-fire sermon that he later published at his own expense. He was quite an author in his own way and also wrote a sizeable body of verse, which has thankfully sunk into the other bogs of Time.

It is strange too, although probably symptomatic of the chauvinism of the time, that he felt the truly creative genius of the family lay in his son Branwell. Branwell mixed with artists and poets in the Bohemian underworld of Bradford and Halifax, dabbling with painting and poetry and even writing to the then poet laureate, William Words-worth, insisting that the latter take him seriously as one of the nation's finest poets. Poor Branwell, he spent more of his time talking about

what he was going to do than doing anything, while his sisters quietly scribbled away between running the household, and teaching and nursing sick relatives. All Branwell's fine ambitions turned to dust and he ended up as the clerk at Luddenden Foot Railway Station, even losing that job through his bad accounting. He ended his life a drunk and opium eater, bribing people to procure laudanum for him from the chemist in Haworth Main Street.

Obsessed by his lack of height, ashamed of his red hair, a discontented dabbler in painting and poetry, he was one of Life's great 'Might Have Been's'. It must have saddened him deeply towards the end of his life to discover that his sisters had succeeded where he had so miserably failed. I have an abiding image in my mind's eye of a seedy little railway clerk writing letters to Wordsworth by the light of the railway booking office lantern, his brain half fudged with drink and dope – very sad.

I climbed to Top Withins, with the new heather purple around me, and although it was towards the end of high summer, it was mid-week and there were very few people about. Fistfuls of high white clouds wallowed above me, a light breeze pushing them on. I thought of all the people at work in factories and offices while I was rambling about like this, and even though I told myself this was work and that I was writing a book, I still felt guilty.

The Pennine Way is easy to follow south of Withins and although it has suffered from some erosion, footpath reclamation work using local stone has started to blend in with the surrounding land. By the side of the trail is a small memorial stone erected in memory of 'E. Wilkinson – A Rambler', who died in 1964 aged thirty-five. The Pennine Way here crosses what Halliwell Sutcliffe, the Yorkshire writer, claimed was 'the most beautiful and characteristic moorland in the West Riding', but signposts by the side of the path tell you that if you stray from it, you will be trespassing either onto the grouse moors of the Saville Estate or the water-collecting lands of the privatised authority, so just watch it! I read recently that the law that included transportation for poaching has never been repealed, so if you find yourself wandering from the path and treading on a grouse by mistake, your next stop would not be Walshaw Dean Reservoirs but Botany Bay where you would be given a nice suit with arrows to wear and a hat with lots of pretty bobbing corks. (I always find it strange that walkers on a moor are said to frighten the grouse whereas men with twelve bores seem to worry them not a bit.)

The reservoirs are a wonderful monument to Victorian engineering. The massive blackened stones of walls, aqueducts and leats meld well into the hillside while the ubiquitous rhododendrons crawl everywhere. But, still and all, the reservoirs are a bit of an eyesore if you can imagine the valleys the way they were, and I'm always glad when they, and the concrete track that leads from them to Alcomden Water, are well behind me. The path from Alcomden follows a gentle green lane rounding under New Laithe Moor and curving above Hardcastle Crags and it is a cracking walk. Abel Cross, the two looming standing stones also known as 'Mourning and Vanity', stand at the spot where I usually stop for something to eat. These mark the old packhorse way that led from Haworth to Hebden Bridge and beyond. They are beautiful polished stones and so much care went into their making that they surely functioned as more than waymarkers.

At Baby House Hill above the lovely valley of Crimsworth Dean, some old ruins stand by the lane. I once found a sheep there, stuck in the fireplace. It had climbed the stairs to an upper floor and had somehow fallen down the chimney where I found it, dazed and, so far as I could tell, unhurt. I pulled it out and let it go – and it ran straight back up and did it again so I gave up. It must have been waiting for Father Christmas, although it had a long wait since it was July at the time. Following down the lane brought me to where the bridge crosses Crimsworth Dean Beck at Grain Water; here I lay on the bank and drank from the cold water, splashing it over me so I should cool

down in the afternoon sun. The bridge is a lovely spot for a picnic and on summer weekends it is crowded with families – children paddling in the water, dads and mums asleep on the grass.

I climbed away from the road and onto the moor to Top of Stairs. The track is quite good but, as if to remind you that you're in 'Heathcliff Country', there are references on the map to Red Dike Swamp and Stairs Swamp, and the boggy-looking holes are filled with bog cotton that shakes its noddy little head even on the calmest of days. It was getting on in the day by the time I reached Top of Stairs and a long light was throwing shadows across the land. Bodkin Lane took me through the afternoon sun up through fields and farms to Tom Stell's Seat and Penistone Hill. Tom Stell was a local man who loved these moors and his seat was carved from a single piece of stone and carted up here by quarrymen in 1932.

Coming back this way, I was reminded of the very first time I crossed these moors on a rainy day in November when I was fifteen years old. I was with an uncle, now long dead who, putting it kindly, was not playing with a full deck. As they say in Lancashire, 'He was a sandwich short of a picnic', or 'The bus was full, but there was no one on top'. He insisted that he knew his way and by map and compass could take us out over the moor to Top Withins and back. Although I was only fifteen, I knew that I was the most competent map reader of the two of us, particularly since, when I asked him what time it was, he looked at the compass and said 'Quarter to two'. I'd had four years in the Boy Scouts which, as well as teaching me never to be alone in the same room as the scoutmaster, had taught me how to line up a map with a compass and how to walk on a bearing. My uncle thought North was North no matter what, and that the little red needle was something to do with the speed you were walking at.

He got us totally and absolutely lost in the mists and rain and winds of November and we wandered round that moor for hours until we met a shepherd in the middle of a bog who pointed us a way off. My

'Heathcliff Country', with the season's new heather softening the bleakness

uncle ignored him and even when we met the man again an hour later in exactly the same spot, he swore it was the shepherd that had moved. When I finally limped off, leaving him, I walked about a quarter of a mile in the direction the shepherd had pointed us and found myself at Ponden Hall, where I ordered a pot of tea and scones and jam. The uncle turned up an hour later insisting that he had known where he had been all the time and that he'd intended to go into a bog up to his arm-pits. Well, he's dead and gone now and is probably wandering round paradise lost, bumping into angels and falling through holes in the clouds.

Coming across Penistone Hill this summer's afternoon by one of the old quarry tracks, I found some old workings that I'd never noticed before, bits of pumping machinery in pits sunk into the moor. Apparently, they have only recently been unearthed and are all that is left of a windmill that powered the pumps that sent water uphill to the quarries. It was dismantled in 1926 shortly after a tragic accident, when a man was caught up in its machinery and killed.

From the hill, I like to follow the lane that brings you into Haworth by the stone-flagged churchyard walk with its iron railings, its great trees above and the ocean of graves below. The graveyard is probably one of the most overcrowded in England, and tragically many of the graves are those of children. Haworth in the eighteenth century was a pestiential village with no sanitation or water supply and the death rate, particularly amongst children, was high. It was a village of lawlessness and godlessness too by all accounts, and when Mad

Parson Grimshaw arrived here in 1742 he found it a fallow field in urgent need of ploughing. And plough it he did with his horsewhip and boot, scourging the men out of the ale-houses and into church, and running the length of the aisle to lay about with his boots at the dogs fighting in God's house. He had a special pulpit made with a sounding board to amplify his voice; on it was painted a blazing sun to echo his blazing sermons. He preached until the congregation dropped with exhaustion and spared neither himself nor the weakest of his flock. He often travelled miles to shrive some poor dying soul, ranting at the bedside until the room shook and the sinner came round to the path of righteousness before the death rattle echoed round the room. He was an obsessive and manic man and threw his lot in with the Methodists while they were still a part of the established church. Thousands flocked to hear him preach, so many that the church was solid with people, while hundreds outside strained to hear his ranting. He hated hypocrisy and on one occasion, when he suspected one of his flock of posing as an almsgiver while really being nothing of the kind, he dressed as a beggar and went to the man's door where, as he expected, he was turned away. The next Sunday, of course, there was 'pop to play' and the offender was ridiculed and exposed before the entire congregation.

Grimshaw's pulpit is still in the church which is worth a visit, a quiet cool place to sit on a hot summer's day for a bit of a think before you venture into the hurley-bulloo of Blackpool-sur-Moor for a pot of tea and a Brontë cream cake.

The Slaughter Stone and Wycoller

The scene is beautiful, wild, sleek, untamed beauty. It is a wilderness of loneliness as primeval as creation almost, and not one good to be lost in. It is an untamed desert. Small piles of rock tooth the summit edge; all else is a gentle curve, smooth flank, rounded rise, slippery hollow, curving swell.

Boshemengro quoted in Titus Thornber: *Taking the Car for a Walk*

MAPS ARE LIKE BOOKS TO ME and I'll often spend hours just poring over them; not just looking for walks I might do, but reading them for themselves. The 1:50,000 is the scale I usually begin with, then, when I find something interesting, I go up to the 1:25,000. The latter, particularly the Pathfinder maps, are exactly what you need for walking since they show not just footpaths, but field-walls and hedges, things of archaeological interest and other details left off the Landranger Series.

One night, looking at the map of the area around Wycoller, I traced a walk that started from Nelson and went by Catlow Bottoms to Coldwell Reservoir; it then went by Will Moor to climb Lad Law on Boulsworth Hill. From there I could head north-east to Wycoller, coming back by field paths to Trawden and Nelson. It looked a fascinating walk through fairly gentle country with much to look at along the way. People often suggest that, having been to the Himalayas a couple of times, walking in the Pennines, in Britain generally in fact, must be pretty small beer to me now. Not so. The scale is different, and the physical effort and danger may be much less but the Pennine hills and dales have a unique character and beauty; it's a difference merely of kind.

It was a grey Sunday in March when Pat and I left Nelson behind and headed towards open country. Nelson was nothing other than a hamlet until the expansion of the cotton industry when, in the space of a few years, it became a major northern Lancashire town. It takes its name from a pub called the Lord Nelson, which cheers me greatly. I like to think of towns called 'Dog and Marshmallow' or 'Pig and Ballbearing'. Nelson boasts the Star Cycling Club, one of the oldest wheelers' clubs in the country, and has a long tradition of dissent and resistance earning itself the nickname Little Moscow for a time because of the large number of left-wingers in the town.

We followed a succession of field paths to Catlow Bottoms, where a water-splash crosses the road and, meeting open country beyond the Coldwell Reservoirs, followed an old green lane to the pack route across Boulsworth Hill. A lone doorway is all that is standing now of a ruined farmhouse and I read that this is called Scotsman's Gate, indicating perhaps that the farmhouse stood once by a drove road used by the wild Scots drovers who spent weeks driving their cattle south to the great fairs of Lancashire and Yorkshire, the burgeoning cotton and wool cities being hungry for meat. Many of the herders spoke only the Gaelic and slept by the fires wrapped in their long filibegs.

Just before the ruin, we started the climb to the summits of Bouls-worth Hill and Lad Law. The rough moorland here was orig-inally open common but is now owned by the Saville Estate. It was enclosed in 1821 and bought from the commissioners by the Towne-leys, one of the first families of Burnley. By all accounts, it has always been a jealously guarded moor, and before and during the grouse season, the keepers of the estate are often on the look out for people who may have strayed from the concessionary path nego-tiated by the Ramblers' Associa-tion in the 1970s.

From the summit of Boulsworth Hill, you can see Pendle, Black Hambledon and Stoodley Pike on a good day, and all around you the jumble of stones that go by the names of the Abbot Stone, the Great and Little Saucer Stones, and, on the very summit of Lad Law itself, the Slaughter or Druid's Stone. This is shaped like a crude altar and has some cup-shaped depressions in its upper surface, similar to those in the stones at Pots and Pans above Uppermill, so maybe it was used as a primitive altar stone. The word *llad* is said to be the Gaelic for 'slaughter', so who knows. The moors around are thick with tumuli and other prehistoric remains; perhaps at one time there was a burial chamber or stone circle here, in which case 'Law' could be a corruption of *low*.

We dropped down from the hill to pick up the packway again that would lead us by Parson Lee to Wycoller. The old packway was so

The Slaughter or Druid's Stone on the summit of Lad Law

important that when the moor was enclosed, a special Act of Parlia-ment was passed, declaring the route a public right of way. Where it meets what is now the road from Colne to Keighley, there stands an inn called The Herders Arms, and behind it is a parcel of land called Herders Common, where the Scotsmen grazed their stock dur-ing their overnight halts, a sure indication that this was the meet-ing of two busy trading routes.

Above the lane to Wycoller is Foster's Leap, a very deep gap between two boulders said to have taken its name from a sheep-stealer who was caught red-handed on the

moors above. Men were hanged for sheep stealing in those times and the luckless Foster was offered his life if he could leap the nine-foot gap. He cheated by leaping it on his horse and they cleared the gap without any trouble. Unfortunately, as they landed on the other side, the poor animal lost its footing and both rider and horse fell to their deaths on the rocks below. The gap has narrowed after two hundred or more years of rock movement and it's now only five feet or so wide, but I still wouldn't like to try it, particularly after a session in The Herders Arms.

The lane soon drops down into Wycoller Dean, where it becomes leafy and overhung with trees, a reminder that at one time this whole area was far richer in woodlands than it is now. It was all once part of the Forest of Trawden, a hunting forest governed by Edward the Confessor. The word 'forest' here is a little misleading since it implies vast acres of woodland; woodland there certainly was in Trawden but a 'forest' then was largely open country set aside solely for the King's pleasure in the sport of the chase. Trawden, Rossendale, Pendle and Bowland all fell under the King's jurisdiction. Reserving the land for game alone was not a profitable usage, so the King and his lords encouraged farming to continue in small pockets. The farms were known as 'booths', 'folds' and 'heys', around which high walls and fences were erected to keep out the deer although, of course, they were of little use. Other walls were erected to keep cows in: long slabs of gritstone, cut locally and dragged into position by ox or horse, they surrounded these mediaeval 'vacceries', as the Norman French called them, and they still stand now around Wycoller and Trawden, the old Vaccary walls.

The lane into Wycoller passes three wonderful bridges. The first, a 'clam' bridge lies across the beck like a fallen log. Probably prehistoric in origin, it is the earliest form of bridge known. When Wycoller was a busy village, full of weavers and weaving, some of the local young bloods held competitions to see which of them could lift the bridge and though many of the big beef-fed Lancashire lads got into the beck and shouldered the stone, none of them managed to budge it.

Further downstream, another ancient bridge, the clapper bridge, was here long before the Romans came. It has been deeply rutted by the iron-shod clogs of handloom weavers, taking their cloth by the fields to Trawden and Colne. A farmer, whose sister slipped off the bridge because of the rut, chiselled it flat. The bridge collapsed and his sister died anyway but the bridge was easier to repair than his sister and was put back into its original position with the addition of another upright. The packhorse bridge, which you meet as you come into the village, probably dates from the seventeenth century and is a lovely two-span, narrow affair built in the warm local stone.

Wycoller, save for one farm, was a deserted village in the 1950s and old photographs show the place as a nest of empty ruins. Following the filming there of a BBC series on the Lancashire witches, the place seems to have looked up and now the village is a conservation area. Quiet only in the winter mid-week, it is at other times packed with walkers and day-trippers. The council have built a car park a few hundred yards from the village, but idiots still drive down the lane, causing chaos, rather than leave their tin-womb in the place provided and walking a couple of hundred paces.

Wycoller Hall was built by one of Lancashire's oldest families, the Hartleys, between 1550 and 1560 and seems to have been one of the foremost halls of Trawden and Calder. Charlotte Brontë is said to have used it as the model for Ferndean Manor in *Jane Eyre*. It remained in the Hartleys' possession until marriage to a Cunliffe brought it into the hands of one of the north's old Royalist families. Once rich and powerful, the Cunliffes had seen much of their land and wealth sequestered by the Puritans and, in much reduced circumstances, they settled at Wycoller after the Civil War. For four generations they lived at the hall and by all accounts they were a rapacious and ale-swilling bunch of rapscallions, becoming noted all over the area for drinking, horse racing and cock fighting. There is a cock-pit still in the woods behind the house and at times there must have been dozens of the county's finest young (and old) bloods, boozing, smoking and cheering as the two birds, with spurs fixed to their legs, fought in the pit, while the men above placed bets on them. The word 'cocktail', according to one source I read, comes from this sport and was a toast to the victor, the number of drinks in the mix being dependent on the number of tail feathers left in the rump of the bird, alive or dead. I don't think the SOED gives this definition.

Local legend has it that the last squire of Wycoller Hall, in his final illness and too frail to struggle to the cock-pit, had the cocks brought into his death chamber so he could watch the bloody battle from his bed. A painting by Lazlett J. Pott called 'Game to the Last' depicts the scene and the story goes that as Squire Cunliffe grew increasingly

Pat crossing the watersplash at Catlow Bottoms

The old vaccary walls at Wycoller

The ruins of Wycoller Hall

feeble and unable to raise his head from the pillow, he had mirrors arranged round the room so he could continue to watch the fights. Mrs Gaskell has a fine account of it in her life of Charlotte Brontë.

When this last cockfighting squire died in 1818, having squandered every penny of the family fortunes (very much as did Hindley Earnshaw in *Wuthering Heights*), the Hall fell into the hands of its chief mortgager, the Rev. John Oldham who sold its doors, windows, roofing timber and stone to recoup his losses and so the building fell into ruin. Local farmers and landowners descended on the Hall like locusts and took bits of it to fettle their own houses and buildings. The beautiful old two-storey porch was taken to Trawden and built onto the front of a house in Church Street belonging to a man called David Bannister, whose grandson, Dr Roger Bannister, was the first man to run a mile in under four minutes. The foundations were lousy and the porch started to collapse, so it was sold yet again and taken to Foulridge where, after having been split in two, it was built again into Ball House.

Like all good ruins, Wycoller Hall is haunted by a spectred horseman and a rustling lady, but not, strangely, by a lot of angry dead cocks with drinks named after them.

The Spectred Horseman visits the Hall once a year. On a moonless night, when the wind is screaming off the moor, he thunders into the village and, dismounting in front of the Hall, he climbs the stairs to where the first storey once stood. Women's screams are heard and then the ghost gallops off into the night. Apparently, one of the Cunliffes beat his wife to death with a horse-whip after finding her in the arms of a man he took to be her lover, but who was in fact a long-lost brother who had returned after having been assumed dead. Because of his foul deed, the horseman is forced to return each year to re-create his crime.

A two-storeyed porch in Wycoller

The Rustling Lady was the wife of Simon Cunliffe who once led the hunt into his wife's bedroom in pursuit of a fox that had gone to ground under her bed. When she protested, he raised his whip to silence 'this wittering wife', but she fell down dead before he could strike. Nice lot, those Cunliffes. At the anniversary of her death, a horn is heard sounding through the Dean and the hills of Trawden. Horse, rider, hounds and all come flying through the night, howling and jabbering. There are screams, then silence, followed by the rustling of the lady's dress as she walks the chamber of death. It's a wonder anybody in Wycoller gets any sleep.

Now the poor old Hall stands, little left but a huddle of walls around a flagged floor. The mullioned windows, the great fireplace and the little key-hole compartment at the right-hand side, where the gentlemen would powder their wigs, are all that remain of this seat of cock-fighting, wife-murdering, true blue-blooded gentlemen. If anywhere was the model for that claustrophobic house boiling with violence – Wuthering Heights – then surely this was it.

because there was a certain amount of road walking involved, so the next time we climbed Boulsworth Hill, we went from the little village of Worsthorne by Thursden to Lad Law. It was a hot summer's day and the moor, toasting under the sun, smelt of peat and summer grass. There is a definite smell to the gritstone moors that differs totally from the smell of limestone country. It is a peaty, almost metallic, nutty smell, whereas limestone is sweeter – or perhaps it's just my nose.

Wycoller, that day, was busy with school parties and families, many of them splashing about in the beck. At the packhorse bridge, a tiny little boy, no more than two years old, in a cap, a tee shirt and wet underpants, was paddling with his sister. He bent down, picked up a stone from the bed and shouted to his parents on the bank, 'Look, mum, it's a bottom!'

'What do you mean?'

'It's got a wrinkle. It's a bottom,' and he burst out laughing, as all small children do at the mention of bottoms or willies.

'It's a rude stone,' he said. 'It's a bottom.'

So I took a photograph of him holding up the Bottom Stone and we decided that from now on the bridge ought to be called 'Bottom Stone Bridge', which made him laugh even more. (Ordnance Survey, please note the change of name.)

Following the path to Trawden, we went by Will o' th' Moor to Coldwell Reservoirs, then by Monk Hall to Worsthorne for a good pint at the Crooked Billet. The village was quiet when we were there, but in the seventeenth century it was infested with boggarts and witches. Naughty children were known as 'changelings' and, until fairly recently, offerings were left at certain stones and wells to appease the sprites and goblins. We left a few quid to appease the landlord and sat outside in the sunshine with our pints and a packet of crisps.

Pat and I stopped at the newly opened tea rooms for a sandwich and a brew before making our way back by Trawden and the fields to Nelson. I decided that I didn't like the beginning and end of this walk

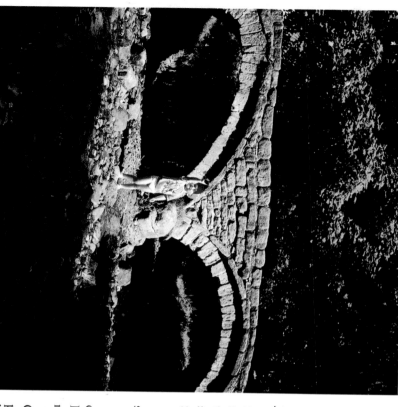

The naming of 'Bottom Stone Bridge'

Sunset over Wycoller, Pendle Hill in the distance

Old Pendle

Pendle Stands
Rownd cop survaiying all ye wild moor lands,
And Malkin Toure, a little cottage where
Report makes caitive witches meete to sweare
Their homage to ye divell, and contrive
The death of men and beasts . . . .

Anon

BEFORE I KNEW MUCH ELSE, I knew that there were witches in
Pendle; it was part of our family folk-lore, together with the
Sandman who made you go to sleep and the Bogey Man who came
and got you for the least excuse. Witches were an important part of
my childhood mythology. They were real and they had cats and rode
broomsticks, and Pendle Hill had a whole coven of them. When I first
cycled round Whalley and Pendle, the place had hardly changed since
the days of Mother Chattox and Demdyke. It's changed a bit since
then. The Clitheroe by-pass runs at the foot of the hill now and there
are ski slopes on the Nick o' Pendle for winter sport, but the villages
are still much the same as when a handful of poor women who
practised the Old Religion were dragged away from their homes and
tortured until they confessed to having babies by frogs and to flying
through solid walls.

Pendle (the name means 'hill' from the Celtic *pen*) is a place that has
great atmosphere, a broad spreading mound rising to 1,831 feet at its
summit with the old villages of Sabden, Barley, Worston, Downham

and Roughlee at its skirts. Sabden, as every northern schoolperson
knows, still has its Treacle Mines which, according to Bede, was a
source of some income to the manor of Whalley in Anglo-Saxon
times. The miners, descendants of the original Celts who first worked
the seams in Roman times, are secretive and silent folk, short of
stature, dark-featured and bearded and they guard the location of both
the mines and the rich seams of *Sacriferous Negribus* jealously. The
treacle, caused by fragmentation of the magma mantle and a concentration of the carbons that form the same chain as sugar and glucose,
oozes naturally from rocks far underground where it is tapped and
collected by miners, many of whose families have lived in the area
since mediaeval times. The first granting of rights to extract treacle
was made to the Abbot of Whalley by King Ulfric of Mercia in 879,
and treacle from Sabden finds mention in the Domesday Book: 'In ye
Saybdin in Pendelle be quaryes of Kodie Muk and Several Mines of
Traycle alle in ye Manore of Wallee – value seven groats.'

In the early eighteenth century, Yorkshire parkin weavers from

Pendle Hill from above Barley

A classic view of Old Pendle on a winter's evening near Sawley

Sarby Brig, furious at the high prices charged by the Sabden miners, came across Trawden from Calder intent on wrecking the mines, and laid siege to Sabden in what later came to be known as the Battle of Dicky's Medder, when coddy-muck cannons were fired across Dicky-Mint Clough and twelve miners and twenty-one weavers died. In some of the houses in Sabden and Whalley, and in the inn called The Wellsprings in the Nick o' Pendle above the village, you can still see, stuck in the east wall, balls of that same coddy-muck.

The shallow drift mines were worked extensively until the turn of the century caused their closure. One of the richer mines has recently been re-opened because of the overseas demand for high quality Sabden treacle and another mine, although not working, is now open as a tourist attraction complete with tea room, toilets and interpretative centre – an ignoble end.

And what of the witches? Well, the basic story is that there were two rival families known to practise 'witchcraft' in the Pendle area. One the family of Old Mother Demdyke, the other that of Old Mother Chattox. We call them 'witches' and 'wizards' today and the image is conjured up of black cats and broomsticks but 'wise women and men' would perhaps be a better description. They were herbalists, plant doctors who knew where the best herbs grew and when they were best gathered.

Some of them were also midwives, and many of them would have practised the Old Religion, tying rags to the branches of sacred wells, perhaps making offerings at the four Sabbats – the old Celtic Festivals of Beltane, Lughnasa, Oimelc and Samhain. Laurie Lee in *Cider With Rosie* remembers one such 'wise man' in his Gloucestershire village in the early years of this century.

So, to get away from Macbeth for a while, let's call them 'wise women'. To save too much confusion, the following family tree might help.

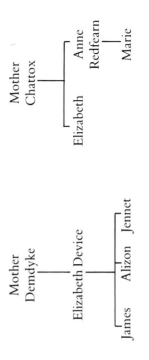

Mother Demdyke
— Elizabeth Device
— James   Alizon   Jennet

Mother Chattox
— Elizabeth   Anne Redfearn
— Marie

The two old women and their families seem to have been at loggerheads for some time. Demdyke, lame and almost blind, lived with her widowed daughter Elizabeth Device and her three children Alizon, James (who was a half-wit) and Jennet who was, at the time, just a young girl. It was Jennet, the youngest who was to damn them all to the gallows.

Chattox, also widowed and, like Demdyke, blind (they probably both had cataracts) had two daughters and a grand-daughter, Marie. The Demdykes lived at Malkin Tower near Blacko and it appears that Chattox, or one of her daughters, broke into the tower and stole some clothes and some oatmeal. The following Sunday, Alizon Device saw Elizabeth Chattox wearing a cap which was one of those stolen from the tower. At that time the law, although it was notified (in the person of Justice Roger Nowell – note the name) was too busy to bother about a bit of larceny in one of the old Pendle Forest villages, so John Device, husband of Elizabeth, went to see Chattox. It is here that the story gets confusing, for, instead of demanding the goods back, he offered to pay a yearly tribute of oatmeal if Mother Chattox agreed not to cause the Demdykes any more trouble.

Whether this was a case of one 'wise woman' buying off another is anybody's guess. However, it appears that the oatmeal tribute was not paid and that soon after John Device sickened and died, blaming

Chattox to the end of his life. After his death, the Demdyke family became beggars, Alizon leading her grandmother round the lanes to beg from door to door. Presumably, since she was a 'wise woman' few would refuse her, perhaps not always out of fear but because of past favours done.

Then in the late 1590s, a man called Robert Nutter of Greenhead Farm fell ill and he too blamed witchcraft for his sickness saying that Anne Redfearn, who lived on Nutter land had bewitched him. It later became known that Nutter had tried to seduce Anne and, when she had refused him, he had sworn to be revenged by turning out her and her daugher. He died soon after, blaming Anne and Mother Chattox until his very last breath.

Ten years later, we find Demdyke's daughter, Elizabeth Device working for a miller, Richard Baldwin. Millers, by tradition, are mean and it seems that Baldwin tried to swindle Elizabeth out of her wages. Whatever the reason, she went with her mother, Old Demdyke, to collect her dues, perhaps feeling that her mother would be a witness or, conversely, that he would be unlikely to thwart a 'wise woman'.

'Get off my ground,' he is reported as saying, 'whores and witches! I will burn the one of you and hang the other.' A few days later, the miller's daughter sickened and died.

Nothing was done about the deaths of either Nutter or Baldwin's daughter but the word soon spread around the villages around Pendle, and when John Law, a pedlar from Halifax, met Alizon Device on 18 March 1612, then the sparks of rumour and enmity that had been flickering about the Pendle Forest gathered to light a fire that was to burn brighter than any beacon and would be seen all over England. Alizon asked the pedlar to give her some pins for nothing and when he refused she cursed him. He had walked no more than a few yards before he fell down helpless. Nowadays it would probably be diagnosed as a seizure or stroke, then there was only one word for it –

This black cat just appeared when I came into the churchyard at Newchurch and led me to the Nutters' graves

'witchcraft'. The affair of the lame pedlar brought the weight of His Majesty's law to bear on the women and Alizon was hauled before the magistrate, Roger Nowell of Read Hall, together with her mother Elizabeth and her brother James.

There are a number of things to consider here. First, 'wise women' (and men) traditionally passed their craft on to their children, in the same way that blacksmiths or coopers would have passed on their skills, so that Alizon claiming she was taught her craft by her mother and her grandmother would be nothing strange.

Secondly, the act of 'cursing' is not something confined to 'witches'. Curses and blessings were used by all country people and vestiges of the old beliefs linger on today – touching wood, saying 'bless you' when someone sneezes, black cats being lucky, wishing someone a safe journey, drinking someone's health; all are shadows of the stronger beliefs of the past. In my own childhood in Manchester there was an old man in the next street who was known to be a 'seer' and a herbalist and anything he said, good or bad, was taken very seriously. The curse or blessing of a known 'wise woman' in the early seventeenth century would of course have been seen as having tremendous potency.

Thirdly, and most importantly, the investigation carried out by Roger Nowell was based on the readings he had made of King James I's book on demonology. King James was obsessed by witches (Shakespeare's *Macbeth* was written as a direct sop to the king) even to the extent that he believed that the storm that delayed his bride-to-be from crossing the sea was caused by 'the Black Arts'. His book gave details of witches' 'teats' and 'spots' and witches' 'familiars'. The 'spots' were dead places on the body where a witch had been touched by the devil and would therefore feel no pain. Pins could be stuck into the flesh and if the witch didn't respond it was a sure sign of her dealings with Satan. Supernumary nipples or warts were another indication of witchery because this was where she fed her familiar, the

devil spirit, often in the shape of an animal, usually a black dog or cat, that would accompany her everywhere.

Armed with this knowledge, and realising of course that finding witches would be a sure way to advance his career, Nowell drew from Alizon Device (perhaps under torture) the confession that her grandmother had introduced a demon to her in the shape of a black dog and that she had let it suck from her. Taking the opportunity to strike a blow for the family, she went on to tell how Old Mother Chattox had bewitched her father to death and how Old Mother Demdyke had churned milk into butter without leaving her bed. All nonsense, of course, and most of it obviously placed in the young girl's mind by Nowell himself, who never once questioned or doubted any of the tales he was told. Mother Demdyke, eighty years old and half dead, was dragged in and readily confessed to having a familiar in the shape of a boy, half black, half brown, and to having bewitched to death Miller Baldwin's child. Under further questioning, she accused Chattox and Anne Redfearn of bewitching Robert Nutter to death. I put it to you that an eighty-year-old dying peasant woman, dragged from her village into the presence of a rich and finely-dressed magistrate in his great hall, would confess to anything that was suggested to her.

All four women were detained to stand trial at the next Lancaster Assizes. From then on the story becomes more bizarre and tragic. Nowell commanded the constable of the Forest of Pendle to make further enquiries and, at Malkin Tower, he found some human teeth (which were supposed to have come from graves at Newchurch) and a clay image. Clay images are used in sympathetic magic and the teeth could have come from anywhere, even poor old Demdyke's own mouth. But the children were dragged before the magistrates (Nowell had been joined by another, Nicholas Bannister) and what really set the cat amongst the familiars was when they questioned Jennet Device, then just nine years old. There had been a coven, she told them, at Malkin Tower that Good Friday, and twenty 'witches' had been present to feast on stolen mutton and to plot murder, and she named every woman present.

Here a little clue drops out of nowhere. One of the women named was Alice Nutter of Roughlee. She was a wealthy gentlewoman, owner of the magnificent Roughlee Old Hall. What was she doing associating with a haggle of peasant women? There are two possibilities: one is that she was involved in the Old Religion, the other that she practised the other 'old religion', Catholicism.

Pendle and the area around remained devoutly and determinedly Catholic throughout the Reformation and, in fact, still has a largely Catholic population. Some families like the Towneleys managed to hold on in spite of all the persecutions but many others lost land and lives. The abbots of Whalley and Sawley, the two monasteries at the foot of Pendle, led what was later to be called The Pilgrimage of Grace for which they were hanged, drawn and quartered and close relatives of Alice Nutter's who had become Catholic priests had been put to death. It is also interesting that, just prior to her arrest, there had been a boundary dispute between Robert Nowell and Alice Nutter which she had won and which had cost him a great deal of money. The fact that Alice Nutter's testimony was never recorded means either that she remained silent to protect other Catholics, or that her words were struck out lest they indicate that Nowell had more than an innocent interest in the case.

Nineteen 'witches' were taken across the Trough of Bowland to stand trial for their lives, and there, on the basis of hearsay and fantasy, Alice Nutter, Alizon Device, Mother Chattox, Anne Redfearn, Elizabeth Device, the half-wit James and a handful of others implicated by Jennet, were sentenced to death and hanged the following day; Mother Demdyke had died in the dungeons whilst awaiting trial. Ironically, Jennet herself stood trial for witchcraft twenty-one years later and was condemned to death; the sentence was repealed, however, and she vanishes at that point from the pages of written history.

There is no doubt in my mind that the true story of the Pendle Witches is that a few 'wise women' practising the old ways were caught up in a mad witch hunt that had swept across Europe and resulted in the horrific deaths of millions; that the same hysteria that took possession of hitherto sensible people during the McCarthy hunts of the 1950s in America and that are paralleled so well in Arthur Miller's *The Crucible*, took place here too. James I, being obsessed with demonology, was also a rabid anti-papist, so the witch hunts of Lancashire served two purposes. They secured preferment for the Justices of the Peace and other gentry involved in the witch hunts, and kept down any opposition or recusancy, since any deviance, moral or political could be seen – since the King was appointed by God and therefore his word was God's word – as coming from Satan.

There is no doubt that the 'Old Religion' is much more tenacious than many people imagine, and has lived on well into this century. The last killing of a witch took place in 1945 at Meon Hill in Warwickshire when an elderly labourer, reputed locally to be a wizard, was found dead with his throat cut and a pitchfork through his chest, ritual ways of 'laying' a witch. The case is said to have baffled Fabian of the Yard. Modern historians, amongst them Dr Anne Ross, believe that in parts of the Pennines, particularly in the Longdendale and Calderdale area, there are still groups of people practising the 'Old Religion' and that Celtic Head cults and Beltane fires are a part of this. The 'wise women' of Pendle didn't vanish with the trials and hangings. In 1875, a woman from Sabden, well known for her spells was taken before the magistrates' court at Colne, accused of assaulting another old woman who she said had been 'hag-riding' her husband. The newspapermen present were forbidden to make reports by the magistrate who said, 'This is the sort of thing that London papers would report at length if they could but learn of it,

Barley village below the summit of Pendle

making some of us appear as ignorant and superstitious chawbacons with not an idea in our heads but weft and twist.'

The 'Old Religion' was, and for all I know still is, the worship of the female Earth mother and the male horned fertility figure. It is basically a form of religion that looks to the spiritual powers of stones, trees and springs and to the healing powers of 'magic' herbal medicines. It has nothing at all to do with devil worship and the pentagram, the reciting of the Lord's Prayer backwards or desecrating of Christian graves which are more to do with the black side of the human psyche and mental illness.

North-east of Sabden is the hamlet of Barley which makes a good base for my favourite walk up Pendle, going by Lower and Upper Ogden Reservoirs, following their feeder stream by Ogden Clough to the summit. It's a great walk and one of the classics of the Pennines. I first came this way as a boy and since then it has been a regular walk, short but full of interest – and in wicked weather it can be challenging too.

One cloudy-bright, bitter-cold day in February I came this way alone to blow off the cobwebs of months of the daily grind. The footpath passes something marked on the map as Buttock Plant. (obviously a short-form for Plantation) which always conjures up a vision in my mind of an enormous tree with lots of bums on it.

A 'Pendle Way' sign near Barley

The gritstone rocks on the banks of Pendle Water were skimmed with frozen spray and although the clough is a safe enough place in most other conditions, there were some very slippy moments and I began calling myself names before anybody else got a chance. Boar Clough is another way up onto the rolling summit of the hill but I've been that way and it is even steeper at the bottom end and I would guess that in very bad conditions it could be more than a bit hairy.

Once on the top that February day, the wind blew me across the tussocks towards Big End – as the summit is known locally – and the trig point, and below me, under racing cloud the Ribble valley stretched to Longridge Fells and the Irish Sea in the west and north-eastward to the Yorkshire Dales and the river's source close by Ribblehead Viaduct. To the north, the mountains of the Lake District were just discernible, Peny-ghent and Ingleborough a smudge before them. To the south and east were Black Hambledon, Lad Law and Stoodley Pike. It was getting very cold, and although there were still hours of day left, the clouds were rolling in and it looked as though there could be snow in that swollen black sky, so I dropped down by Robin Hood's Well and followed the footpath across the slopes of the fell to Pendle House and Barley.

Robin Hood's Well, named after the Celtic (or proto-Celtic) Robin Goodfellow, was a holy well and a place of Easter pilgrimages from

Clitheroe, Burnley and Colne. It is also called Fox's Well, because it was on Pendle Hill that George Fox, the founder of the Quaker Movement had the vision which inspired him to preach the word of friendship and quiet meditation to the world.

As we travelled we came near a very great high hill called Pendle Hill and I was moved by the Lord to go to the top of it, which I did and with much ado it was so very steep and high. When I came to the top of it I saw the sea bordering on Lancashire. From the top of this hill the Lord let me see in what places he had a great people to be gathered. As I went down the hillside I found a spring of water and refreshed myself.

It was on a summer's day a few years back that Pat and I did the round of Pendle from the Nick. It's a fine walk but, if you like a quiet time, it's best done mid-week because at weekends it gets pretty crowded.

The dew was still on the grass and our boots were wet as we climbed from The Wellsprings Inn to Apronful Hill and Badger Wells. Years and years and years ago I appeared at the folk-club at The Wellsprings. It was a fairly regular gig for me and good crack it was too. But I remember one occasion when I stopped the show and sat down for ten minutes. The reason was that the stage in the pub room stood in front of a big window which looked westward over miles of the Ribble Valley towards the Irish Sea. It was a glorious summer evening and the sun was dropping through curdled clouds that had turned into an ocean of boiling magma, molten and bubbling, the magenta and deep plum of the clouds was shot through with raging bronze and splashes of bloody fire. It was the sort of sky that would have had Turner running for his Winsor and Newtons and there was no way I could compete with that, so I called a break and sat down with the rest of the audience (who, in any case, had been paying more attention to it than me) to watch the sunset. Then, when it had finally gone dark and the last flush had left the sky, I got on with the show. Nature is a hard act to follow.

Pendle witches in Downham

The Apronful of Stones on Pendle's shoulder is all that remains of what seems to have been a Bronze Age tomb. Old Nick is held responsible for dropping the apronful after lobbing the rest of the stones at Clitheroe Castle and leaving a hoofprint at Deerstones Quarry; and, as so often, the burial site is on the hill's edge looking out to the west. I often wonder whether the people who made these tombs employed the same principles of geomancy used by the Chinese today, to whom 'aspect' in the choice of a grave is all important. The right aspect means that air and water and wind and earth must all be in harmony. The fact that so many of these tombs seem to be on shoulders of hills where they look down on valleys and where the air is in constant motion leaves me wondering if there may not be something in it.

Above Badger Wells at Black Hill we contoured round to the head of Ashendean Clough and then followed the gently rising footpath along the edge to the boundary stone. It's a great edge path with the flank of Pendle falling away to the Ribble Valley and below the hamlets of Pendleton, Worston and Downham. Pendleton is a bonny, little visited village with a stream running through the middle, and Downham, equally bonny is much visited while Worston has a house with a witch's window.

We climbed from the cairned path to the site of the beacon on Big End that linked Pendle to the chain of fires which were lit across the country to warn of invasions or to celebrate a Coronation. Walking down from the summit, we made our way to Sabden by Lower

Sabden Fold and Hob Wood, where yet another group of pixies must have made their home, and from there, after a cup of tea, it was a gentle slog up the hill to the Nick.

When you stand on the summit of Pendle Hill, do not go imagining toads and broomsticks, spells and cauldrons. Leave those poor maligned women to their rest, and if you are looking for villains, look no further than the corrupt Roger Nowell and his master, James I, 'the wisest fool in Christendom'. Instead, enjoy the views and the very special atmosphere of the place, and if you're looking for a spiritual experience, think of George Fox and the peaceful Quaker movement he founded, think of the Holy Well and of the hill's Celtic links, and the Beltane and Samhain fires that have been burnt there but most of all enjoy it for what it is, one of the most beautiful places on earth, for to walk Pendle in clear fine weather with a good companion is to taste the wine of days.

Pendle Hill from near Sawley

Index

[244]